Rethinking World Politics
Series Editor: Professor Michael Co

In an age of increased academic specialization where more and more books about smaller and smaller topics are becoming the norm, this major new series is designed to provide a forum and stimulus for leading scholars to address big issues in world politics in an accessible but original manner. A key aim is to transcend the intellectual and disciplinary boundaries which have so often served to limit rather than enhance our understanding of the modern world. In the best tradition of engaged scholarship, it aims to provide clear new perspectives to help make sense of a world in flux.

Each book addresses a major issue or event that has had a formative influence on the twentieth-century or the twenty-first-century world which is now emerging. Each makes its own distinctive contribution as well as providing an original but accessible guide to competing lines of interpretation.

Taken as a whole, the series will rethink contemporary international politics in ways that are lively, informed and – above all – provocative.

Rethinking Global Governance

Mark Beeson

BLOOMSBURY ACADEMIC
LONDON • NEW YORK • OXFORD • NEW DELHI • SYDNEY

BLOOMSBURY ACADEMIC
Bloomsbury Publishing Plc
50 Bedford Square, London, WC1B 3DP, UK
1385 Broadway, New York, NY 10018, USA
29 Earlsfort Terrace, Dublin 2, Ireland

BLOOMSBURY, BLOOMSBURY ACADEMIC and the Diana logo are trademarks of
Bloomsbury Publishing Plc

First published in Great Britain 2019 by Red Globe Press
Reprinted by Bloomsbury Academic 2022

A catalogue record for this book is available from the British Library.

A catalog record for this book is available from the Library of Congress.

ISBN: HB: 978-1-137-58861-6
          PB: 978-1-137-58860-9

To find out more about our authors and books visit www.bloomsbury.com and sign up for
our newsletters.

For Simon and Karl:
The best of brothers

Contents

Abbreviations

APT	ASEAN Plus Three
ARF	ASEAN Regional Forum
AFC	Asian financial crisis
AIIB	Asian Infrastructure Investment Bank
APEC	Asia Pacific Economic Cooperation
ASEAN	Association of Southeast Asian Nations
BCBS	Basel Committee on Banking Supervision
BDB	BRICS Development Bank
BIS	Bank for International Settlements
BRI	Belt and Road Initiative
BWIs	Bretton Woods institutions
CCP	Chinese Communist Party
CSCAP	Council for Security Cooperation in the Asia Pacific
EAS	East Asia Summit
ECB	European Central Bank
EFH	Efficient markets hypothesis
ENGO	Environmental nongovernmental organizations
EPA	Environmental Protection Agency
EU	European Union
FDI	Foreign direct investment
FSB	Financial Stability Board
GATT	General Agreement on Tariffs and Trade
GFC	Global financial crisis
GGOs	Global governance organizations
GPE	Global political economy
GPNs	Global production networks
IASB	International Accounting Standards Board
IFIs	International financial institutions
IMF	International Monetary Fund
INGOs	International nongovernment organizations
IOs	International organizations
IPCC	International Panel on Climate Change
IPE	International political economy

IR	International relations
MNCs	Multinational corporations
NAFTA	North American Free Trade Agreement
NATO	North Atlantic Treaty Organization
NICs	Newly industrializing countries
NIEO	New International Economic Order
NPM	New Public Management
OECD	Organisation for Economic Co-operation and Development
PBC	Peoples' Bank of China
PRC	Peoples' Republic of China
PTAs	Preferential trade agreements
QSD	The Quadrilateral Security Dialogue
R2P	Responsibility to protect
RBIO	Rules-based international order
SCO	Shanghai Cooperation Organization
SEA	Single European Act
SOEs	State-owned enterprises
TPP	Trans Pacific Partnership
UN	United Nations
UNCLOS	United Nations Convention on the Law of the Sea
UNCTAD	United Nations Conference on Trade and Development
UNFCCC	United Nations Framework Convention on Climate Change
UNSC	United Nations Security Council
WIPO	World Intellectual Property Organization
WTO	World Trade Organization

Foreword

When I first launched the series 'Rethinking World Politics' well over ten years ago I had two broad goals in mind: one was to challenge what I saw then as the tendency amongst many academics towards writing more and more books of an increasingly specialized character which fewer and fewer people were actually bothering to read; and the other was to try and do something about it by encouraging scholars to reflect on their subject in ways that allowed them to write in the broadest terms possible and in ways not encouraged – indeed actively discouraged – by universities increasingly dominated by metrics and all the other controlling paraphernalia that now shape life in the academy. Perhaps I was tilting at windmills; and I hardly think the series has changed the world. But it has led to the publication of several great volumes that have, over the years, rethought some of the big issues in world politics. I am also pleased to report that the majority of them have reached a very wide audience too!

In this new book in the series – written by an established authority on Asia – Mark Beeson has authored a daring and, dare I say, a very well-written and engaging study on the past, present, and future of global governance. It is certainly not the first book on the subject. Indeed, when I first arrived at the LSE many years ago it was very much in vogue. But times change, and so too do academic fashions, and over the last few years even if the topic has not disappeared entirely, it does seem to have been displaced by other concerns, and now, by that long awaited – and for some much dreaded – 'return of realism' which has had a field day of late talking about the rise of China, the return of Russia, the demise of the West, the ascent of the East, and of course that old favorite, the decline of the United States.

It is one of the many strengths of this volume that the author manages to bring together both the 'real world' of power shifts and economic change on the one side and the issue of global governance on the other. The volume ranges far and wide, from the origin of the state to the nature of modern capitalism, from regionalism to the environment. But one big question remains central, namely how will the big changes now taking place in the international system impact on how 'we' try and manage the world? The author provides no easy answers and no comforting words. Thus, while China may have been 'one of the principal beneficiaries of the so-called "rules based international order"', Beeson is none too sure it will want to remain a rule taker forever. And while we might all agree that the US-led created order is on the wane – more so than ever in the age of Trump – would it be good for the world as a whole if 'many of the international institutions that were created under the auspices of American hegemony' in a previous age were to disappear entirely? He is doubtful. In the end, Beeson comes up with no pat answers; and he certainly offers no easy solutions. But he does at least face the challenge that at this 'precise moment in history' global governance has never been more necessary – in fact in his view 'we' are unlikely to survive without some type of effective global governance; on the other hand, given all the changes now taking place, effective governance is going to become ever more difficult to sustain. Clearly some very testing times lie ahead. Hopefully, this fine volume will help readers understand why.

Professor Michael Cox
General Editor and Director of LSE IDEAS
London School of Economics and Political Science, UK

Introduction

Anyone trying to make sense of international affairs, especially in the early stages of the twenty-first century, faces a number of challenges. First and foremost, perhaps, is the difficulty of separating long-term transformations in the way the 'international system' operates from the short-term impact of particular events and actors. The reemergence of China as a great power and the relative decline in the influence of the United States is an example of the former. The presidency of Donald J. Trump is possibly an example of the latter. Presidents come and go, and many people assume that the American political system will outlast its unpredictable leader and we will all return to geopolitical business as usual. This seems increasingly unlikely, however, and not simply because of the behavior of President Trump.

If arguments about the erosion of American primacy are correct, then this has major implications for the sorts of things the United States can actually achieve in foreign policy terms. As other 'rising powers' like China assume a more prominent position in regional and even global affairs, this necessarily means that America's ability to shape the international system in the way it has for half a century or so is going to be reduced. One response to this emerging reality is a Trumpian tantrum, and an abandonment of the highly institutionalized multilateral order that the United States played a pivotal role in creating and running. But even a different, better informed, less impulsive American leader will have to deal with the reality that her country may not be able to act in quite the way it once did.

Because the United States has played such a central role in the operation and development of the international system since the Second World War, it necessarily occupies a central place throughout this book. These days, however, it is far from alone. Much of the following discussion focuses on China, too, and not simply because of its growing material importance – although that *is* why we're all interested in it, of course. A growing number of people, especially in China itself, think it offers a different way of thinking about some of the most fundamental and taken-for-granted issues in international relations and development. The 'China challenge' highlights many of the long-term changes that are undermining the institutional and even ideational foundations of the old order. This doesn't mean that the world the United States helped create will disappear overnight, but it does mean that it is likely to change in ways that many in the West are likely to find disconcerting, if not alarming.

Having said that, it is also clear that China has been one of the principal beneficiaries of the so-called 'rules-based international order' (RBIO) that emerged under the auspices of American leadership. Whatever one may think about the impact and operation of this order it allowed at least some countries, especially in East Asia, to develop and prosper. In combination with the growing impact of 'globalization', the highly institutionalized postwar international order has led to long-term changes in the way many international activities are conducted. The principal manifestations of such developments are in part technological and organizational, but in large part can be seen in the continuing transformation in the way many formerly state-based activities are conducted. Such developments pose an equally fundamental challenge for the growing number of authoritarian powers who seek to simultaneously benefit from and control forces associated with globalization. As a consequence, what we have come to think of as global governance may not look quite as some of us imagined.

Global governance

Yet global governance *still* seems like a good idea. What, after all, is there to object about something that sounds as if it will bring order to an international system that has been distinguished by a degree of chaos and uncertainty of late? The very idea of 'governance' suggests that there is an element of potential intentionality and purposiveness in the way human affairs are managed that is inherently attractive, even necessary. It is not entirely fanciful, either. Despite some of the high-profile horrors and failings in the practice of contemporary international relations, much of what happens outside of the confines of the domestic political sphere remains surprisingly orderly, rule-bound, and predictable (Weiss 2013). Or it has done for half a century or so in what is rather loosely described as 'the West', at least. It is the possible simultaneous existence of order and anarchy – at least in the formal sense adopted by scholars of International Relations (IR) – that makes global governance both so desirable and so elusive.

The central – and it must be said, rather paradoxical and unsatisfactory – argument of this book is that at this moment in history global governance is both increasingly necessary and unlikely. If we think of global governance as *the conscious, goal-oriented collective actions of state and nonstate actors to develop new responses to problems that are both transnational and beyond the capacity of individual governments or organizations to resolve,* we immediately become aware of the nature of the challenge. While efforts at cooperating internationally are not unprecedented, as we shall see, they have arguably never been more important and urgent. Sadly, they are not getting any easier to achieve. On the contrary, the development of commonly supported norms, ideas, and practices, which many see as a key aspect of putative global governance, is becoming more difficult rather than less – all of the talk about so-called globalization notwithstanding. Rather than an inevitable convergence of ideas about the best way of conducting political, economic, or even social life, there are growing differences about how national and transnational affairs should be conducted. There are also profound differences in the relative capacities of different actors to influence the way such practices are actually realized.

Indeed, while much of the world is still surprisingly orderly in many important respects, parts of the planet remain particularly vulnerable to crises, governance failure, and chronic insecurity. International development, especially in the economic sense, remains a very uneven business. The consequences of such unevenness are not simply to be found in the all-too-familiar persistence of poverty, but in the nature of political institutions and relationships at the domestic level, too. Intuitively, if this really is a global age, as some have claimed, then we might expect to see greater similarity in the way that the world is organized and the sorts of lived experiences people have in different parts of the world. Nothing could be further from the truth, however. Not only are there still striking differences in the lifestyles, living standards, and values held by different people in various parts of the world, but there is also little sign that they are disappearing in the way some expected.

If processes associated with global governance are actually real and consequential, however, they ought to be happening across national borders and affecting people in broadly similar ways. Indeed, there ought to be something about the international system today that is distinctively different from the way international relations have been organized in earlier periods of human history. While there clearly *is* something different about the way the world works at the beginning of the twenty-first century, it is more difficult and contentious to claim that this adds up to something we might want to call 'global governance', or even the more descriptive idea of globalization. As we shall see throughout this book, there are different ways of thinking about these key concepts. While both have their limitations, they have risen to conceptual prominence because they capture something potentially important about the contemporary states system, as well as some of the economic, political, and strategic dynamics that have made it what it is.

One way of trying to get greater purchase on what global governance might amount to, and whether it is even any longer possible, is by trying to unpack its component parts and placing them in some sort of historical context. Chapter 1 provides an overview of the history of greater international cooperation and integration, which turns out to be a surprisingly long-standing affair. Indeed, some argue that 'globalization' has been developing for decades if not centuries. This chapter reviews some of the more important manifestations of these processes such as Western colonialism, the universalization of the nation-state, and the growth of international institutions. I also detail the circumstances in which China's rise has occurred and the implications this may have for extant governance practices.

Some observers think there is a certain inevitability about the continuing integration of not only economic, but also political processes. Cosmopolitans, world government theorists, and analysts of globalization more generally have all made important contributions to the debate. So, however, have the skeptics. The role and possible transformation of the state is a vitally important aspect of this process, especially given its centrality in the rise of China and other powers. Chapter 2 reviews some of the more important theoretical debates in order to provide some sort of conceptual framework for the more general discussion of global governance as a theoretical and practical possibility.

The institutional architecture created under the auspices of American hegemony is arguably the nearest we have come to something approximating global governance, and this provides the main focus of Chapter 3. Whatever its merits as a template for international order and development, and no matter how incompletely it was realized, it remains a potent force in international affairs. Its durability has been a result of distinctive geopolitical forces and an institutionalized order that may no longer exist in quite the way they did. I pay particular attention to the impact of the administrations of George W. Bush and Donald Trump as these have arguably done more to undermine 'American hegemony' than anything else.

American primacy, leadership, or domination – the choice of noun is not insignificant – faces its greatest challenge in the form of the seemingly unstoppable rise of China. The key issue here is the fact that not only is American power seemingly in relative decline, but China is also promoting an alternative institutional order and even values. Chapter 4 considers the nature of this challenge and the debate around the Washington vs. the Beijing consensus, and the specific institutional and geoeconomic initiatives that have emanated from China.

Much attention has been given to the emergence of new actors, be they newly powerful states or nonstate actors in the contemporary international order. There remain striking divisions and differences of opinion between the 'North' and 'South', however, which make any transition to truly global governance inherently unlikely. Chapter 5 assesses the capacity of new actors, especially other potentially 'rising powers', to contribute to (or obstruct) international cooperation in new forums such as the G20.

One of the more striking features of the international system is that it has a strong regional accent. Despite all its current problems, the European Union remains the most compelling example of this possibility and the closest the world has come to effective transnational governance. Other parts of the world also continue to demonstrate a strong interest in developing regional solutions to collective action problems – including global ones. Chapter 6 explores regionalism's place in a global order, with particular reference to the European crisis and China's capacity to play a hegemonic role in East Asia.

The global economy is increasingly crisis-prone and unpredictable. Chapter 7 sketches the evolution of transnational production and economic integration before considering the nature and implications of recent crises for efforts to promote wider processes of international cooperation. It also considers whether America's problems have actually undermined its ability to play the sort of hegemonic role some thought essential to putative forms of global governance. The key question here is whether China will be able to either offer an alternative vision or help to preserve the current patterns of international cooperation.

The global environment presents a notoriously 'wicked' policy problem and arguably the definitive test for putative forms of global governance. It may ultimately prove to be the quintessential driver of international relations – for better or worse. The principal focus in Chapter 8 is on formal interstate efforts to respond to climate change, and some of the possible obstacles to successful environmental management more generally. A lack of leadership in this issue area is a major impediment to collective action. I also explain and assess China's brand of 'environmental authoritarianism' as an alternative to the current regime.

Managing security is another fundamental test of global governance, and one that is partly dependent on the way it is defined. Chapter 9 employs the encompassing 'security governance' framework to explore strategic issues and their management. The key question here is whether forces generating insecurity in different domains are actually becoming ungovernable. Does the existence of such disruptive forces mean that security governance will inevitably be partial and only realized within specific issue areas, regions, or individual states at best? More pertinently, what are the implications of a relative shift in the balance of power between the United States and China?

The final chapter reviews the debate about global governance and offers some rather sobering observations about its future as a practical and theoretical enterprise. The significance of the difference between long- and short-term developments, and their possible interaction, is a key consideration in this context. While there are some encouraging indicators – interstate war is still rare – the deterioration of the environment, and the limited amount of time available to do anything about it, provides an implacable bottom line with which all other cooperative initiatives must contend. It is simply impossible to imagine how security issues or even economic development can be guaranteed, unless action is taken to avert the potentially catastrophic implications of global warming.

Before the casual reader throws the book aside with a sigh, however, let me make the case for carrying on. Yes, some of the issues and developments that are considered in the following pages are by turns depressing, frustrating, baffling, and at times difficult to believe, but that's no reason to ignore them. Only by trying to make sense of how we got to where we are and what the potential of global governance actually is can we hope to make 'progress'. Even the possibility that such a thing is any longer possible will strike some readers as naïve and fanciful. They may be right. But nothing is more certain than that their beliefs about the future will come to pass if we all subscribe to similar views. Understanding some of the impediments to reform of any sort is still essential – and not without interest!

1

The Forerunners of Global Governance: A Brief History

There are two initial things to consider in any discussion of global governance: first, can we agree on what it actually means? Second, even if it is a meaningful concept, when did it actually begin and how has it evolved over time? The next chapter takes up the theoretical debate in more detail, but for now it is worth repeating my provisional definition: *the conscious, goal-oriented collective actions of state and nonstate actors to develop new responses to problems that are both transnational and beyond the capacity of individual governments or organizations to resolve.* The rest of this chapter is dedicated to trying to establish when a more global approach to governance began to emerge, and how and to what extent a concomitant sense of interconnectedness among political actors has developed.

Although much of what follows is descriptive and designed to provide a context for the subsequent discussion of specific aspects of global governance, it is not atheoretical – or value free, for that matter. The issues I highlight or neglect inevitably reflect my biases and sense of what is important in trying to develop a plausible explanation of complex and contested processes. In this regard, I am conscious that earlier generations of scholars often took a highly eurocentric view of historical development that neglected the significance of economic and political relations outside of the Western 'core' economies and imperial powers (Blaut 1993). Recently, such absences have been recognized and to some extent overcome, not least because it has become increasingly difficult to ignore the historical significance of China as a long-term influence on its region, if not the world (Frank 1998; Hobson 2004). It is no coincidence that concerns about possible Western bias and the neglect of alternative understandings of history have underpinned the emergence of distinctive Chinese readings of IR and historiography (Qin 2011; Zhang 2015).

1

Attempting to adopt a genuinely global perspective also highlights questions about the nature of interactions between different parts of the world, something else that has recently begun to attract the attention and recognition it merits (Anievas and Nisancioglu 2015). One of the key questions in this regard is why Europe rather than East Asia generally, or China in particular, has become the driving force of international development. Even more specifically, why didn't China's comparatively advanced civilization provide the impetus for global expansion and even domination in the manner subsequently adopted by the Europeans? Unsurprisingly, the answers to these sorts of questions are contested and not easily answered, but they provide an important context in which to try to make sense of not only the course of historical developments, but also the legacy of their impact on contemporary IR.

In the beginning

Knowing quite how far back to look for the origins of global governance and the closely related notion of globalization is not straight forward. Although it makes sense to think of contemporary forms of global governance as having been consolidated and institutionalized in conjunction with the development of American hegemony, it is possible to trace 'global' impulses and patterns over a much longer time frame. 'World systems theorists' have long claimed that not only is the world an enclosed, interactive entity, but such processes have been occurring for thousands of years, since the earliest civilizations emerged in the Middle East and what we now think of as China (Frank and Gills 1996). Given that world system theory is predicated on Marxist ideas it is no surprise that it has a strong emphasis on the material basis of human interactions (Wallerstein 1979). There has recently been an upsurge of interest in Marxian accounts of history that recognize not only the impact of areas outside the West, but the 'uneven' consequences of the economic impact of such interactions (Anievas and Nisancioglu 2015).

Be that as it may, for our purposes what is significant is the growing interaction and awareness of human beings over time and especially across space. The central point to make about the spatial aspect of nascent global processes is that they initially occurred in a far less politically and geographically demarcated arena than they do now. The political and institutional architecture that we have come to take for granted, is a very new phenomenon. Even nation states are a comparatively recent development and despite their continuing contemporary importance, there is absolutely no guarantee that they will endure. On the contrary, this historical record strongly suggests that states are the exceptions rather than the rule when it comes to the organization of political and social life.

Nevertheless, states have assumed a dominant position in the contemporary system and are potentially a major part of – as well as obstacles to – any effective form of global governance. Significantly, China is an especially prominent champion of state sovereignty (Tang 2018), something that is explained by its distinctive history and its current political regime. It is, therefore, important to say something about the way states came to be such a central feature of the modern international system. Before we do, however, it is also helpful to remind ourselves of what preceded that state, especially as some observers think we are currently moving toward forms of governance that more closely resemble feudal patterns of political order and control (Cerny 1998).

Before the state

We have become so accustomed to thinking of ourselves as part of geographically demarcated communities of fate that it is difficult to imagine anything else. Indeed, this is one of the fundamental difficulties facing those who advocate the transcendence of state forms and the often-debilitating sovereignty claims that are associated with them (Held 2000). It is seemingly impossible for many policymakers to imagine or – more consequentially, perhaps – give up a system of governance that confers distinct advantages, especially for those who find themselves at the apex of nationally based structures of power. And yet for most of human history states did not exist; or certainly not in the sort of formally recognized geographically distinct forms that states have notionally assumed today. I say 'notionally' because the reality is, of course, that even in an international system theoretically composed of similar states, in reality states are very different, in terms of their relative capacities, values, and goals. History can explain some of this continuing differentiation, too.

In humanity's long collective transition from bands of hunter-gathers through to the sorts of complex forms of institutionalized interdependence that distinguish the contemporary international system, there have been some significant milestones. Importantly, in pre-modern, nonglobal times such transitional moments were reached at very different times and this had major long-term consequences for political, strategic, and economic relations between different parts of the planet. There is a noteworthy 'path dependent quality' about many historical processes, in which enduring patterns of institutionalized and/or routinized behavior shape, if not determine, possible future outcomes (Pierson 2000). Such processes of 'uneven development' were especially noteworthy following the development of capitalism as the Western European states that pioneered these distinctive patterns of social relationships often enjoyed significant 'first mover' advantages (Smith 2008). Because of the path-dependent nature of development generally, such advantages often endured and help to account for the very different positions and roles some parts of the world occupied in an increasingly interconnected world.

The fate of Australia's aboriginal population dramatically highlights the potentially calamitous consequences of interaction between communities with very different capacities and resources at their disposal (Hughes 2012). Australia's indigenous community is also a reminder of the pioneering, 'globalizing' role of hunter-gatherer societies as they fanned out across the world. For our purposes, however, it is the emergence of distinct sedentary communities that is of principal interest here as it marks the beginning of increasingly self-conscious *political* communities that were distributed across space and existed in potential opposition to each other. At one level, this led to the development of distinctively different notions of identity. Less happily, such differences also provided the basis for possible sources of conflict, of course, a force that has remained one of the most fundamental drivers of human development – especially as social collectivities – ever since (McNeil 1982). The key transition here was the emergence of chiefdoms and hierarchical patterns of political organization as agricultural development encouraged greater social stratification – and the creation of an economic surplus that could be plundered (see Buzan and Little 2000).

As societies became more complex, expanded in size and developed a coercive capacity, the outlines of the sorts of modern forms of political and economic organization begin to emerge more clearly. Bayly (2004: 42) suggests that what he describes as a form of 'archaic globalisation' was driven by three general principles: 'first, universalizing kingship; secondly, the expansive urge of cosmic religion; and thirdly, humoral or moral understanding of bodily health.' Trade, diplomacy, and conflict were encouraged by the formation of more consolidated forms of kingly rule, but religion was also a driver of global movement and migration. The exchange and movement of ideas, peoples, and cultural products such as medicines, tea, tobacco, and – most consequentially for China, perhaps – opium, helped drive higher levels of interconnectivity (Findlay and O'Rourke 2007). While this sort of social interchange was plainly a major driver of social development across Europe and Asia, there was, according to Abu-Lughod's (1989: 12, emphasis in original) influential reading of the world before European hegemony, 'no *inherent historical necessity* that shifted the system to favor the West rather than the East'. And yet the reality is that that is precisely what happened; a process that has had the most profound path-dependent consequences, from which China in particular has only recently reemerged.

While we might take for granted the fact that Europe came to dominate the international system as a consequence of its technological and social innovations, it is still important to ask why – especially as many of the key competitive advantages of Western civilization had 'Eastern origins' (Hobson 2004). After all, China in particular had actually developed or invented many of the key innovations and institutions that were borrowed and deployed to such devastating effect by the European powers. The key questions here are consequently about China's 'failure' to develop a fully-fledged capitalist economy despite the presence of markets, a paper currency and other important technical innovations; and conversely about why Europe did. How did a relatively backward and peripheral part of the globe come to dominate so much of the world, strategically, economically, and politically?

One of the problems with many of the prevailing explanations of long-run historical processes is a failure to take contingent differences seriously. Indeed, some forms of 'Western' scholarship, especially in the field of international relations (IR), seem to wear ahistoricism as a badge of honor, preferring to focus instead on supposedly timeless and universal abstractions that supposedly account for state behavior everywhere. There a number of fundamental problems with such approaches, however. First, as has been suggested, the state is a relatively recent phenomenon and its future is far from certain. Second, as Teschke (2003: 124) points out, 'the universal logic of geopolitical competition has to be filtered through the social forces within polities'. In other words, IR, globalization, or any of the other tropes that are routinely deployed to explain or conceptualize complex, multidimensional processes, are ultimately realized and manifest in contingent social circumstances. Given the centrality of states in mainstream IR theory it is ironic that it frequently offers impoverished explanations for the rise of the very phenomenon it regards as so theoretically and practically pivotal.

The rise of the state

It is important to highlight the manner in which the state became the dominant political institution across the world for two reasons: firstly, for better or worse, it remains a critically important element of any potential form of global governance. Secondly, it provides a powerful illustration of the way in which particular ideas about optimal forms of governance and political order can be transmitted – or imposed – across time and space. Despite its European origins, the nation-state has become the default political form all over the world. Indeed, no part of the globe is *not* demarcated by notionally sovereign borders, even if some states have much greater capacity to police and operate within such geographical borders (Jackson 1990). Yet, with the noteworthy and currently fragile exception of the European Union, states – especially in the East Asian region of which China is such a central part (Beeson 2014a) – remain fiercely protective of their sovereignty and independence. Rather problematically for supporters of global governance, effective transnational cooperation, let alone sovereignty pooling of the European sort, remains the exception rather than the rule.

Perhaps it is fitting and unsurprising that the region that pioneered the state's rise has also been at the forefront of efforts to reform it (Sabel and Zeitlin 2010); even to fundamentally undercut the foundations of national sovereignty that many IR scholars assume to be the sacrosanct and non-negotiable foundations of an international system that is supposedly anarchic. I shall consider the theoretical basis of such assumptions and their relevance to particular patterns of regional evolution and the prospects for transnational governance in subsequent chapters. The point to consider at this stage is why the state rose to prominence in Europe rather than Asia, especially given China's status as one of the earliest, and certainly the most enduring, civilizations on the planet.

Francis Fukuyama's (2011: 150) explanation for China's failure to consolidate the sort of effective, highly institutionalized state form that distinguished Europe was that 'it created a modern state that was not restrained by the rule of law or by institutions of accountability to limit the power of the sovereign'. This is a theme that continues to resonate in debates about China's relative strengths and weaknesses, and its consequent potential role in global governance (World Bank/DRCSC 2012). It is also an idea that reflects a particularly 'Western', even teleological, view of history and theory, for that matter (Hobson 2007). Be that as it may, the point to consider at this point is why the Europeans did manage to develop such a powerful state form, and why it was subsequently they that imposed themselves on China and the rest of the world, rather than vice versa.

Henrik Spruyt (1994) argues that the state triumphed in a process of institutional selection in which it eclipsed, and ultimately rendered redundant, rival medieval organizational forms such as the Holy Roman Empire or the Hanseatic League. The rise and fall of the Holy Roman Empire is a long and complex story spanning centuries, but it illustrates the enduring influence of papal authority and the importance of organized religion in an era before states (Wilson 2011). Ironically, wars of religion actually helped to consolidate the state form and the importance of national rather than transnational authority. Likewise, the Hanseatic League, which was a confederation of merchant guilds across northern and central Europe from the twelfth to fifteenth centuries, was designed to offer the sort of physical protection for trading activities that states would ultimately come to provide much more successfully.

In this context, Spruyt (1994: 28) argues that the state had three major institutional advantages: first, the state's internal organizational logic had fewer deficiencies than its rivals; second, state sovereignty provided an effective mechanism for the conduct of external, interunit relations; and third, sovereign states 'delegitimized actors who did not fit a system of territorially demarcated and internally hierarchical authorities'. The other critical dynamic that underpinned the state's ascendance was war. As Tilly (1990) famously observed, war made the state and the state made war. Put differently, there was an inextricable, mutually constitutive relationship between capital and coercion, or economic development and security. What McNeil (1982) describes as the 'bureaucratization of violence' was a key part of state formation and the 'efficiency' of European forms of warfare.

The European state's potential to survive and prosper in an environment of chronic insecurity and unremitting violence made it irresistibly attractive to other actors facing similar threats or harboring similar ambitions. Such factors help to explain its eventual export around the world in a process that is one of the more striking and important aspects of political history over the last few hundred years. In reality, other less 'developed' or militarily capable states had little choice other than to emulate the European model if they wanted to survive or resist colonization. The very different historical experiences of Japan and China are instructive in this context: both countries faced similar exogenous challenges, and yet their responses to the challenge of European imperialism and expansion were very different. In Japan's case, it proved an assiduous pupil of European modernization and rapidly borrowed and adapted many of the key institutions that had reinforced European power (Morris-Suzuki 1996). The more insular and complacent Chinese empire, by contrast, failed to recognize, much less respond to, the challenge of Europe and were consequently plunged into a century of internal convulsion and external predation (Beeson 2014a; Fairbank et al. 1965).

The state goes global

Thus, the state emerged in conjunction with the development of capitalism in Western Europe, especially Britain. So far, so uncontroversial perhaps. There is, of course, a long-standing debate about the causes of this social and institutional transformation, and the transition from feudalism to capitalism, which I cannot hope to add to here (see Anderson 1996; Aston and Philpin 1987). Suffice to say that the 'agrarian revolution', which seemed to trigger a distinctively capitalist mode of accumulation and a concomitant transformation in social relationships (Wood 2002), was intimately bound up with the consolidation of the distinctive state form that would go on to effectively eliminate all its potential rivals through a rather Darwinian process of institutional competition. This is not only an important consideration when thinking about this historical process and crucial aspects of contemporary 'globalization', however. On the contrary, the universalization of state forms – in principle, at least – provides an important illustration of the way other forms of governance could conceivably be transmitted and institutionalized across time and space.

The fact that capitalism was one of the key driving forces in both the state's consolidation as the master political institution in Europe and its subsequent expansion across the world was, and is, a crucial part of the story of globalization. Having said that, we should also recognize that some observers, such as Giovanni Arrighi (1994: 32), point out that 'the close historical tie between capitalism and the modern interstate system is just as much one of contradiction as it is one of unity'. Capitalism, in short, is a specific mode of production-characterized commodification, private ownership, and the existence of potentially antagonistic social classes (Hunt 1979). Equally importantly for the current discussion, capitalism is inherently expansionary and encourages the growth of trade and other forms of economic interdependence that are central to the contemporary story of globalization. As we shall see, however, the expansion of a capitalist mode of production (and with it the sovereign state) was not a seamless or peaceful process. On the contrary, European imperialism was often brutal and necessarily exploitative.

There are a number of competing explanations for the existence of, and motivations for, the European empires of the nineteenth century, but most agree that mutual rivalry, prestige, and the economic imperatives provided by underlying, expansionary capitalist dynamics were central. The fact that the Europeans were able to overcome potential sources of local opposition to their rule through the technological superiority of their collective war-making capacities was also critical, of course. Abernathy (2000: 235) argues that colonized peoples were subject to a 'triple assault', perpetrated by governments, profit-oriented companies, and missionary bodies, the combination of which gave the Europeans a capacity to 'organizationally outflank other societies'. The key feature of empires in this context is that they are 'relationships of political control imposed by some political societies over the effective sovereignty of other political societies' (Doyle 1986: 19).

It is not simply that such a relationship represents a mechanism for political domination and economic exploitation, but that it may engender long-lasting feelings of resentment and outrage among subsequent generations about their treatment at the hands of colonial oppressors. This is plainly part of China's contemporary efforts to reassume what many of the population consider to be its rightful position at the center of regional and international affairs. Recognizing what a humiliating period this was for China in particular helps to explain why it generates such strong feelings to this day (Kaufman 2010). It is important to remember that China lost its effective sovereignty, endured a calamitous civil war, and – most gallingly of all, perhaps – was invaded and subjugated by Japan, its great regional rival. While China may be an extreme case, it is far from alone; the reality is that the decolonization process was often a violent, drawn-out and unhappy precursor to the eventual creation of independent sovereign states. Even then, the differentiated historical reality of this process meant that some states are significantly more powerful and capable than others.

While much IR theory treats states as essentially identical elements of an overall international system, the historical reality is very different. Contingent, historically specific 'national' circumstances meant that proto-states often faced very different circumstances when they eventually achieved independence. Some nations were 'granted' sovereignty, others had to fight for it; some had the basis for potentially effective internal governance, some were woefully ill-equipped for the challenges of independence. When the Democratic Republic of the Congo achieved independence in 1964, for example, only sixteen members of the entire population had university degrees. Less extreme, but no less illustrative, the leaders of modern Indonesia not only had to fight for their freedom, but they also had to create a nation where none had existed before – to say nothing of encouraging economic development and maintaining internal and external security at the height of the Cold War (McMahon 1999). The point to stress is that while something like the universal adoption of the state form is clearly significant in its own right and as a possible precursor to other forms of political development, it is highly uneven and contingent.

Uneven development

The legacy of 'uneven development' remains to this day and is one of the most important potential obstacles to the adoption of universal forms of governance. Many states feel understandably aggrieved at their unfavorable positions in what is an unambiguously hierarchical international system that continues to be characterized by profound asymmetries of power and inequality (Donnelly 2006). Understanding how this came about is central to any attempt to remedy such problems and the sense of injustice they foster. Once again, the historical experience and its path-dependent legacy is a crucial part of the story and one that is not easily overcome.

Some of the most important and innovative analyses of uneven development have emerged from a broadly Marxist tradition, with economic geographers leading the way (Smith 2008). Interestingly, such perspectives have had relatively little impact in contemporary China, despite their potential importance in explaining uneven development within China itself. Nevertheless, the emphasis placed on the significance of the geographical dispersion and interconnection of economic activities and the increasingly international division of labor that underpins them is crucial: not only does such a perspective potentially account for the radically different developmental paths that have distinguished different parts of the globe, but they also help to explain why some features of the historical evolution of capitalism have proved so resistant or difficult to change. As we shall see, some of the expectations about the impact and nature of 'globalization', as well as the prospects for global cooperation, are profoundly circumscribed by such enduring historical legacies.

That the world is an uneven place and a long way from converging on some sort of common template of development is painfully evident, not least in the seemingly irremediable problems of what Paul Collier calls the 'bottom billion', or the world's poorest people, and the failure of capitalist development to take hold. Interestingly, Collier (2007: 157) argues that 'citizens of the rich world are not to blame for most of the problems of the bottom billion; poverty is simply the default option when economies malfunction'. The precise relationship between the developed and underdeveloped parts of the global economy remains a subject of debate, with some scholars favoring long-term 'structural' explanations derived from Marxist premises (Wallerstein 1979), while others, especially powerful institutional expressions of the contemporary international order, stress failures of 'agency' in the form of poor governance (World Bank 1994). Either way, the historical process of economic development is geographically contingent and reflects the interaction of an 'overall pattern of development [that] must comprise an uneven distribution both of socio-cultural forms and of material capabilities among coexisting human populations' (Rosenberg 2010: 183).

This may be a form of 'globalization', but it is a long way from the sort of essentially progressive, 'win-win outcome' – to borrow a phrase from Xi Jinping (2014a) – that many prominent advocates and analysts of greater economic integration claim. Consequently, we need to unpack what this 'essentially contested concept' actually means.

Globalization

The concept of globalization has been so frequently invoked by so many people to describe such a variety of underspecified processes that it is in danger of becoming completely meaningless. Nevertheless, for anyone interested in the prospects for global governance, it is important to say something about the sorts of structural transformations and historical developments that have seemingly made the world such a different place. Consequently, it is important to map some of the more salient empirical features of the globalization phenomenon so that we can better understand why it has proved so contentious, and why observers come to radically different conclusions about its nature and significance.

As we have seen, there is a good deal of scholarly debate about how to periodize supposedly global processes. Such differences are partly explained by the theoretical assumptions that are made about globalization and the very processes that might constitute it. Whether it actually makes sense to use a pronoun like 'it' to describe a set of complex, multifaceted political, economic, social, and even strategic process is itself a moot point. However, we need to start somewhere and Held and colleagues' (1999: 15) definition usefully highlights some potentially key features of the concept:

> Globalization can be taken to refer to those spatio-temporal processes of change which underpin a transformation in the organization of human affairs by linking together and expanding human activity across regions and continents.

The parallels with theories of uneven development are striking, even if there is less emphasis on capitalism as the primary historical driving force and a more open-ended sense of what global processes might actually lead to in developmental terms. Many observers are united in the belief that there is something qualitatively and quantitatively different about the way that the international system has evolved recently that distinguish it from all previous eras (Wright 2000; Slaughter 2017). Of course, in some ways they are undoubtedly correct: the nature and extent of interconnectedness today really *is* different from anything we have seen before in human history. And yet we also need to recognize at the outset that judgments about the significance of globalization rather hinge on what is taken to be a measure of the process(es) itself. Hirst and Thompson (1996) famously pointed out that when measured in terms of economic integration, globalization was more developed before the First World War than it was in the immediate aftermath of the Second.

Indeed, it would take several decades and the creation of the Bretton Woods system (discussed in Chapter 3) to reach similar levels of integration. Another initial point to keep in mind, therefore, is that globalization can go backwards as well as forwards and there is nothing inevitable about its possible future trajectory (James 2001). With these caveats in mind, it is useful to unpack some of globalization's constituent parts as they will help to determine the prospects – perhaps even the *need* – for a concomitant process of global governance.

The world trade made

Trade has been one of the great drivers of economic expansion, growth, and human interaction. Adam Smith (1981: 671 [1776]) was the most articulate and influential advocate of the idea that trade is beneficial, and ultimately enhances human happiness: any country that inhibits foreign trade 'necessarily hurts its own interests', he argued. This quintessentially liberal reading became the conventional wisdom among policymakers in the Western world, even if it was not always acted upon in practice. It still isn't: trade relations have become one of the great potential flash points between China and the United States over recent years and they remain a potential obstacle to global governance. Nevertheless, there is little doubt that global trade has expanded dramatically over time, and especially in the period since the Second World War when it became the object of specific and arguably highly effective policy interventions designed to keep markets 'free and open' (Frieden 2006).

While the desire of postwar policymakers to maintain an open international trade regime in the aftermath of the Great Depression may have been understandable (see Chapter 3), we need to recognize that even with all its inherent 'comparative advantages' trade has never been an unalloyed good.

On the contrary, one of the initial drivers of large-scale international commerce in the modern era was the slave trade between Europe, Africa, and the plantation economies of the 'New World', relationships that had long-term institutional and path-dependent consequences (Acemoglu et al. 2001). The chronic underdevelopment of the African continent and its troubled subordination to external powers can be traced back to this period (Acemoglu and Robinson 2010). Likewise, many of the factors that created the conditions for China's dynastic crisis were brought about by its trade relations with imperial Britain, which were dictated by the hegemonic power of the era. The opium trade in particular, which was systematically encouraged by Britain as a way of addressing its trade deficit with China, clearly illustrates the logic of uneven, interconnected development:

> opium not only bound together China, India, England, and the United States in a quadrilateral trade, but also played a central role in sustaining Britain's industrialization drive and the revolutionary nineteenth century expansion of the world economy. (Pomeranz and Topik 1999: 105)

While China's trade-induced dynastic crisis and decline may be familiar, less widely recognized is the situation before the Europeans imposed themselves on East Asia. Prior to the European intrusion, China had already developed a flourishing system of trade relations with what we now think of as Southeast Asia. Indeed, Frank (1998: 117) goes so far as to suggest that Ming China was the driving force of trade in the early modern period and that 'the entire world order was – literally – Sinocentric'. It is only the subsequent eurocentric rewriting of history that has obscured this point. It is not one lost on Chinese scholars, however.

The general point to make about trade over the last half century or so, though, is that it has grown significantly. Defenders of American influence and of the potentially positive role of the so-called Bretton Woods institutions (BWIs) would argue this is no coincidence. The establishment of powerful agencies such as the General Agreement on Tariffs and Trade (GATT), which was later replaced by the World Trade Organization (WTO) in 1995, were clearly instrumental in encouraging states to reduce tariff barriers in particular and promoting trade liberalization more generally. Whether this has been an unambiguously 'good thing' is a matter of continuing dispute: some countries, the argument goes, were locked into subordinate positions in a global economic hierarchy in which their principal role was providing a particular commodity, or acting primarily as a source of cheap labor in an increasingly complex, transnational division of labor (Fröbel et al. 1977).

No doubt this reflects precisely the sort of specialized division of labor – in which increased specialization and expertise enhance productivity – that the likes of Smith and David Ricardo argued would increase overall economic welfare, but it often failed to recognize the underlying logic of international production. One key structural constraint was the fact that some economic commodities and products were significantly more valuable than others: producers of primary agricultural products, for example, often received low prices, not least because of residual protectionism in the 'developed' economies of North America and Europe, which wished to protect their own primary producers. Even states such as Saudi Arabia, which was fortunate enough to specialize in cheaply produced oil, found themselves subject to variants of the so-called 'resource curse', in which national resource wealth was captured by domestic elites in order to prop up what were often corrupt, parasitic regimes predicated on patronage (Ross 1999).

'Critical' scholars argue that the failure of much mainstream economic theory to recognize the sometimes pernicious effects of trade reflects the fact that 'the "reality" examined by trade theory is itself partly constructed by trade theory' (O'Brien and Williams 2010: 157). As we shall see in more detail in the next chapter, the possibility that our notions of political, economic and even strategic reality are socially constructed is an increasingly prominent part of debates about the theory and practice of IR. While a recognition of the socially constructed nature of reality may – in theory – be a potentially liberating and positive possibility, as the example of the often-impoverished trade debate demonstrates, it can often be unrecognized and unhelpful. Worse, some critics argue, it can often be a cynically constructed discourse designed to entrench the position and power of extant elites.

Be that as it may, the incontrovertible empirical reality is that the nature of trade has changed profoundly since the time of Smith and Ricardo. No longer does 'trade' occur between discrete national economies via the exchange of different commodities. Two of the biggest developments over recent years have been the growth of intra-industry and intra-firm trade (Dicken 2011). Countries, especially the established industrialized economies, often trade in precisely the same things. The proverbial person from Pluto might wonder why remarkably similar goods are transported across the Pacific and the Atlantic in both directions. Europe both imports and exports several million cars a year, for example, and something like 30 or 40 percent of 'trade' in manufactured goods occurs between parent companies and subsidiaries in various parts of the world (O'Brien and Williams 2010). Such is the supposedly beneficial logic of global competition; it is also one of the structurally embedded impediments to developing a collective approach to managing climate change and creating a sustainable environment. The other noteworthy feature of intra-firm trade that occurs within the confines of a single multinational corporation (MNC) is that it opens up opportunities for 'transfer pricing' and profit shifting in the process (Sikka and Willmott 2010).

State-business relations

Global and/or regional production networks are another of the distinctive features of the contemporary global political economy (Yeung 2016; Gereffi et al. 2005). They are simultaneously both an expression of the efficiency gains brought about by modularization, containerization, and general technological development on the one hand, and a fundamental challenge to the autonomy and capacities of individual states on the other. One of the challenges for national governments everywhere is to ensure that 'their' economic space and 'national champions' are situated advantageously in production processes that often have an implacably transnational logic. The auto manufacturing and electronic industries are quintessential examples of industries that have been transformed by the possibility of disaggregating the production process and locating individual parts of productive activities where the competitive advantages are greatest (Dicken 2011). Crucially, the economic logic underpinning corporate strategies is often transnational and identification with – much less loyalty to – a particular national jurisdiction is frequently a secondary consideration. 'Winning' a trade war is consequently much more difficult than some people would have us believe (Farrell 2018).

Or it is in many Western economies, at least, where there is notionally an arms-length relationship between states and private sector business. In China and East Asia more generally a very different tradition prevails. Not only is there a long-standing tradition of state 'interference' in economic activity, but the relationship between the state and indigenous business is often much closer and more collusive than it is in the West (Gomez 2002). Indeed, as we shall see in more detail in subsequent chapters, the continuing existence of state-owned enterprises (SOEs) in China and the government's desire to maintain close oversight, if not control, of what it judges to be 'strategically' important parts of the economy (Szamosszegi and Kyle 2011), has profound implications for the content of public policy at the national level, and increasingly at the *transnational* level as China becomes a more active player in processes associated with global governance, and the ideas and institutions that shape it.

The so-called 'varieties of capitalism' literature has usefully drawn attention to the very different ways that broadly similar capitalist processes are organized in Western Europe, the 'Anglo-American economies' and much of East Asia (Hall and Soskice 2001). Not only are economies and relationships between business and government frequently organized in very different ways but such differences show no sign of disappearing and this presents a potential hurdle to the development of all-embracing international regulatory frameworks. Ideas about the appropriate role of the state, for example, are very different and often at odds with some of the assumptions about the nature of economic development. The 'developmental state' tradition pioneered by Japan is predicated on the assumption that the state can *and should* play a proactive role in encouraging the course of economic development (Tabb 1995). While they may be loath to admit it, China's economic planners have learned many important lessons from Japan about the benefits of state interventionism (Heilman and Shih 2013). Such developmental strategies underpin some of China's distinctive ideas about the sort of regulatory frameworks that might be appropriate at the transnational level.

These issues assume a wider importance when we consider that many observers think the authority and competence of the state – especially in the West – is being profoundly undermined by a variety of forces and challenges that are associated with broadly conceived processes of globalization. Not only are MNCs frequently larger than many individual states when measured as economic entities, but they have a potential mobility that nationally based political actors do not. Despite a growing interest in the possibility of international cooperation, one of the most enduring features of the contemporary international system is that there is a fundamental difference between the dynamics of political and economic space: political actors are still overwhelmingly nationally based and with a concomitantly limited frame of reference and action. Many economic actors, by contrast, are often potentially mobile, and able to play off one national jurisdiction against another in a process of 'regulatory arbitrage' (Rodrik 1997).

Such pressures have become especially acute in the financial sector, which has even greater potential mobility than firms that may have long-term investments in the 'real' economies of various states. In addition to the inherent mobility of financial sector actors and their highly fungible assets, international money markets, and the ratings agencies that offer advice on the credibility of various government policies can exert significant pressure on individual governments (Sinclair 2005). In an environment of market-determined exchange rates and high capital mobility, states are especially vulnerable to the adverse judgments of powerful market actors. The relationship between states and the private sector is especially significant in this context, and not just at the national level. On the contrary, much of the regulation of international financial markets and other important elements of the international commercial system are under the control of unelected private sector actors who are only accountable to their members (Braithwaite and Drahos 2000). Despite the fact that (some) states may have helped create this regulatory environment, the reality is that many of the bodies that now provide some form of global governance are beyond the control of (most) states.

Private sector regulatory bodies are not the only actors challenging and seeking to influence state policy, of course. The precise impact and significance of the rise of international nongovernmental organizations is a matter of some debate, as we shall see in the next chapter. That they have become more visible, significant, and numerous is not in doubt, however. Some observers argue that there is a functional necessity driving the emergence of so-called international nongovernment organizations (INGOs) and that they have expanded in tandem with the globalization of the nation-state because they are 'oriented to intellectual, technical, and economic rationalization' (Boli and Thomas 1999: 45). These issues and their theoretical implications are taken up in more detail in the next chapter. What is noteworthy at this stage is that there is a growing number of actors placing pressure on states that are simultaneously trying to satisfy the rising expectations of the populations they claim to represent, while their capacity to tax footloose economic actors is being continually challenged and eroded. The so-called 'fiscal crisis of the state' may not be a new phenomenon (O'Connor 1979), but it is one that is being exacerbated, not least because policymakers are reluctant to shift the burden onto their relatively immobile populations.

Political power beyond the state

The possibility that there may have been a long-term shift in the balance of power between broadly-conceived states and markets is important not simply for practical reasons. One of the more noteworthy manifestations of, and potential contributors to, global governance has been the emergence of 'global civil society' (Keane 2003). As we shall see in more detail in the next chapter, some observers claim that if global governance is to be achieved it will be dependent on complex emergent patterns of 'networked relations among different kinds of actors with different kinds of authority and power that are embedded in both formal and informal arrangements'

(Barnett and Sikkink 2009: 75). The underlying idea is that as global forces and transnational interconnectedness become more established and universal, political space outside the space will continue to expand and the scope of civil society will become global. Yet even before the recent resurgence of nationalism and populism raised profound questions about the extent and depth of global civil society, admirers of the concept conceded that 'empirical analysis of global civil society is tied up with normative agendas and associated contests over the meaning and significance of particular practices and ideas, including the idea of global civil society itself' (Dryzek 2012: 112).

Collective efforts to manage the natural environment also highlight another aspect of the evolving international order that have played an important historical role: the rise of international organizations (IOs) and the potential for multilateral regimes to contribute to international cooperation and global governance. As with INGOs, IOs have grown significantly in number; they have also had a significant impact on, and formal responsibility for, problem solving and encouraging cooperation in a number of important issue areas. One of the initial causes of the development of IOs was the sheer technical necessity of developing mechanisms that would allow growing international interconnectedness to actually occur. As early as the nineteenth century, a range of new IOs, such as the International Telegraph Union in 1885, the International Railway Congress Association in 1885, the International Bureau of Weights and Measure in 1875, and the Universal Postal Union in 1874, emerged to establish common technical standards and imperial rules (Mazower 2012; Howland 2015).

The United Nations (UN) is, perhaps, the best known and most important of the surge of IOs that emerged in the twentieth century, and it highlights many of the strengths and weaknesses of such organizations (Starrs 2017). Significantly, the UN was born in the aftermath of the Second World War and the abject failure of its predecessor, the League of Nations, as we shall see in later chapters. For many IR scholars, especially one of the founders of modern realism (Carr 1998 [1939]), the failure of the League was confirmation of the limitations of international cooperation and the continuing primacy of national interests. This is a major claim that will be addressed in subsequent chapters. What is significant at this stage is that the establishment of the UN and other key IOs, and other security organizations such as the North Atlantic Treaty Organization (NATO), as well as economic institutions like the World Bank and the International Monetary Fund (IMF), marked a noteworthy commitment to the potential for international cooperation in order to pursue common goals.

Unsurprisingly, no goal was considered to be worthier of pursuit in the aftermath of the Second World War than the pursuit of peace. Significantly, the UN was, like the failed League of Nations before it, predicated on the idea that security might most sustainably be pursued on a *collective* basis. The UN also enshrined certain principles and goals – human rights, freedom of religion and the like – that were judged to have universal applicability and relevance (Gareis 2012). It is also important to recognize that, unlike the nineteenth century, the incentives for interstate cooperation and the constraints on autonomous state action were shaped by forces that simply did not exist in earlier epochs. The horrors of the Second World War and the subsequent rapid emergence of nuclear weapons has a sobering impact on the foreign and strategic policy calculations of political elites everywhere (Deudney 2007; Mueller 1989).

Yet one of the central challenges facing the UN and any other regime or body seeking to coordinate the actions of states through multilateral auspices has been overcoming the sacrosanct nature of sovereignty (Krasner 1999). Respect for national sovereignty was built into the operational principles of the UN from the outset, creating a fundamental potential obstacle to cooperation above and beyond some of the unique impediments that have dogged the UN, such as the highly unrepresentative, but very powerful, Security Council. While it may be true that sovereignty is ultimately a socially constructed idea as some IR scholars claim (Glanville 2013), this does not make it any less of a potential stumbling block when it comes to encouraging cooperation between states that have very different ideas about how or whether to address particular issues. This was true before the so-called 'rise of the rest' that I discuss in Chapter 5; it is doubly so now.

The travails of the EU are the most dramatic illustration of how difficult it is to move beyond the sovereignty question, even for the best-intentioned and successful IOs. While it is undoubtedly the case that the EU pioneered new forms of sovereignty pooling that seemed set to permanently alter the actual practice of IR in one important part of the world, at least, recent events have thrown such assumptions into doubt. As I explain in more detail in Chapter 6, internal divisions within the EU, a lack of popular support for a more powerful federal structure, and widespread doubts about the EU's capacity to deal with major economic and social crises have undermined confidence in, and the credibility of, the world's hitherto most successful and fully developed form of collective governance. The question that confronts advocates of global governance as a consequence is this: if collective governance is not even achievable and sustainable on a regional basis, what hope is there for the global variety?

Concluding remarks

That the world has changed is not in doubt. Deciding quite when the most significant changes occurred, what drove them, and how they might be significant is far less certain, however. Nevertheless, it is clear that some of the most important institutions and the social relationships that ultimately constitute them have evolved over time, and that their behaviors are different as a consequence. This is not to suggest, however, that there is something teleological about the direction of such changes. As the discourse about the 'end of history' reminds us (Fukuyama 1992), there is nothing inevitable about the direction of historical development or the consequences of international change, no matter how fundamental, transformative, and even desirable they may seem at the time.

This is an especially important consideration for advocates of global governance. There is noteworthy normative commitment on the part of many admirers of 'cosmopolitan' approaches to complex transitional problems, which argue that human beings share a common humanity that transcends national borders and which notionally gives them similar rights (Cabrera 2006). Such values and views are generally not shared by the populations of states such as China, however, which is currently in the midst of a nationalist revival that frequently spills over into chauvinism. Nor is China alone in this regard, of course. As I explain in Chapter 5, the 'rise of the rest' is threatening to overturn many of the most firmly held assumptions about the nature and direction of political change and development in the world, placing major impediments in the way of possible global governance. Even in the so-called 'developed' world, which has done most to create the institutional framework and normative context for greater cooperation, some populations and policymakers are turning away from collective projects and potentially vital IOs are coming in for sustained criticism.

And yet, paradoxically enough, it is clear that the international system is integrated and interdependent to a degree that has never occurred before, and even the most nationalist of governments must come to terms with the reality of what that means. North Korea may be fiercely protective of its national autonomy, but its aberrant behavior is largely driven by its response to external pressures. While it may be the practical consequences of 'rogue' state behavior that understandably dominates the debate, trying to understand the underlying drivers of even 'normal' state behavior requires more than a simple accounting of the facts. Consequently, the next chapter considers the way in which the changing international system has been understood by the academic community.

2

The Theoretical Debate

Although some readers and many policymakers may be incredulous, theoretical debates about global governance are important for two principal reasons. First, given that the object of theory is to help us understand the world, theoretical developments are potentially illuminating. It might seem unnecessary to point this out, but one of the most common complaints about IR theory in particular is that it is not 'relevant' and/or accessible. This is possibly less of a problem for more narrowly conceived theories of governance, which are often self-consciously oriented toward problem-solving, but even debates about governance are not immune from criticisms about introspective self-absorption and irrelevance. But as Chris Reus-Smit (2012: 530) points out, 'it is unclear why we should be any more concerned about this than physicists or economists, who take theory, even high theory, to be the bedrock of advancement in knowledge'.

At the outset, I should admit that I subscribe to a rather traditional view of intellectual activity that is premised on the idea that it is actually possible to develop more plausible accounts of 'reality' – even the social variety. Having said that I am also conscious of the fact that the sort of political reality I am particularly interested in is a social construction and consequently susceptible to all of the ontological and epistemological complexities that implies. This leads directly to the second reason for taking theoretical debates about governance seriously: the increasingly politicized nature of the concept of 'governance' provides an illuminating window through which to view some of the most important policy debates of the last few decades. As Robert Cox (1986: 207, emphasis in original) famously pointed out, 'theory is always *for* someone and *for* some purpose'. In other words, knowledge – especially in the social sciences – is never value-free or politically innocent, but reflects a particular perspective and may be consciously designed to serve a political purpose. China's rise and the debate about and *construction* of domestic and foreign policy in that country reminds us that these questions remain valid and are taking on renewed geopolitical significance.

This chapter traces the evolution of the debate about governance and its increasingly global focus, before considering how ideas about governance and public policy have developed in China. One question to keep in mind throughout the subsequent discussion is about the relationship between knowledge and power. It is not necessary to be a follower of Michel Foucault (1980; 1991) to recognize that there is an important connection between the most influential ideational discourses of an era and particular modes of governance. At the international level, the dominant power of the era the ruling hegemon can also play a major role in promoting and normalizing certain ideas (Lipschultz 2005). Britain's ideas about free trade and the gold standard were highly influential in the nineteenth century, for example, just as America's ideas about economic and, to a lesser extent, political liberalism were instrumental in shaping the postwar international order.

Significantly, China's policymaking and scholarly communities are becoming increasingly interested in developing their own distinctive ideas about the way we think about the international system and development, which reflect their own unique historical experience. The question to consider in this context, therefore, is whether China's material dominance will bring about a similar increase in its ideational influence. In short, will China, like the United States, have the capacity to promote distinctive ideas about governance, IR, and the normative and regulatory principles that should underpin the international system? Before trying to answer these questions, however, it is worth providing a brief reminder of assumptions that inform some of the most influential strands of IR theory as they continue to inform academic debates and – in the case of realism, at least – the actual practice of interstate relations.

The conventional wisdom

Realism is by far the most influential paradigm among the international policymakers in the West and in China (Booth 2011). It is also the oldest. Some of its adherents claim that precisely the same kinds of underlying dynamics that were supposedly at work when Thucydides reported on the Peloponnesian War in the fifth century BC continue to shape international behavior now. States, the argument goes, live in a condition of anarchy, with no transnational authority to impose order, much less justice. Consequently, individual states – the key actors in the system – are involved in a constant struggle for survival in which the accumulation of power, especially the military variety, is the only guarantee of security. It is a self-help system in which states must look after and pursue their own interests. Conflict is always a possibility in such a system. The only way of avoiding or postponing such an outcome is by establishing a credible balance of power, in which the material resources of states, acting singly or in alliances, can counter the offensive potential of possible rivals and enemies. The 'Concert of Europe' in the nineteenth century is the quintessential example of a successful balance of power. Its subsequent breakdown led – almost inevitably many realists would argue – to conflict. This rather pessimistic, zero-sum view of the world has had some notable champions and practitioners in the United States, including the likes of Henry Kissinger and George Kennan.

There are some long-standing powerful criticisms of realism and its progeny, 'neorealism', which provides a rather abstract, ahistorical reading of international relations. Neorealism claims that state behavior is a consequence of the international system itself (Waltz 1979). Such 'structural' readings of state behavior are not good at accounting for the very different forms of politics, economics, and even strategic thinking that inform the actions of policymakers in countries with strikingly different attitudes to security issues and much else. To be fair, some early and influential advocates of realist theory, such as the German émigré Hans Morgenthau (1973), did take national differences seriously, as does so-called classical realism. However, realist theory entirely failed to predict the end of the Cold War, or the fact that it led to a period of unipolarity and relative stability, rather than conflict and a new balance of power directed at the incumbent hegemon. It was an outcome that was difficult to explain in a world of supposedly 'like units' afflicted by chronic insecurity.

Indeed, what Richard Ashley (1984) famously described as the 'poverty of realism' became even more apparent in the 1990s. It is no surprise, perhaps, that this led to a growing interest in the role of institutions and ideas both in maintaining a remarkable and durable interstate peace and in shaping the behavior of policymakers. At least some states seemed to recognize the contradiction implicit in the 'security dilemma', which highlighted the fact that no amount of defense spending could guarantee security if possible rivals were guided by the same assumptions about the possible need to provide for their own security (Booth and Wheeler 2008). Accounting for different state behaviors led to a growing interest by liberal theorists in particular in the role of international organizations and their capacity to provide collective goods and realize positive-sum outcomes (Keohane 1989). Many of the insights derived from this liberal view of the world have fed directly into debates about global governance and the way that it might be constituted and understood.

In contrast to realists, liberals tend to be far more optimistic about human beings and their capacity to learn and address so-called collective action problems – or issues that cannot be resolved by individuals (be they people or states) acting alone. The provision of national defense is a classic example of this problem but so, too, is the provision of the sort of regulatory framework and agreements that allow an interconnected, transnational economy. It was precisely such observations that underpinned a growing interest in the theory and practice of 'liberal institutionalism', which focused on the role of states and IOs in creating new regimes in particular issue areas such as economic and security cooperation, and more recently the environment. Not only do many liberals believe that international cooperation is possible, mutually beneficial, and actually capable of cooperatively managing particular problems, but many thought that such ideas would ultimately triumph because they were in the national interest as well as the collective variety (Moravcsik 1997).

It is partly because of what is seen as the inherent attractions and benefits of liberalism as the bedrock of the postwar international order that some scholars believe it will endure, no matter what either the United States or China may do. John Ikenberry is one of the most prominent and influential champions of the value and durability of the liberal international order:

> there is no competing global organizing logic to liberal internationalism. An alternative, illiberal order – a 'Beijing model' – would presumably be organized around exclusive blocs, spheres of influence, and mercantilist networks. It would be less open and rule-based, and it would be dominated by an array of state-to-state ties. But on a global scale, such a system would not advance the interests of any of the major states, including China. The Beijing model only works when one or a few states opportunistically exploit an open system of markets. But if everyone does, it is no longer an open system but a fragmented, mercantilist, and protectionist complex – and everyone suffers. (Ikenberry 2011: 63)

These are important claims that need to be kept in mind when thinking about ideological content of global governance as well as its practical realization. As we shall see, there is no doubt that both the United States *and* China have benefited from the postwar international order, but this is no guarantee of its durability or resistance to change. Not only is China developing a rather different political economy at both the domestic and international levels, but even in the West there are growing doubts about – even hostility toward – some forms of broadly liberal policies. *Neo*liberalism is often associated with the sometimes brutal imposition of economic policies that are associated with growing inequality, diminished social welfare, and the demise of a sense of community even at the national level (Harvey 2007; Boas and Gans-Morse 2009). Some scholars have employed the Foucauldian idea of 'governmentality' to argue that the populations of 'advanced liberal' societies are especially prone to being manipulated by governments (Rose 1993), and that even the seemingly most 'progressive' expression of new social movements at the international level are complicit in reproducing the status quo (Lipshultz 2005: 55).

Whatever the merits of such arguments, attention to the way the people in general and policymakers in particular thought about themselves, their relationships, and the way that they might act has become an increasingly prominent focus of attention. Thinking about 'what makes the world hang together', as Ruggie (1998) put it, became a major priority of a rapidly developing school of constructivism. The key focus here was the role that ideas and norms might play in the social construction of reality. Although some of these basic insights and claims had been around for some time (Berger and Luckman 1967), the supposedly post-ideological environment that prevailed in the 1990s led to a growing interest in the way intangible factors might influence the identity and behavior of actors, and not just state-based ones either. On the contrary, constructivists have been keen to draw attention to the role of transnational actors and social movements in shaping the zeitgeist (Checkel 1999; Blyth 2002). Quite how successful they have been in this endeavor is a matter of some debate, but whatever one may think about the relative merits of these different theoretical approaches it is worth keeping them in mind when thinking about the practice, even the possibility of global governance.

Governance

Historical context is important even when thinking about something as apparently abstract and timeless as theoretical concepts. And yet the way scholars think about questions of governance, the issues that are considered to be amenable to analysis, and even improvement as a consequence of placing them in a governance framework has expanded significantly. The achievement and management of security, for example, is now considered to be – in part, at least – a problem of effective governance. Likewise, the evolution, integration, and interdependence of the international system has brought about concomitant changes in the way scholars think about the nature of governance in a global era. Before considering these theoretical innovations in any detail, however, it is important to remind ourselves of what the basic concerns of governance theory actually are.

Conceptualizing governance

One fairly standard but useful definition of governance (of the nonglobal variety) is provided by Kooiman (1993: 2) who suggests that 'governing' involves 'all those activities of social, political and administrative actors that can be seen as purposeful efforts to guide, steer, control or manage (sectors or facets of) societies'. More specifically and pointedly, Fukuyama (2013: 350) argues that governance should be thought of as 'a government's ability to make and enforce rules, and to deliver services, regardless of whether that government is democratic or not'. The key point here is that effective governance is not necessarily exclusively associated with, or dependent on, democratic forms of political organization. Indeed, a growing number of scholars have begun to argue either that there is potentially something 'functionally' superior about meritocratic, even authoritarian regimes (Bell 2015) or that democratic polities are incapable of addressing contemporary problems and should learn from their nondemocratic Asian counterparts (Berggruen and Gardels 2013).

Historically minded economic theorists may be right to argue that the West managed to develop property rights of a sort that allowed economic and political development in the first phases of capitalist transformation (North and Thomas 1973), but the world is a very different place now and such 'first mover' advantages may no longer apply. Indeed, it has been persuasively argued that there are potentially distinct advantages to 'late development', if states have the capacity and the political will to realize them (Gerschenkron 1966). This is, in many ways, the story of East Asia's 'miraculous' development in the period since the Second World War (Kohli 2004). Some would argue that the failure to absorb possible historical lessons and to establish the preconditions for economic take-off helps to explain the slower pace of development in Latin America and Africa (de Soto 2000; Acemoglu and Robinson 2012).

One of the key determinants of effective governance at the national level, whether the state in question is democratic or not, is 'state capacity'. In this context, Polidano (2000: 810) distinguishes between 'policy capacity' (which he defines as the ability to structure the decision-making process, coordinate it throughout government, and utilize informed analysis) and 'implementation authority' (which he suggests is the ability to carry out decisions and enforce rules). A key determinant of the effectiveness of the state is not simply the expertise and competence of the individuals who ultimately constitute 'the state', but the state's institutionalized relationship with the society of which it is a part. 'Strong' states in this context are those that can 'extract, regulate and appropriate' (Migdal 1988: 4), something that is in turn profoundly affected by the existing social structures within which a particular state is embedded. Some states confront inherently more challenging problems than others simply because of their unique inherited constraints and potentials.

If states cannot raise taxes, for example, the prospects for effective governance are slim – and vice versa, of course (Hobson 1997). States need to have both the ability to mobilize the nationally demarcated populations and the wherewithal to underwrite policies and the personnel to implement them. For a state to function effectively it needs what Michael Mann (1993: 59) called 'infrastructural power'. Infrastructural power is the 'institutional capacity of a central state, despotic or not, to penetrate its territories and logistically implement decisions. This is collective power, "power through" society, coordinating social life through state infrastructures.' Like Fukuyama and Polidano, Mann is agnostic about whether a democratic or a despotic state is likely to be better equipped to achieve this. The possibility that Chinese forms of governance may actually be functionally superior is a possibility that is being actively championed by a growing number of scholars in China (Shih and Huang 2013), not to mention by China's president, Xi Jinping (2014a), of course.

Significantly, there is a good deal of historical evidence to support claims about the importance of the state's role and the attitudes of its policy elites in East Asia, especially in determining economic outcomes (Wade 1990; Kohli 2004). In East Asia in particular, the historical experience of the so-called developmental state not only illustrates the potentially efficacious role of the state in planning the course of economic development and mobilizing social resources, but also highlights the contested and politicized nature of the debate about what the state's role *should* be. For many Western economists, as well as officials in powerful agencies such as the World Bank, the success of East Asia's 'miracle' economies was a challenge to mainstream ideas about economic development and the appropriate role of the state (Wade 1996).

Even after the World Bank (1993, 1997) eventually acknowledged that the state had played an important role in accelerating the course of economic development in first Japan and then a number of other East Asian states that emulated its successful developmental strategies, this did not mark the end of ideological contestation between rival Western and Asian intellectual camps. On the contrary, as we shall see, such debates continue and have assumed renewed importance in light of China's recent development and the highly 'interventionist' role of the state in that process. Significantly, it is a role that the current generation of leaders shows no sign of wanting to relinquish, despite claims about the declining capacity of China's own governance regime (Pei 2016).

Despite the fact that 'statist' readings of international politics and development have become decidedly unfashionable in some academic circles these days, China's rise in particular highlights the continuing importance of nationally based political structures and forces. Some observers may not like the idea of powerful authoritarian states and the nationalistic discourses that accompany them, but this is not going to make them go away. On the contrary, with 'the West' apparently in retreat (Luce 2017), some have argued that 'China is not becoming more like us; we are becoming more like them' (Kuttner 2018: 284). But before we consider the role of China's political practices and ideas in any detail, it is important to say something about the way debates about governance have evolved.

The rise of 'good' governance

Some ways of governing are clearly better than others. Even those scholars that drew attention to the historically crucial role of the state in facilitating economic development also recognized that patterns of governance varied significantly and 'strong' states could be vehicles for corruption, predation, and general misrule. Much depended, according to one of the most prominent theorists in this area (Evans 1995), on the degree of 'embedded autonomy' enjoyed by any state: if policy elites were too close to the business interests they sought to influence for the collective good, then they risked 'capture'. This is a debate that continues to this day, albeit in new forms that explicitly acknowledge the global dimension of contemporary governance practices (Underhill and Zhang 2008). It also forms part of the backdrop for the intellectual and policymaking revolution that swept through the so-called Anglo-American economies from the 1980s onward.

It is clear that the forceful, ideologically committed leadership of Ronald Reagan and Margaret Thatcher played an important role in championing new ideas about economic management and political order during the 1980s. And yet such ideas had been around for decades without having any discernible impact on the widely accepted Keynesian consensus that underpinned the broadly based liberal order that emerged in the period following the Second World War. I explain these changes in more detail in the next chapter. The point to emphasize here is that the apparent exhaustion of the Keynesian model and the concomitant 'fiscal crisis of the state' opened up a political space in which powerful political actors such Reagan and Thatcher could promote a new political and economic agenda (O'Connor 1979; Hall 1989). In other words, there is a close relationship between long-term structural change and the relative effectiveness of agency in determining policy outcomes. This is a complex dialectical process in which structural constraints play an important role in determining what actors can actually do (Beeson 2017a). As Stephen Bell (2011: 899) puts it, 'structures (or institutions) are produced by the thoughts and actions of agents over time, but, at any given time institutions are not simply reducible to agents or what they think'.

It is important to revisit the period in which these new ideas about domestic governance took hold because they continue to influence contemporary debates about the most 'efficient' forms of government and the appropriate role of the state, and not just in the Anglo-American economies where they largely originated. The scare quotes are merited because the very idea of efficiency is ultimately a socially constructed concept and one person's notion of what that could or should refer to may be very different from another's (Heilbroner 1990). Indeed, there is an increasingly acrimonious if unresolved debate about what sorts of functions governments ought to be responsible for in the first place in an era when, despite all the criticisms that are leveled against professional politicians – in the West, at least (Hay 2007) – expectations about the sorts of services states provide continue to grow. These potentially unrealizable and incompatible expectations form part of the backdrop for the rise of what came to be known as neoliberalism in the 1980s (Harvey 2007).

For our purposes, what is crucial about neoliberalism and its championing of 'small' governments, free markets, and an open international political economy is that it became something of a universal template for governmental best practice; or it did in the Anglo-American economies, at least. The implications are captured by Andrew Gamble and it is worth quoting him at length. For Gamble (2009: 5), neoliberalism

is not just one standpoint among many in the political marketplace, but in part reflects and justifies the fundamental structures that underpin and circumscribe that marketplace. If neoliberalism were just another doctrine, it would be easier to dismiss it, but it also reflects something much more fundamental in the political economy of modernity – the recognition that there are certain characteristics of modern society, such as the extended division of labour, individual property rights, competition and free exchange, that have to be accepted as givens rather than choices. In this sense, the main dispute in political economy in the modern era has been settled, and settled substantially in favour of neoliberalism.

Even in the few years since these words were written, though, a number of developments – especially the rise of China and the growth of economic nationalism, not least in the United States – have raised doubts about the continuing primacy of neoliberal ideas; as they have about the primacy of the United States itself. Nevertheless, neoliberal thought was instrumental in underpinning the rise of 'New Public Management' (NPM).

Although NPM is a more nuanced and policy-oriented framework than neoliberalism, its central concerns sprang from a dissatisfaction with existing forms of government and the 'overloaded' nature of the state. Two aspects of NPM theory were especially important: marketization and managerialism, or the introduction of corporate-style incentive structures into the internal operations of the state. The underlying assumption informing both these initiatives was that market forces are the best ways of allocating resources and driving growth, and that the private sector is inherently more efficient than its public counterpart (Self 1993). The selling-off of formerly state-owned assets was given a veneer of intellectual credibility through the discourse of NPM despite its inherently ideological origins. The fact that impoverished states could benefit from the windfall gains that the privatization of key parts of national infrastructure generated was another attraction of the new conventional wisdom in much of the so-called Anglosphere (Vucetic 2011).

Yet whatever the inherent merits of NPM theory may or may not have been – and recent history has produced some spectacular failures of 'outsourcing' strategies (Ford 2018) – it has had a limited impact in many parts of the world. Indeed, NPM theory has had relatively little impact in China. On the contrary, China's 'communist' government not only retains control over the 'commanding heights' or strategically important elements of the domestic economy (Szamosszegi and Kyle 2011), but under Xi Jinping's leadership the state is also trying to assume an ever-larger place in a more centralized political system (Callick 2017). This is an especially important consideration when trying to assess the impact of foreign ideas on China, and whether states in other parts of the world have the capacity to replicate the sorts of public–private partnerships that have proliferated elsewhere – even supposing the political will to do so existed in the first place.

In one of the most influential formulations of the 'new' governance, Rhodes (1997: 15) suggested that it should now be thought of as 'self-organizing, interorganizational networks characterized by interdependence, resource exchange, rules of the game and significant autonomy from the state'. The possibility that networks of one sort or another might play a new, positive, and productive role in complex governance relationships has rapidly become an established idea, in part because of the pioneering work of Manuel Castells (1996). Yet the idea that political space within which governance occurs should be expanded and that nonstate actors should play a larger role in policymaking is generally an anathema to most of the rising states that are invariably authoritarian and not interested in power-sharing arrangements (see Chapter 5). Even if they were, the limited institutional infrastructure outside the state in many of the rising powers means that developing that sorts of 'policy networks' that feature so prominently in the Western literature is inherently problematic (Beeson 2001).

Nevertheless, policy networks have been a prominent part of the theoretical and practical development of governance in the West (Marsh and Smith 2000). Generally, policy networks revolve around particular issue areas with a view to generating policy. They are composed of government and nonstate actors, who may be drawn from civil society, NGOs, or private sector business interests. Governance in Western polities is frequently seen as occurring through, or with the assistance of, these networks, which may be drawn upon because of their supposed expertise in specific policy domains. The overall significance of the policy network approach was to draw attention to the informal relationships within policy communities, and their horizontal rather than hierarchical nature, as was traditional within state-dominated policymaking processes (Kenis and Schneider 1991). In fact, there is a common assumption in the literature that the entire policymaking process is becoming more decentralized, with significant implications for the state's power, authority, and even its internal architecture (Bevir and Rhodes 2010).

One of the biggest drivers of changes in the state's role and the nature of the governance processes in which it is involved, the argument goes, is globalization. If correct, it has implications even for those states that jealously guard their sovereignty. This would be a potential challenge for those states that were unenthused about the sorts of neoliberal policy ideas that were being promoted – and imposed – by powerful external agencies like the World Bank (1994) under the guise of 'good governance'. As we shall see, much of the conventional wisdom about optimal economic policies for would-be developing states proved inappropriate and counterproductive. The general point to emphasize is that contingent historical circumstances are important determinants of developmental outcomes, and debates about appropriate policy are likely to be contested, politicized, and reflect different national experiences and values (Taniguchi and Babb 2009). Such possibilities are important to keep in mind in the context of any move toward global governance.

Governance goes global

As political, economic, and security relations have globalized, the concepts we use and the way we think about governance have tried to keep pace. The fact that so many of the global processes described in the preceding chapter are new and/or intensifying means that they are inherently historically unprecedented in their scale, scope, and impact. This makes the task of making sense of these changes challenging, especially for realists who claim that drivers of the international states system are essentially unchanged and revolve around competition and the pursuit of national security. And yet, one of the pillars of the international system – the state – has been at the epicenter of many of these changes. While some IR scholars have made important contributions to the ensuing theoretical debate, it is noteworthy that realists have remained remarkably unmoved by such developments, despite the fact that the ontological status of the state is nothing like as secure as it was. The state's very ability to provide basic security is under challenge as never before, in large part because some threats – such as climate change – are implacably transnational in nature. Consequently, the empirical status of the state, especially when measured in terms of its capacity, competence, authority, and legitimacy, has been transformed at best, radically undermined at worst.

Even before the global environment became the defining collective action problem of the era, many scholars thought the state was 'in retreat' (Strange 1996), or being overwhelmed by global forces it was increasingly powerless to control – on its own, at least. Significantly, much of this early literature on the possible decline of the state was inspired by perceived changes in the relationship between economic and political activity. We have become more accustomed to the possibility that there are many losers as well as winners associated with globalization (Rodrik 1997; Kuttner 2018), but it is important to remember that some globalization enthusiasts thought that the 'borderless world' would be an unequivocally positive development and the state's declining role and importance would be beneficial. In true Smithian fashion, the likes of Kenichi Ohmae (1990) argued that the state's role should be restricted to providing education and infrastructure and allowing market forces and the enlightened self-interest of business to work their magic.

Such views looked overly optimistic and at odds with a rapidly evolving reality even at the time; now they look naïve. On the one hand, the state has simply failed to wither away. On the contrary, as we shall see, rising powers are doing all they can to reinforce state power and sovereignty. On the other hand, the state's relationship with its external environment has become significantly more complex and differentiated. Broad assertions about 'the state' make little sense when we recognize the enormous differences in the historical circumstances, capabilities, and power resources of various states in what is in many ways a very hierarchical system that is not populated by 'like units' (Hobson and Sharman 2005), as some of the most influential formulations in neorealist theory would have us believe (Waltz 1979). Such differences are especially stark and consequential in the security arena, but it was the emerging school of international political economy (IPE) that made some of the most important conceptual breakthroughs in the way we think about international system and the nature of, and potential for, global governance.

Governance and political economy

Remarkably enough in retrospect, the disciplinary study of politics and economics prior to the 1970s was a highly siloed affair with little mutual interest or recognition. For some in the economics profession it still is (Quiggin 2012). But things began to change in part because of Susan Strange's (1970) clarion call for reform, and in part because sheer material reality was proving too difficult to explain without recognizing the mutually constitutive impact of economic and political processes.

One of the most important early contributions to what would eventually become the major new field of IPE was Keohane and Nye's (1977) *Power and Interdependence: World Politics in Transition.* The key insight here was not simply that the actions of individual states were frequently shaped by their external environments, but that changes in what would come to be called the global political economy (GPE) were exerting new pressures and creating new relationships of 'interdependence' and vulnerability.

Importantly, Keohane and Nye drew attention to both the growing importance of economic forces and actors in such processes and the relative decline in the role of military power. Other scholars built on such ideas to argue that Japan represented the dawn of a new era of trading states in which success would be measured by economic development rather than by traditional military conquest and self-assertion (Rosecrance 1986). It is revealing and noteworthy that Japan actually illustrates the changing logic of state behavior and international competition, having achieved through foreign investment after the Second World War what it could not manage through conquest before it (Hatch and Yamamura 1996; Beeson 2014b). Debates about the importance of economic leverage are coming to the fore once again as China's growing use of 'geoeconomic' power is reinforcing its international importance and status (Zhang and James 2017).

As we saw in the previous chapter, globalization is associated above all with economic forces, and it is no surprise that it is increasingly commonplace to think of capitalism as a global phenomenon (Frieden 2006). However, it is one thing to consider that capitalism has become planetary in its scale and impact, it is quite another to suggest that some of the mechanisms and relationships that seek to govern it have achieved a similar universality and presence. Even those scholars who argued that the global economy was becoming more governable recognized that the sorts of institutions and initiatives that played a part in such processes continued to reflect domestic political pressures and a concomitant sense of national interests (Kapstein 1994) – no matter how discursively realized and contingent the latter might be. The challenge for the scholarly community was to develop conceptual frameworks that were sufficiently alert to the complexity of possible governance arrangements, while still having something meaningful to say about the way such processes actually worked and impacted on the international system.

One of the most important contributions in this context was made by James Rosenau who developed the highly influential idea of 'governance without government', which adumbrates many of the key ideas that have come to be associated with global governance. Rosenau (1992: 5) argued that what he called global order 'consists of those routinized arrangements through which world politics gets from one moment to the next'. In this context, he suggested that order and governance are mutually constitutive: 'there can be no governance without order and there can be no order without governance' (Rosenau 1992: 8). Importantly, Rosenau (1992: 14) offered a valuable way of unpacking and analyzing three distinct, yet interrelated elements that together made up a specific global order: ideational (what people understand about governance); behavioral or objective (what people routinely do); and the aggregate or political level (where governance occurs through rule-oriented regimes and institutions).

Rosenau was no starry-eyed Utopian, however. Despite offering a groundbreaking analysis of the possible mechanisms of global governance, he was under no illusions about quite how difficult it would be to achieve. He was particularly concerned about the possible forces that could undermine cooperation and the realization of sustainable international security (Rosenau 1990, 1995). For other observers, the ideational order and the routinization of social practices and norms that Rosenau drew attention to were actually a central part of the problem and of the maintenance of an irredeemably inequitable international order. Craig Murphy (2000: 789), for example, claimed that a form of global governance that was essentially predicated on economic liberalism and a faith in the efficacy of market forces was 'incapable of shifting resources from the world's wealthy to the world's poor, pro-market, and relatively insensitive to the concerns of labour and the rural poor'. The intergovernmental organizations created under the auspices of American hegemony, discussed in Chapter 3, were, many observers claimed, instrumental in reproducing and institutionalizing a particular set of ruling ideas (Hurrell 2001).

Two aspects of this general critique of especially liberal forms of putative global governance are worth emphasizing: the role of IOs and the possible class basis of the interests that were served in the creation of a liberal international order. One of the great ironies of contemporary scholarship in this area is that the most influential Marxist-inspired accounts of global governance and the possible role played by a transnational capitalist class have come from outside 'communist' China (Gao 2018). Yet for some critical scholars, such as Robert Cox, class forces were a central part of explanation of the durability of American hegemony and the creation of the postwar liberal order. Drawing on the work of the Italian Marxist, Antonio Gramsci, Cox argued that hegemonic orders were created by specific 'historic blocs' that were products of particular moments in the evolution of capitalism. An important and distinctive part of this process was the emergence of a 'transnational managerial class' that was embedded in key IOs such as the IMF and the World Bank (Cox 1987: 359). Other Marxist scholars made similar claims, arguing that 'transnational state cadres act as midwives of capitalist globalisation' (Robinson 2004: 101).

These views merit emphasis not only because Marxist ideas are ostensibly taken seriously in China, but because China's historical experience offers an important test case of the continuing validity of these sorts of claims. I take up these issues in more detail in Chapter 4, but even at this stage it is clear that China offers support as well as potential problems for these sorts of perspectives: to be sure, the Chinese economy and its own domestic governance practices have been profoundly affected by the country's incorporation in a global capitalist economy; at the same time, however, the Chinese state is fiercely nationalist and protective of domestic sovereignty and policy autonomy. This is where the role of IOs becomes important and potentially politically contentious.

Chinese policymakers have become interested in developing their own IOs, which are not dominated by the United States but which potentially reflect *their* ideas and interests. The motivations for such initiatives are not hard to discern: IOs are more than simply functional, problem-solving mechanisms designed to impartially realize the common good. On the contrary, as Barnet and Finnemore (1999: 700) argue,

> Global organizations do more than just facilitate cooperation by helping states to overcome market failures, collective action dilemmas, and problems associated with interdependent social choice. They also create actors, specify responsibilities and authority among them, and define the work these actors should do, giving it meaning and normative value. Even when they lack material resources, IOs exercise power as they constitute and construct the social world.

Whatever the class basis of the officials who populate and ultimately constitute IOs may be, one of the most important determinants of their impact and efficacy is the *authority* they enjoy and the consequent perceived *legitimacy* of their actions.

One of the perennial problems facing IOs is their legitimacy and accountability deficits (Kahler 2004). As we shall see, this is one of the most debilitating problems facing regional IOs such as the EU. IOs are composed of unelected officials who are not accountable to the general public. While this may be less of a problem in authoritarian states, in democracies it has become a major source of voter discontent, especially when the potentially legitimacy-conferring expertise of their personnel has also been undermined by a conspicuous failure to get to grips with important public policy issues of a sort that are detailed in subsequent chapters (Grant and Keohane 2005). It is important to remember that one of the original justifications for a more 'technocratic', expertise-based approach to problem-solving was the perceived limitations of professional politicians who couldn't be trusted to deal with politically sensitive issues such as interest rates (Fischer 1990). It is no coincidence that central banks were one of the first areas to be transformed by such changes (Polillo and Guillen 2005); they are also quintessential examples of a putative 'transnational managerial class'.

While the existence of so-called 'epistemic communities' of like-minded experts might be considered to be the quintessential expression of technical rationality and efficiency, the reality has been rather different of late. Even before the current rise of populist anger against 'unaccountable elites', followers of Michel Foucault had drawn attention to the way in which particular forms of knowledge might be used to enable forms of social control and regulation (Rose and Miller 1992). Recent events suggest that this is a much more complex and uncertain process than some analysts supposed, especially in the 'advanced' liberal economies that tended to be the principal focus of attention (Snyder 2017). Equally importantly, there are also clear limits to the potential influence of epistemic communities in promoting particular ideas about optimal policy reforms – a possibility that was especially clear in the attempted promotion of neoliberal economic reforms in the Asia-Pacific region (Beeson and Islam 2005).

What many of these approaches have in common is an implicit or explicit concern with power, which remains the most important concept in political science, albeit one of the most difficult to conceptualize at any level. One of the most useful and influential attempts to define the nature and impact of power in evolving forms of global governance has been developed by Barnett and Duvall (2005), who suggest that there are four distinct types of power at work in global governance: compulsory, institutional, structural, and productive.

Compulsory power is the stuff of traditional realist approaches, generally state-centric, and potentially involves coercion and the overcoming of resistance. Institutional power, by contrast, frequently occurs at a distance and indirectly; IOs and private regimes feature in this context. Structural power refers to the 'determination of social capacities and interests' (Barnett and Duvall 2005: 18). Class positions are one of the clearest theoretical examples of structurally embedded historical circumstances that can determine differential capacities, identities, and interests; so, too, are the long-term inequalities and asymmetries of power that continue to distinguish a highly uneven international system. Finally, productive power is concerned with 'the social processes and the systems of knowledge through which meaning is produced, fixed, lived, experienced and transformed' (Barnett and Duvall 2005: 20). The sorts of discursive processes highlighted by constructivists are central to this form of power. Overall, this framework helps to explain not just the obstacles to global governance, but the unambiguous reality that the international *system* is just that: it is neither anarchic, entirely ungoverned, nor without significant ordering principles that influence the behavior of states.

Governance – and the state? – transformed

Despite the possible obstacles to the seamless promotion of political ideas and economic policies that have been primarily associated with and developed by Western polities (Walter 2008), much of the academic debate about global governance focused on the degree of policy and institutional 'convergence' that might be occurring as a consequence of globalization (Baldwin 2016; Drezner 2005). Even with all of the caveats noted above, there clearly was something important happening at the level of what Fernand Braudel (1992) described as the *longue durée* and the underlying structural transformation of material civilization. The fact that China has now become a capitalist economy in all but name, is far more significant than the fact that China's version of capitalism is very different to the sort found in the Anglo-American economies (Peck and Zhang 2013).

For understandable reasons, however, much of the debate about the policy implications of globalization and the theoretical possibility of global governance has tended to focus on the here and now, even if that encompassed the last few decades. A number of features of the evolving scholarly debate in this context are important and worth unpacking. On the one hand, much contemporary research has focused on the ways some ideas have been 'diffused' through policy networks and social processes, which have become increasingly transnational (Dobbin et al. 2007; Stone 2008). On the other, a good deal of attention has been paid to the way the state has been affected by the possible erosion of national sovereignty and the concomitant need to cooperate with other states and nonstate actors to address collective action problems (Cerny 2010). These processes are clearly interconnected, to some degree mutually constitutive, and ultimately social. One of the key questions that emerges from both literatures is whether there is a certain degree of inevitability about such developments. Alternatively, do states – such as China – retain the capacity to act autonomously, or even to shape global processes to suit their own very specific, essentially national interests?

As one might expect with a topic as inherently complex as globalization there are a range of possible explanations for possible policy diffusion processes from sociology, political science, and IR (Dobbin et al. 2007). Some scholars emphasize the degree of 'learning' that may be occurring as less 'developed' states seek to copy the best practices of their more successful –

invariably Western – peers (Meseguer 2005). This idea always looked rather Eurocentric; now it looks like wishful thinking. In the aftermath of the so-called global financial crisis (GFC) that had its origins in the domestic failings of the American political and economic system, and which only really affected the United States and the EU countries, confidence about the supposed superiority of the Western model of capitalism looks woefully misplaced. More fundamentally, perhaps, the ideational status of the American economic system was seriously undermined, especially in comparison with the 'Chinese model', which proved remarkably resilient in the face of a crisis that was unambiguously made in the United States (Breslin 2011a).

More plausible explanations for the enduring influence of neoliberal ideas generally and of the so-called 'Washington consensus' of economic liberalization and reform in particular may be found in the activities of the IOs, on the one hand, and the increasing prominence and power of private sector actors, on the other. In a process that Sarah Babb (2012: 273) describes as 'coercive isomorphism', IOs continue to encourage particular types of policies by 'rewarding adoption (and punishing non-adoption) through various means, including the selective channeling of resources'. Less powerful states – rule takers – may have little choice other than to acquiesce to the demands of powerful IOs and the states that influence them – rule makers (Mastanduno 2009). This is learning of a sort, but not the sort of freely undertaken outcome of rational calculation that underpins much mainstream economic and even political theory.

It is also important to point out that the Washington consensus when translated into actual policy represented a very demanding list of reforms. Whatever the merits of fiscal discipline, trade and currency liberalization, privatization, tax reform, and the other staples of what Williamson (1993: 1334) – who coined the term Washington consensus – considered to be the 'common core of wisdom embraced by all serious economists', there were always questions about its appropriateness and viability in much of the 'developing world'. The fact that the principles of this doctrine were often imposed on reluctant (or incapable) governments, via 'conditionality' clauses that demanded far-reaching policy reforms from indebted governments in return for lending from the likes of the IMF and the World Bank, made them unpalatable as well as difficult to achieve (McMichael 2012). As we shall see, the 'Beijing consensus' presents no such challenges or obligations.

Generally, however, the rise of an increasingly powerful and footloose financial sector means that even the most powerful and capable of governments have become susceptible to the adverse judgments of private sector actors, such as rating agencies. Indeed, as Simmons and Elkins (2004: 173) point out, 'governments that resist ideational trends face reputational consequences that cast doubt on their approach to the economy and potentially the legitimacy of their governance'. One of the most consequential ideational trends and theoretical assumptions in this regard is the possibility that effective governance in a global era actually *necessitates* new types of relationships between states and other domestic and transnational actors. Indeed, even the very distinction between the domestic sovereign sphere and some notional 'external' sphere of action appeared to be breaking down and becoming less useful as the basis of addressing or making sense of policy challenges. In what Levi-Faur (2005: 13) described as a 'new chapter in the history of regulation',

> a new division of labor between state and society (e.g., privatization) is accompanied by an increase in delegation, proliferation of new technologies of regulation, formalization of interinstitutional and intrainstitutional relations, and the proliferation of mechanisms of self-regulation in the shadow of the state. Regulation, though not necessarily in the old-fashioned mode of command and control and not directly exercised by the state, seems to be the wave of the future.

Wolfgang Reinicke made a similar argument in an early analysis of the implications for *global* public policy. Reinicke claimed that sovereignty has lost much of its external significance as public policy is transformed by global forces. He suggests that 'the spatial reorganization of corporate activity leads to the emergence of a single, integrated economic geography defined by the reach of corporate industrial networks and their financial relations'. The net effect of these changes, Reinicke (1998: 7) contends, is that these new relationships challenge 'the operational dimension of internal sovereignty, as governments no longer have a monopoly of the legitimate power over the territory within which these private sector actors organize themselves'. While there is some question about how universal these changes are, there is less doubt that – in much of the West, at least – authority and legitimacy have shifted from states to unelected actors from the private sector. Indeed, David Lake (2010: 588) argues that 'in a world of global governance, states have no special authoritative status. Like all authorities, they negotiate their rights.'

Paradoxically, states have been responsible for many of these changes and have created the circumstances in which authority and real power have shifted from national governments. As I shall explain in more detail in the next chapter, the rise of global financial markets, and the independent governance of important institutions such as equity markets, has come about with the blessing and assistance of at least some states (Helleiner 1994). Nevertheless, no matter how the transfer of authority and responsibility may have occurred, the reality is that actors other than states now play a prominent part in international policy initiatives and their implementation. As a result, some observers argue that it now makes more sense to focus on the actors that are actually making consequential decisions, rather than simply assuming that it will be states or their representatives. As a result, Avant and colleagues (2010: 2) suggest that we should focus on what they call 'global governors', or 'those authorities who exercise power across borders for the purposes of affecting policy'. The key attribute of global governors is that they can 'create issues, set agendas, establish and implement rule or programs, and evaluate and/or adjudicate outcomes'.

This sort of approach usefully focuses attention on agency and the actual process of governing, even if such processes are not always entirely effective or uncontested. While the idea of global governors helps to explain the manner in which private sector actors have become more authoritative and even able to create what Cutler and colleagues (1999: 13) describe as 'private regimes', especially in economic issues areas governing business practices, it is important to emphasize that this is not necessarily an unproblematic process. On the contrary, the concentration of power in the hands of unelected, unaccountable (other than to their members), and self-regulating authorities begs crucial questions about who benefits. As Mattli and Woods (2009: 16) point out, there are fundamental asymmetries of information, financial resources, and technical expertise that encourage forms of 'regulatory capture', exacerbating the differences between – and the benefits that accrue to – insiders and outsiders. The potential damage that may result from such self-serving practices was painfully clear in the GFC, which was a product of a toxic combination of perverse incentive structures and poor oversight by state authorities who had effectively abrogated their former responsibilities (Baker 2010; Tett 2009).

Given the consequences that have flowed from some of the Anglo-American attempts at domestic and international governance reform, it is not surprising that there is often diminished enthusiasm for replicating them. Some less powerful states may have little option other than to adopt a form of 'mock compliance' so as to maintain good relations with important IOs and more powerful states (Walter 2008). A more fundamental consideration, even for states such as China with the capacity to vigorously resist policy reform if its leaders choose to do so, is that some forms of the new governance represent an existential threat to national sovereignty and the very institutional architecture of the state itself. Kanishka Jayasuriya (2004), for example, has argued that the role of neoliberal states has been reduced to insulating economic activity from political 'interference', a process that involves a transformation of the state itself as some regulatory functions are outsourced and/or transnationalized. While there is plainly something in this argument, it is also apparent that the fate of the state – especially powerful ones with the political will to maintain a degree of authority and autonomy – is in its own hands. As Bell and Hindmoor (2009) point out, states still matter because they have a capacity for 'metagovernance' in overseeing, coordinating, and steering governance relationships – should they choose to exercise it. Clearly, China's leaders, especially under Xi Jinping, are still very interested in metagovernance, which is what makes Chinese ideas about governance and IR so important.

Theory with Chinese characteristics?

One of the reasons that American international relations theory has been so influential, it is argued, is not necessarily because it is the best, but because the United States enjoys a hegemonic position that reinforces its ideational influence (Smith 2002). The relatively narrow, self-referential scope of much American IR and the prestige attached to publishing in prominent American journals tends to both entrench the dominance of perspectives that emerge from the United States and encourage a rather uncritical approach to key issues, such as great power contestation and the rise of China. As Levine and Barder (2014: 870) point out, 'the continuous emergence of sophisticated methodological tools to uncover the general patterns, causal relationships, or recurrent practices that largely constitute neo-positivist epistemologies and methodologies already presuppose an entire set of cognitively and historically constituted objects that remains unproblematized'.

Clearly there are exceptions to such criticisms, but it is striking that some of the most influential forms of scholarship in the United States start from the premise that, on the whole, American hegemony is a good thing, and that it ought to be preserved. Unsurprisingly, the rise of China is primarily seen as a threat to the established order, and not just by security specialists based in the United States. On the contrary, some of the most prominent American IR scholars go to great lengths to defend the broadly liberal international order the United States created. The possible links between national identity, theoretical perspectives, and the foreign policies of individual states is an interesting and under-researched area (Beeson and Zeng 2017), but one that has a potentially important place in discussions about global governance. Are scholars consciously or unconsciously reproducing perspectives that reflect or help to inform a distinct national position? Moreover, as China's power and influence continue to grow, will distinctive 'Chinese' perspectives emerge that not only reflect their unique historical experience and circumstances, but which explain and even legitimate China's foreign policy?

The answer to the last question would increasingly seem to be 'yes'. Before considering what some of these perspectives look like, however, it is important to acknowledge that, just as in the United States, not everyone subscribes to perspectives that reflect or champion a distinctively national orientation. For example, Tang Shiping (2013) of Fudan University, one of China's most prominent and innovative IR thinkers, not only engages primarily with the Western IR canon, but argues that a Darwinian perspective should be utilized to provide a universally applicable explanation of the evolution of the international system. Whether one agrees with Tang's perspective or not, this is precisely what one might expect of someone disinterestedly involved in the pursuit of truth. Whether or not the reader thinks such an endeavor is any longer worthwhile or even possible, Tang may be a noteworthy exception to an emerging trend in China. A distinctively Chinese approach to IR is emerging that may help to explain that country's attitudes to cooperation, global governance, American hegemonism, and much else.

All under heaven

By far the most distinctive and original idea to emerge from IR scholarship in China has been the concept of *Tianxia*, which is generally translated as 'all under heaven'. According to Zhao Tingyang, perhaps the most influential exponent of the concept's reemergence from Chinese history, *Tianxia* is a way of thinking about the world as a whole which has three meanings:

> (1) the Earth or all lands under the sky; (2) a common choice made by all peoples in the world, or a universal agreement in the 'hearts' of all peoples; (3) a political system for the world with a global institution to ensure universal order. This semantic trinity indicates that a physical world is far from being a human one. (Zhao 2009: 9)

Significantly, the *Tianxia* concept emerged during China's period of regional hegemony and the development of a 'tributary system' during the Tang dynasty (618–907). Unlike dominant Western IR scholarship, Chinese perspectives then (and now) recognize the reality that hierarchy, rather than notional sovereign equality, is the defining feature of international political activity (Kang 2010). Even if the idea of the 'international' may not have made a great deal of sense in premodern China, the possibility that order may be maintained or imposed on different peoples by a benign hegemonic state personified by the emperor was an attractive one (Dreyer 2015). In this formulation, Chinese dominance or hegemony was not something to be feared but – just like its contemporary American counterpart – an essential element in the preservation of a durable, mutually beneficial order.

To say that *Tianxia* is at odds with some of the more influential strands of Western IR would be putting it mildly, however. Even liberals assume that states are rational egoists intent on pursuing national interests, even if they recognize that cooperation and effective institutions might help them reach their goals. The conceptual distance from the pared back 'structural' orientation of neorealists who assume an anarchical world driven by competition and the struggle for survival could hardly be more dramatic. Even those observers who have serious doubts about the historical lineage and theoretical credibility of *Tianxia* recognize that does not necessarily undermine its importance. On the contrary, as William Callahan (2008: 759) points out, 'the power of Tianxia comes less from nuanced argument than from its strategic placement in China's discursive networks of power ... the success of The Tianxia System shows that there is a thirst for "Chinese solutions" to world problems, and a hunger for nationalist solutions to global issues, especially when the promote a patriotic form of cosmopolitan.'

So, does this mean that we can simply dismiss *Tianxia* and other ideas from Chinese culture and history as novel ways of legitimating China's hegemonic pretensions and 'assertive' foreign policies? Not really. Or no more than we can simply dismiss American claims to 'exceptionalism' or being what Madeleine Albright famously described as the 'indispensable nation', at least. Such discursive tropes are important if only because of their power to justify and even inform the actions of policymakers. It is also important to understand why so many scholars in China might take distinctively Chinese approaches to IR so seriously. Not only will Western interlocutors gain something from understanding ideas that may become increasingly consequential if China's rise continues, but they may actually have something to tell us about the way the current and possible future orders are constituted.

Qin Yaqing of the China Foreign Affairs University has made a twofold contribution to the debate about, and development of, Chinese IR. First, Qin has provided an overview of the development of IR in China since it opened up. The dominance of American perspectives during the formative period of IR studies in China is remarkable and striking (Qin 2009). Unsurprisingly, given at least some aspects of China's own intellectual tradition, broadly realist perspectives of the international system have been dominant (Johnston 1995). Realism's prominent place in China explains the popularity of prominent American scholars such as John Mearsheimer (2010), despite his notoriously pessimistic views about the implications of China's rise. Significantly, China has its own prominent realists, such as Yan Xuetong, who attracted much attention in the United States by provocatively outlining how China might defeat the United States in any new conflict (Yan 2011a). And yet Yan's realism is influenced by Chinese conceptions of international interaction, especially when he suggests that 'the basic cause of shifts in international power lies in the thought of the leaders rather than material force' (Yan 2011b: 67–8).

Qin's second contribution to China's emerging school of IR develops ideas about the possible importance of morality in world politics. Qin's 'relational' theory of world politics is very different from the conventional epistemological and ontological wisdom that informs Western traditions of thinking broadly, let alone in IR. The crucial idea that informs his work, which is built on and draws extensively from earlier Chinese scholars such as Confucius and Mencius, is that if we are to understand the world we need to focus not on individuals, but on the relations between them. This emphasis is significant not only because it is entirely at odds with the sort of 'methodological individualism' that is so pervasive in economics and more recently IR, but because it has potentially major implications for the practice of international relations, too. For Qin (2018: 335) what he calls relational governance is 'a process of negotiating socio-political arrangements that manage complex relationships in a community to produce order so that members behave in a reciprocal and cooperative fashion with mutual trust evolving over a shared understanding of social norms and human morality'. While this may seem like wishful thinking and a long way from international relations as they are currently practiced, it should not be dismissed out of hand. Not only does it actually point to a neglected but important element of cooperative international relations, but elements of these ideas can be found in the declaratory rhetoric of some of China's leaders, too.

Xi Jinping (2018) has made much of the idea of a 'shared future for mankind' and the need to 'uphold inclusiveness and seek harmony without uniformity … [and] to promote mutual learning among civilizations as it will help us build bridges of friendship, drive social progress, and safeguard peace for the region and beyond'. Skeptics may find it difficult to reconcile such noble sentiments with the reality of China's continuing militarization of the disputed South China Sea region, or its crackdown on ethnic populations in areas such as Xinjiang (Clarke 2018). Similar criticisms could be made about the gap between the United States' claim to be the guardian of liberty and the guarantor of international stability (Bacevich 2005), of course, but the point is that such criticisms *can* be made. This cannot be said about contemporary China, where the intellectual climate is becoming increasingly restrictive and where ideological conformity and social control are the order of the day (Chin 2018; Mitchell and Diamond 2018).

It is important to recognize that, as in the United States, not all 'Chinese' commentators accept the benign interpretation of Chinese history. Zhao Suisheng, for example, argues that the Chinese empire was maintained 'as much by military force as by virtue', and that 'Chinese intellectuals and political leaders not only selectively remembered but also often reconstructed history to advance the current political agenda of the Chinese government and justify their concept of justice and their view of China's rightful place in the world' (Zhao 2015: 981). Likewise, Pei Minxin (2016: 264) is a high-profile critic of the Chinese political system and argues that 'the practical effect of the decay of the critical institutions of the Chinese party-state leads not only to deteriorating governance, but also to elite disunity and power struggles'. Significantly, however, both of these scholars are based in American universities. There is currently a noteworthy absence of scholars based in China itself who are willing to openly criticize the state in general, much less the CCP of Xi Jinping in particular (but see Mo 2018).

Concluding remarks

Robert Cox's famous aphorism quoted at the outset of this chapter looks as valid as ever: 'theory is always *for* someone and *for* some purpose'. The benign view of American hegemony was vigorously contested by Cox who pointedly suggested that the United States' domestic and foreign policies reflected and furthered the interests of a particular class, which was becoming ever more transnational and interconnected. While there may be some doubt about just how transnational the global bourgeoisie actually is at a time of growing populism and national self-assertion, Cox's point about the possible political purposes to which theory might be put still seems sound. Ironically, however, it may highlight the limits to which essentially nationalist discourses can be put. Yan Xuetong (2011: 99) argues that

> a superpower may be a humane state or a hegemonic state. The difference between the two lies not in the greatness of their power but in their moral standing. If China wants to become a state of humane authority, this would be different from the contemporary United States. The goal of our strategy must be not only to reduce the power gap with the United States but also to provide a better model for society than that given by the United Sates.

It is difficult to make a persuasive argument that China currently provides such a model.

Indeed, *Tianxia* looks rather like a theoretical or even ideological justification for hegemony with Chinese characteristics. This is not to suggest that the current American model of politics or economics necessarily offers a more compelling alternative either. Part of the underlying problem, perhaps, is that our principal theoretical models have been developed by, and primarily in order to make sense of, the experience of the dominant power of the era. Understandable as this may be, it necessarily forecloses and marginalizes contributions from 'the rest'. It is not obvious that China's rise is going to break with this tradition, even if elements of Chinese perspectives on governance and international relations are distinctive and based on their own unique history.

The possible consequences of America's relative decline and China's growing ambitions are considered in greater depth in subsequent chapters. Before doing that, though, it is worth pointing out that a supposed international leadership deficit is a source of growing concern and leading to calls for so-called 'middle powers' to play a greater role in international affairs (Rachman 2018a). This is an area that has already developed a substantial, if somewhat neglected, literature (Cooper et al. 1993; Cooper 2011), which makes the case for diplomatic activism on the part of lesser powers acting in concert. The possible advantage of this approach would be to overcome the diplomatic logjam that has developed either as a consequence of greater power rivalry between the United States, China, and other emerging powers or as a result of incapacity, as with the EU. Middle powers could potentially offer novel solutions for long-standing problems and act as 'honest brokers' between the great powers.

That, as they say, is the theory, at least. In reality, middle powers are often reluctant to seize the moment because of their ties to one great power or another, or are just as incapable of acting collectively as everyone else (Beeson and Higgott 2014). Nevertheless, if global problems are to be addressed, leadership has got to come from somewhere. Middle powers have the advantage that their actions and ideas are potentially less divisive than those of their more powerful and established peers, and are more likely to be treated on their merits as a consequence. Whether they are capable of influencing the entrenched positions and interests of the likes of the United States, China, or even Russia is another question. However, the continual failure of the UN Security Council to reach agreement on, much less act in response to, urgent issues, or the WTO to resolve the current trade war, is testimony to the failure of global governance as it currently stands. The theoretical debates around global governance at least help us to understand where the problems lie, even if they are less convincing about how to fix them.

3

The World the United States Made

Any discussion of contemporary practices of governance at a global level has to pay particular attention to the role played by the United States since the Second World War. Whatever one may think about its impact, the international order that emerged half a century or so ago was one that was primarily made in America. 'American hegemony' has, for better or worse, been a decisive force in international affairs for longer than most people who are alive today can remember. Consequently, and without wanting to plunge into unfathomable epistemological waters, it is impossible to have an entirely 'objective' view about the United States and its hegemonic role in international affairs. Nevertheless, if we want to understand what is at stake as a consequence of the possible decline of the United States, the repudiation of its former leadership role under the erratic stewardship of Donald Trump, or the rise of China, then we need to unpack the way we were.

To understand how much the international system changed in the period following the Second World War we need to place these developments in historical context. This remarkable period of institution-building cannot be understood without reference to the period that preceded it however. If the period after the Second World War represents the highpoint of efforts to self-consciously construct a 'new international order', the period between the First and Second World Wars marks its nadir. This was, after all, not simply the period that saw the greatest economic crisis the world has seen thus far, but one that also saw the rise of fascism and the failure of the League of Nations. For some observers, the interwar period and the failure of the League was a confirmation of realist claims about the competitive, intractable nature of interstate relations (Carr [1939] 1998). For others, the period between the wars was primarily characterized by an absence of international leadership, something that exacerbated the economic crisis and led directly to the catastrophic political and strategic consequences that followed in its wake (Kindleberger 1973). The net result was that, when the war finally ended, the United States found itself in an unprecedentedly powerful position and with a desire to use that power to ensure that some of the 'mistakes' of the interwar period were never repeated.

Before we consider how the United States went about fulfilling what it has come to see as its historical mission (Smith 1994; McDougall 1997), it is important to emphasize one aspect of the emergence of what we might describe as 'American hegemony' that has relevance for this chapter and a number of others: the goal of postwar reconstruction and development was not simply a technocratic or altruistic exercise in economic management and political reform. On the contrary, the pivotal influence and driver of American policy, and one of the principal reasons the United States was prepared to invest quite so much economic and intellectual capital in the project, was because of the unique geopolitical context it confronted. Even before the guns had fallen silent in the Second World War, the outlines of the next potential conflict were coming into view. The fact that the Cold War never involved a direct conflict between the principal protagonists should not blind us to the fact that questions of 'grand strategy' dominated the thinking of the newly empowered American policymakers who effectively constructed the postwar international order (Gaddis 1982). In other words, the foundations for what approximates for global governance in the contemporary period were laid down in especially fraught geopolitical circumstances.

Crucially, the fact that the struggle between the United States and the Soviet Union remained 'cold' meant that ideology assumed an unprecedented importance, something that helps to explain the potentially pivotal role of the Bretton Woods institutions in stabilizing and eventually promoting liberal capitalism. For the purposes of this discussion, the period is important not simply because it put in place many of the key components and practices we associate with global governance, but because it highlights how ideas about political order and management were powerfully shaped by an overarching geopolitical context. The point of this chapter, therefore, is to explain why the United States was able to exert such a powerful and enduring impact on the international system and to provide a context in which to consider the very different circumstances that exist today.

Before hegemony

The Bretton Woods regime established in the aftermath of the Second World War has come to epitomize the pursuit of the institutionalized, multilateral order established under US auspices. But before considering how this came about, it is important to remember what went before it and account not just for the rise of American power, but also for the desire to actually create a particular sort of international system. Two sets of events are especially relevant here, one economic, one political, both of which are interconnected and both of which had profound geopolitical consequences. The failure of the League of Nations seemed to mark the end of what were seen as naïve and utopian efforts to create a cooperative international order. The prospects for international cooperation of any sort were, however, made considerably more difficult by the greatest economic crisis of the twentieth century, something that contributed to the League's problems and created the preconditions for the rise of the extremist politics that would lead inexorably to war. Although both are the antithesis of global governance, they were crucial influences on the evolution of the postwar international order.

The Great Depression

The relationship between structure and agency, or material reality and ideas about how political and economic life could or should be organized, is a complex one. This does not mean that we have to privilege economic forces as the explanation of the interwar crises. As Keynes ([1919] 2004) famously pointed out, some of the actions that were taken in the aftermath of the First World War – especially the decision to punish Germany by demanding ruinous reparations – were very much a consequence of agency, and ones with all too predictable results. However, it is also clear that some economic and political circumstances are more likely to produce the conditions in which expectations about the very possibility of cooperation are more likely than others. It was Norman Angell's ([1910] 2012) great misfortune to publish his masterpiece *The Great Illusion* on the eve of the First World War. The thesis of Angell's book is a familiar one: greater economic interdependence had made war unthinkable for rational policymakers as they simply had too much to lose. Such ideas continue to resonate today and can be seen in the 'capitalist peace' thesis (Gartzke 2007), and in the belief that the behavior of China and the United States is constrained by their mutual interests; a view that is also shared by some in China (Wang and Zheng 2010).

Two points are worth highlighting about such ideas. First, it is important to remember that Angell's optimism was not as baffling as it might seem; as globalization skeptics have pointed out, levels of economic interdependence before the First World War (among the core economies, at least) were very high and would not be reached again until the 1970s (Hirst and Thompson 1996). In other words, there really *were* grounds for thinking that the calculus of conflict had fundamentally changed in a European continent that had found generally effective ways of managing interstate relations among the great powers (Mitzen 2013). And yet the second point that is painfully apparent from the interwar period is that globalization can go backwards as well as forwards. Indeed, as James (2001) points out, the 'chain of linkages' in the financial sector that seemed then (as now) to be the essence of globalization were actually a potentially fatal flaw with the potential to trigger an unpredictable cascade of unwanted and unforeseen consequences. As we shall see in Chapter 7, not much has changed.

There were, however, some features of the Great Depression that were unprecedented and unique, not the least being the scale and appalling impact of the economic downturn: unemployment hit 25 percent in the United States in 1933, while Germany suffered a crippling form of hyperinflation that directly contributed to the rise of fascism. In other aspects, however, the Great Depression has some strikingly familiar features, not least the prominent role played by poorly regulated financial institutions in creating credit, fueling speculation, and the willingness of the economics profession to give the excesses its blessing (Colander et al. 2009). It is also important to note that the United States before the Crash was characterized by very high levels of economic inequality and concentrations of wealth – structural conditions that have returned to present-day America and which may make the contemporary economy similarly unstable and difficult to manage (Hacker and Pierson 2010). What really distinguishes the Great Depression, however, and the reason it still deserves its title, is the sheer length of the downturn, if this is an adequate way of describing the misery that was unleashed.

The retrospective conventional wisdom is that policymakers between the wars made 'mistakes' that exacerbated the crisis and which help to explain its intensity and duration. The outbreak of 'beggar-thy-neighbor' trade policies, such as the notorious Smoot–Hawley Act of 1930 that unilaterally raised tariffs in the United States, made a dire situation much worse and international trade – and by implication, demand – rapidly turned down. American policy and the pursuit of autarky were particularly important as the United States had rapidly become the largest economy in the world and a major trading partner for other countries – especially the Europeans who had suffered so egregiously during the war. The other particular problem that made the crisis unnecessarily severe was the continuing adherence to the gold standard. The key point to emphasize about the gold standard here is that the belief in the need to underpin the value of money with gold was as much an ideological position as it was a technocratic one. Whatever the technical merits of the policy, the net effect was that the only economic adjustment measure available to countries that found themselves running trade deficits (and thus owing gold) was deflation – something that added to the chronic lack of demand that was the hallmark and intractable problem of the period (Temin 1989).

The key problem, Charles Kindleberger (1973) argued in a very influential analysis of the Depression, was that the United States failed to provide the sort of leadership its new economic importance not only permitted but in his view demanded. For Kindleberger (1973: 11), a stable, well-functioning international economy needed

> leadership, a country that is prepared, consciously or unconsciously, under some system of rules it has internalized, to set standards of conduct for other countries and to seek to get others to follow them, to take an undue share of the burdens of the system, and in particular to take on its support in adversity by accepting its redundant commodities, maintaining a flow of investment capital, and discounting its paper.

Britain had played this role to a large extent during its own hegemonic moment in the nineteenth century. Despite the United States' rapid economic ascent, however, its long-standing desire to avoid 'entangling relations' was not overcome until after the Second World War in a 'decisive' break with the past (Lake 1999). The consequences of this absence of leadership were both predictable and by implication avoidable – a profoundly important assumption that underpinned American postwar policy. Before considering what this looked like in any detail, however, it is important to make some brief remarks about another distinctive feature of the interwar period.

The League of Nations

If there is one organization that symbolizes the failure to achieve international cooperation, even in a relatively embryonic form, it is the League of Nations. The failure of the League of Nations is particularly illuminating for the purposes of this discussion precisely because it was quite unambiguously an attempt to move toward what we might now describe as global governance. The fact that it failed tells us something about both the particular contingent historical circumstances in which it was embedded and the more general obstacles confronting those who wish to encourage greater international cooperation. The reluctance of the United States to actually join the League is a powerful reminder of the difficulty that even the most enlightened and progressive leaders may face when trying to overcome domestic opinion. No individual was more redolent of this possibility than Woodrow Wilson.

In the history of the pursuit of global governance few individuals loom larger or illustrate both the potential of and the constraints on agency. There is little doubt that Wilson's personal involvement in the inauguration of the League was 'absolutely critical' (Mazower 2012: 118). Even by 1919 it was clear that the United States was a potentially pivotal actor in international affairs, something its involvement in ending the First World War demonstrated decisively. But Wilson played a crucial role – in the diplomatic sphere, at least – in trying to overcome the United States' isolationist policy and give momentum to a project that might otherwise not have developed at all. Significantly, however, Wilson was not interested in the bureaucratic or diplomatic machinery with which the League might act, but in the vision the League embodied. The lack of American membership would prove to be a fatal flaw that Wilson was unable to overcome. Given the history that preceded the League's inauguration it is not hard to understand why its ideals and goals might have seemed more important than the minutiae of policy development and implementation.

This lack of attention to detail helps to explain why the League's guiding Covenant was 'vague in many of its clauses' and why 'the emphasis from first to last was on voluntary cooperation' (Northedge 1986: 68). It is a failing that has continued to dog other institutional initiatives down the years as they have struggled to reconcile the desire to maintain sovereign autonomy with the possible benefits of greater cooperation. The problems that confronted the League in this regard are well enough known to need little recapitulation here. Suffice to say that Japan's invasion of Manchuria in 1931 provided the League's first major test, which it conspicuously failed. Given the rather dismissive, not to say racist, treatment the Japanese had received at the hands of some of the League's most important members over the years, there is no small irony in this. Indeed, Japan's behavior, and its rather overenthusiastic adoption of the 'Western standard of civilization' (Gong 1984) – up to and including the establishment of its own European-style empire in East Asia (Beeson 2009a) – rather highlights the gulf between domestically driven political imperatives and international obligations. Indeed, no country then – or now, for that matter – highlights just how much domestic politics can constrain foreign policy options than the United States did. In his typically disdainful style Wilson had conspicuously failed to ensure that there was sufficient domestic support in the United States to underwrite his foreign policy goals.

Then, as now, there were powerful forces in the United States that remained highly suspicious of foreign entanglements and deeply opposed currents of thought about quite what America's international role should be (Mead 2001). While the League's goals were in many ways admirable and understandable artifacts of the era, Wilson's failure to pay attention to the quotidian realities of domestic politics and the continuing salience of sovereignty, meant that the prospects for international transformation remained slim. Nevertheless, in the aftermath of yet another war – this one even bloodier, more destructive and widespread than its predecessor – the preconditions for transformative change and the development of effective international institutions were finally in place.

Embedding hegemony

It may not be politically correct to say so, but when judged in the long sweep of history, the United States had a good war. Not only did the Second World War devastate some of the United States' key peer competitors, but it also had the welcome effect of restarting its stalled economy. Indeed, so transformative was the war on the relative economic standing of the major powers that in the immediate aftermath of the war the United States alone accounted for something like 30 percent of global GDP (Maddison 2007: 381), a historically unprecedented state of affairs. This is not to suggest a crude, materially determined account of history here – American policymakers still had to actually do something with all this potential leverage, after all – but material power is plainly not unimportant either. Indeed, the reason we are all so interested in China is primarily because of its unprecedented economic growth. The point to emphasize about the American experience is that there was a confluence of what were seen as geopolitical imperatives, abilities and opportunities. The rest, as they say, is history. It is, however, a history that merits spelling out, not least because it offers clues about the challenges facing China if it is to play a more prominent role in global governance.

Institutionalizing influence

While the Second World War may have enhanced and revealed the extent of its primacy, the sheer fact of American dominance did not dictate policy. Unsurprisingly, one of the most important influences on the thinking and actions of the policymakers who shaped the immediate postwar order was a 'preoccupation with the past' (Gaddis 1972: 31). The connections between economic crisis and political catastrophe were deeply embedded in the minds of America's policymakers who had witnessed the horrors unleashed by genocidal European fascism. Other, less traumatic lessons had also been taken on board. Keynes was no longer a disregarded voice in the wilderness, and his ideas would play a critical role in the shaping of the postwar economic order (Ikenberry 1992). There was, however, an even more compelling reason for trying to engineer a durable, stable and attractive postwar economic order: there was an alternative that appeared bent on global expansion.

In the aftermath of the Cold War and the dissolution of the Soviet Union, it is easy to forget what a powerful and credible force it once was. Importantly, it was not only the more obvious power of the Red Army and the Soviets' growing military technology that gave 'the West' generally and the United States in particular pause for thought; unbelievable as it may seem at this distance, the socialist model represented a strikingly successful alternative to a capitalist system that was seen as responsible for the worst economic crisis the world had ever seen, to say nothing of the accompanying horrors of international conflict on a truly global scale. For many aspiring developing countries in what would come to be described as the 'Third World', the Soviet model looked attractive and potentially relevant – especially if it came with Soviet aid (Zubok and Pleshakov 1997).

One of the most striking features of the American response to the ideological and material challenge presented by the Soviet Union was that broadly conceived economic initiatives were largely separate from strategic concerns, even if they were largely dedicated to the same ultimate goal – the 'containment' of Soviet expansionism. Indeed, by the time George Marshall articulated the contours of the Marshall Plan in his celebrated speech at Harvard in 1947, George Kennan's ([1947] 1997) analysis of the nature and ambitions of the Soviet Union had become the accepted view of 'virtually all the top policymakers' (Hogan 1987: 44). The point to emphasize here is that the origins of what would ultimately become the European Union, which remains the most ambitious and – all of its current travails notwithstanding – still the most effective example of intergovernmental cooperation and political integration, can be found in the unpropitious crucible of Cold War geopolitics (Beeson 2005; Pollard 1985).

Not only is it possible to discern quite distinct influences and rationales for the strategic and economic components of America's emerging postwar policy, but there were also important *internal* influences on policy which meant that the very conception of national security was shaped by domestic forces and experiences (Smith 1994). It is possible to read unprecedented initiatives like the Marshall Plan as flowing directly out of America's own experiments in economic stimulation under the New Deal (Hogan 1987). Indeed, it is important to remember that the New Deal itself was 'the first wholly secular reform movement in American history' (McDougall 1997: 149), and emblematic of the extensive internal transformation that the long twentieth century was working on the US itself. Significantly, America's postwar planners 'sought to project these principles onto the world as a macrocosm of the New Deal regulatory state' (Burley 1993: 125). In other words, without a major internal reorientation of American attitudes about the possible role of government and appropriate responses to wider geopolitical events, a very different form of hegemony might have developed.

Enlightened unilateralism?

Realists might claim that American responses to the emerging bipolar order were a product of the structure of that order itself and the US's pivotal role within it, but the precise nature of American policy is still somewhat surprising. While the strategic doctrine of postwar President Harry Truman may have embodied an uncompromising commitment to support 'free people' and reflected Kennan's hardheaded, realist analysis of the Soviet threat, there was also a recognition of the need for widespread aid to support European reconstruction 'for the more urgent purpose of alleviating social and economic conditions which might breed communism' (Gaddis 1972: 317). Even an apparently selfless and multilaterally based initiative like the Marshall Plan was always tightly controlled by the United States, furthered American grand strategy, and was essentially 'unilateralism in the clothing of multilateralism' (Kunz 1997: 33). Significantly, the predominantly bilateral disbursement of aid in the postwar period actually established a general pattern for the next thirty years, one that reinforced America's position at the center of a distinctive 'hub and spokes' security architecture that became the model for US engagement outside Western Europe (Milward 1984: 113–14).

In the aftermath of the Second World War, therefore, American policy was part of a broadly based effort to create an interlocking, multilateral institutional structure with which to facilitate not just European reconstruction, but also the international integration of economic and political activity more generally. True, America may have been the prime mover in the emerging order and arguably its principal beneficiary, but as Ikenberry (2001) notes, it was an order that not only offered payoffs for allies, but one that provided potentially important, institutionalized constraints on the US and the unilateral application of its power. There is also no doubt that American policy was broadly successful in reviving capitalist economies not just in Europe, but in East Asia, too. Indeed, it is simply not possible to understand the entire history of the so-called 'East Asian miracle' without recognizing the pivotal role played by American foreign policy in particular and the geopolitical imperatives more generally (Stubbs 2005).

However, it is not simply that the postwar international order that was so successfully reconstructed under the auspices of American hegemony was capitalist that is significant; it also reflected a 'particular shaping of the political and social entities or spaces in which one lives through practices, principles, and institutions associated with liberal governance, rights, markets, and self-determination' (Latham 1997: 14). Put differently, from its inception the international order that emerged following the war was not simply a 'technical' solution to the problem of reconstruction and international economic management, but a profoundly political project that was as much ideational as it was an expression of American power in a more conventional sense.

The importance of ideas from both an ideological and a more narrowly conceived policy perspective is evident in the manner in which the new international order was envisaged by its architects. The Bretton Woods Agreement, which led to the establishment of the World Bank, the IMF, and the GATT, may have had the clear goal of restoring stability and prosperity to the international system, but the specifics of the Agreement reflected an important ideational struggle. British and American economists led by John Maynard Keynes and Harry Dexter White were able to exploit a uniquely fluid historical moment to influence the policy agendas of their respective national governments entrenching the Keynesian notion that governments could play a potentially crucial and effective role in regulating economic activity (Ikenberry 1992).

It is also important to stress that the postwar international order has evolved 'internally'. The logic that underpinned the Bretton Woods Agreement and the role of what have come to be known as the international financial institutions (IFIs) played within it has changed significantly. At its inception, the postwar international system was characterized by what Ruggie (1982) famously called the 'compromise of embedded liberalism' in which a balance was struck between the goal of maintaining an open international economic order and the wish to retain a capacity for domestic economic policymaking autonomy. Consequently, for the first couple of decades following the Bretton Woods Agreement, there were noteworthy limits to the extent of the liberalization process. Significantly, the new economic order deliberately restricted the mobility of capital and the extent of currency trading – a system which owed much to the dominance of Keynesian ideas. But the original, highly regulated Bretton Woods regime that underpinned social welfare capitalism was ultimately undermined by a unilateral assertion of American power in the early 1970s when the United States experienced major budgetary and competitiveness problems (Block 1977). The net effect of the so-called 'Nixon shock' was to overturn the established system of managed exchange rates, reduce national policy autonomy, and pave the way for the globalization of financial markets – an emblem of the contemporary 'globalized' era (Pauly 1997).

What made the original Bretton Woods regime vulnerable to unforeseen change was an especially fraught geopolitical context. Paradoxically enough, the United States' efforts to rebuild successful capitalist economies in Western Europe and Japan had proved all too successful, and its once dominant economic position and balance of trade suffered as a consequence (Block 1977). Even more immediately, the United States was involved in fighting a costly war in Vietnam that was adding to its overall balance of payments problems. This might have been a problem at any time. What made it potentially transformative in unpredictable ways was the fact that the United States remained the lynchpin of a system of fixed exchange rates in which the American dollar could notionally be exchanged for gold. As the Vietnam War dragged on and as America's trade partners began to accumulate ever greater numbers of dollars, it became apparent that key elements of American hegemony were becoming unsustainable (Guttman 1994).

More detailed consideration of the operation of specific organizations such as the IMF and the GATT, which went on to become the WTO, will be provided in subsequent chapters. At this point I want to highlight not just the scope of US ambition for the institutional architecture that it did so much to create, but the fact that the United States was also able to flout its norms and rules when it chose to do so (Beeson and Broome 2010). The ambiguous role played by the United States in simultaneously underpinning and exploiting the institutional architecture it did so much to create has generated important debates about the nature of hegemony and leadership which are taken up later. What merits emphasis here is that while the United States took the lead in building *multilateral* institutions, including alliance structures such as NATO as well as the Bretton Woods economic institutions, the injunction to behave multilaterally always applied more to the junior partners in these organizations than the hegemon itself. Indeed, a hallmark of US hegemony in this period was the development of institutions binding on others, but in which the hegemon was effectively only ever 'self-binding'.

Thus, the Bretton Woods system reflected what Ikenberry (2003) called an institutional bargain. This bargain, underwritten by a combination of US power and resources, enlightened self-interest, and liberal values, albeit it leavened by a dose of technocratic Keynesianism, allowed the creation of a set of collective goods providing institutions acceptable to both the United States and its Cold War allies. In retrospect, therefore, American hegemony in the immediate postwar period is characterized by some significant continuities with, and differences from, the contemporary era. The confrontation with the Soviet Union was clearly a major material constraint on American freedom of action, but one which – somewhat fortuitously – provided the legitimating domestic rationale for an expansionary fiscal policy both at home and abroad (Kunz 1997: 331). Likewise, and despite the criticisms that they have subsequently received as a consequence of the evolution of their agendas beyond their initial remit (see, for example, Woods 1999), the Bretton Woods institutions marked the institutional expression of the 'Big Idea' that, according to Bacevich (2002: 88), has continued to inform American strategy: openness.

Although Americans may not always have practiced domestically what they preached abroad, the idea that America had a special historical mission to make the world a better place has been a continuing theme in American foreign policy, and one that was given direct expression in the Marshall Plan (McDougall 1997: 209). Even if America's postwar policy is seen as ultimately self-serving and part of a larger strategy to secure American interests and dominance, there is no doubt that initiatives like the Marshall Plan contributed not just to the reconstruction of Europe, but to the latter's long-term political stability and integration (Hogan 1987: 438). Under the administration of George W. Bush in particular, however, this strategic calculus began to change. Although the world is currently intently focused on the seemingly aberrant and anomalous presidency of Donald Trump, we need to remember that some of the biggest changes in the application and effectiveness of American power and influence occurred under George W. Bush. The comparative significance of this period and its attempts to 'securitize' foreign policy during the so-called 'war on terror' is so important that it merits a brief recapitulation.

Securitizing hegemony?

It has become something of a cliché to note the 'hubris' of the Bush regime. Remarkably enough, however, Donald Trump has an even greater sense of his ability to reshape the world and appears to have learned nothing from this period, or any other for that matter. Nevertheless, while the Bush administration's optimism about its capacity to impose its will on the world may look wildly misplaced in retrospect, it is important to remember that it was entirely in keeping with the rhetoric of the time. Conservative American commentators were quick to announce the inauguration of an era of unipolarity following the abrupt, almost entirely unexpected, demise of the Soviet Union, and urged the US administration to seize the moment to reshape the international system (Krauthammer 1990–1991). Many thought American primacy was not only unprecedented in scale and extent (Ferguson 2004), but likely to last indefinitely (Wohlforth 1999). As in the economic sphere, some international relations specialists not only abandoned any pretense of objectivity, but became cheerleaders in urging on the Bush administration in their efforts to reshape the world. As we know, this was a regime that needed little encouragement, but in this respect at least they were to some extent a product of the time. On one thing, at least, boosters and critics seemed to agree: there had been an important redistribution of power in the international system and it was having tangible consequences that were manifest in the shift from multipolarity to unipolarity (see Ikenberry et al. 2009; Jervis 2008).

Multipolarity creates incentives for economic integration and cooperation between allies as well as enhancing economic interaction as a major instrument of cooperative statecraft. By contrast, the type of bipolarity that prevailed during the Cold War era encouraged the separation of economics and politics. The sort of unipolar order that many thought had developed during the Bush era, on the other hand, seems to confirm Michael Mastanduno's (1998: 827) argument that a unipolar structure will see the hegemonic state organize economic policy and practice 'to line up behind and reinforce its national security strategy'. In short, given the right structural preconditions and an administration bent on exploiting them, there would appear to be a correlation between the degree of dominance of the international system by the United States in military terms and the manner in which it uses economic policy as an arm of security policy. An empirical reading of US policy in the Bush era shows how a unipolar moment – in the domains of both trade and finance, and at both multilateral and bilateral levels of policymaking – may tempt the hegemon to integrate economic and security policy more closely than under conditions of multipolarity. US economic policy, rather than being a mere instrument of economic relations and statecraft, became a part of the armory of influence that the United States used to develop a strategy toward potential challengers. While Donald Trump may be interested in attempting something similar, he has a weaker hand to play than his predecessor, not least because of the counterproductive impact of Bush's unilateral approach.

The point to emphasize here is that at the outset of his administration, some of the more radical policies and interventions envisaged by the Bush administration were to be underwritten by American military power, and not by the collective approval of a wider 'international community'. As the National Security Strategy made clear, '[w]hile the United States will constantly strive to enlist the support of the international community, we will not hesitate to act alone' (US Government 2002: 6). As Rhodes (2003: 136) notes of the Bush era, 'America's sovereign responsibilities supersede its commitment to international institutions'. While the United States has a history of pragmatic involvement in the development of specific international institutions, there has always been a subconscious ambivalence in the minds of many Americans about the benefits of multilateralism. Donald Trump is part of an enduring tradition.

Multilateralism à la carte?

The United States has had an ability to make choices about which – if any – multilateral institutions it chooses to engage with. It is a privilege that, some argue (Patrick 2009), was under threat from the rise of new powers, even before the emergence of Donald Trump. To assess such claims, it is important to be clear about how multilateralism has been understood. In the theoretical literature, multilateralism relates to the management of transnational problems with three or more parties but operating with a series of acceptable 'generalized principles of conduct' (Ruggie 1993: 11). That is, the principles of behavior should take precedence over interests. But we need to distinguish between multilateralism as a principled institutional form of behavior in international relations (Ruggie 1993: 8) on the one hand, and the actual development and operation of formal international organizations as the centerpiece of multilateralism as policy practice on the other.

The distinction between multilateralism as a principled form of behavior and multilateralism as the conduct of foreign policy through international institutions is often confused in practice. For many observers and practitioners of US foreign policy, the use of multilateral institutions is believed to be but one policy option among many, rather than driven by any sense of obligation to operate in this manner. US policy had always been either 'instrumental multilateralism' (Foot et al. 2003) or 'driven by an understanding of US "exceptionalism"' (Luck 2003). Consequently, a key element in the contemporary theory and practice of global governance – the evolution of global networks at the expense of international hierarchies (Slaughter 2017) – was an anathema to many of those in the Bush administration. Networks pursue their activities by using systems of sprawling, horizontally interconnected, networks of private power and authority (Rosenau 2002; Stone 2008). Notwithstanding US military and economic preponderance, the changing structures of authority – or more accurately power – reflected in the growing salience of network governance under conditions of globalization were at odds with the thinking and practice in US foreign policy that prevailed in the Bush era in particular, and which have resurfaced in the Trump era (Wagstyl et al. 2017).

The blurring of the borders between what is domestic and what is international in the policy process has challenged traditional US understandings of the national interest (Trubowitz 1998). This is especially so in those policy domains where transnational decision-making – for example, on issues such as the environment and climate change or the application of international law – clashes with US domestic law or runs up against dominant American conceptions of national security. Multilateralism for large sections of the US policy community, at best, implies the opportunity for others to free ride on the United States' material support. At worst, it implies sovereignty dilution and unwanted entanglements. This is not simply to argue that the United States has repudiated multilateralism as a principled institutional form of governance in its entirety. Rather, the United States has become more instrumental in its choice of issue areas in which it will adopt a multilateral approach as a matter of preferred policy practice. Unilateral action, backed by American military power, became the modus operandi of the Bush administration with disastrous consequences not only for Iraq, but for international cooperation more generally. Trump's enthusiasm for bilateralism over multilateralism suggests that this legacy endures (Stokes and Waterman 2017).

Generalizations should not be made about US foreign policy purely on the basis of a reading of the Bush era alone, especially regarding attitudes toward multilateral institutions. But the Bush administration's policies did highlight the possibility that the implicit bargain of hegemonic restraint in return for cooperation had come undone since the end of the Cold War as American administrations either cast off unwelcome economic obligations as they did under Nixon or progressively sought to free themselves from institutionalized constraints (Beeson and Higgott 2005). The Bush era in particular weakened the foundations of the postwar international order that American power helped create, and which largely reflected American goals and interests.

The administration of Bush's successor, Barak Obama, gave much stronger rhetorical support to the idea of participating in, and actively supporting, multilateral institutions and this helped to restore America's standing in the world. Unlike Bush and Trump, Obama saw multilateralism as a key part of the way American power might be most effectively exercised (Lindsay 2011). However, Obama was from the outset preoccupied with addressing the consequences of problems Bush created. Whether it was the global financial crisis or the seemingly endless conflicts in the Middle East, Obama was hemmed in by problems that were arguably not of his making. Understandably enough, he was careful not to 'do stupid shit', as he memorably put it. His cautious approach to the seemingly endless conflicts in the Middle East and his reluctance to be drawn into the conflict in Syria have been widely criticized as symptomatic of an inherent indecisiveness (Dueck 2015), however, not as informed calculations of what was feasible.

Indeed, when the United States is thought by many to be in a state of at least relative decline and facing paralyzing domestic political problems (Layne 2012; Mann and Ornstein 2012), there are real doubts about its capacity to provide the sort of leadership the likes of Kindleberger regarded as critical for a stable international economic order – even if the Trump administration or its successors change course and decides that this is, once again, in America's national interest. The implications of some of these claims and possibilities for global governance generally and for America's role in promoting or obstructing it will be taken up in more detail in later chapters. Before doing that, however, it is important to draw out some of the theoretical implications that emerge from this brief overview of the nature and development of 'American hegemony'. Did it ever make sense to describe the postwar order in this way, or should we describe the United States as simply taking a less pejorative 'leadership' role, as a number of influential scholars in the United States prefer to do (Daadler and Kagan 2016)?

Leadership or hegemony?

It is clear that the international system is changing from one in which the United States was unambiguously the dominant power to one in which other powers, especially China, are competing for influence. Indeed, some observers think we may be seeing the beginning of a process of hegemonic competition or even transition, in which a genuine peer competitor challenges American ascendancy. Martin Jacques (2009), for example, argues that it is only a question of time before 'China rules the world'. Other observers have argued that the potential for conflict between a dissatisfied rising power and a declining hegemon is growing as a result of the so-called Thucydides' trap (Allison 2017), a possibility discussed in Chapter 9. Before we attempt to assess the merits of such claims, it is useful to consider them in the context of extant debates about the nature of international dominance and/or leadership. What are the qualities that have allowed the United States to play such an influential role and what implications might any change in them – or even the United States' replacement as the hegemonic power – have for the international system?

For a generation of American scholars in particular, there was something about the United States, its norms and values, and the overall attractiveness of its culture and society that meant it was 'bound to lead' (Nye 1990). It is no coincidence, of course, that such views not only reflect an American sensibility, but are influential primarily because of the United States' position in the world. For all the attention that has understandably been paid to the United States' ideational influence and 'soft power', the original foundation of its dominance was crudely material. The reason we are all currently preoccupied with China is precisely the same: most observers think that, all other things being equal, China is on track to overtake the United States as the world's largest economy sometime in the next decade or two (Patton 2016). A key question for scholars of international relations in particular that emerges from China's possible challenge to the United States is how we understand this conceptually. Even in the currently unlikely event that China could provide increased 'leadership' (Beeson 2013a), would this necessarily mean that it also increased China's 'hegemonic' influence?

The question of China's possible leadership ambitions and credentials is taken up in the next chapter, but its possible importance is clear: Kindleberger's seminal analysis of the Great Depression argued that one of its principal causes was an absence of leadership. Because the UK was incapable and the United States was unwilling, no country provided the sort of leadership that he thought was necessary to prevent the international economy breaking down as a consequence of protectionism, competitive currency devaluations and beggar-thy-neighbor policies. The big lessons that America's postwar policymakers took from the economic catastrophe of the interwar period were, first, that it must never happen again, and, second, there were potentially ways of ensuring that it didn't. In this context, leadership can usefully be distinguished as 'the use of power to orchestrate the actions of a group toward a collective end' (Ikenberry 1996: 388). In other words, *leadership* is a quality associated with the self-conscious application and utilization of material and ideational capabilities for particular purposes and goals. Powerful states act in the international system in ways that allow them to influence the behavior of others.

The creation of the Bretton Woods institutions is a quintessential example of this possibility. The United States was unambiguously the most powerful state in the world in the aftermath of the Second World War and it used its influence, status and leverage to encourage other states to join it in creating a specific world order. Leaders need followers and the United States had many – a reality that was reinforced by the geopolitical imperatives of the escalating Cold War confrontation with the Soviet Union. Crucially, however – and one of the most distinctive features of American hegemony – the fact that this impulse to create a new international order was expressed institutionally meant that American power and 'leadership' were permanently embedded in the notionally independent Bretton Woods organizations and the particular vision of economic and political order they supported (Latham 1997). Hegemony, in other words, is a more enduring, institutionally embedded form of power that provides influence – even leadership – but in ways that go beyond the simple foreign policy initiatives of powerful states. Even at the height of the Bush regime's undoubted unpopularity, there was little desire to completely overturn the international system which the United States continued to dominate – and no clear sense of what an alternative might actually look like either. Similar conclusions may yet be reached by the so-called 'adults' in the Trump administration (Mann 2017).

The ideological contest that so distinguished the Cold War period gives an important clue to the difference between leadership and hegemony (Hunt 1987), and to the manner in which the latter exerts a continuing influence. The United States also undoubtedly exercised leadership when it decided to prod the Western Europeans into greater cooperation in the postwar period: not only were the war-weary, weakened Europeans receptive to a little prodding (Lundestad 1986), but in the Marshall Plan the United States had a powerful set of incentives that actually made cooperation immediately worthwhile. Consequently, as even radical critics have noted, institutionalized American hegemony offered long-term incentives and payoffs that made it attractive in its own right, even to states that might not have been traditional allies, such as Japan (La Feber 1997). Hegemony may, as Robert

Cox (1987: 11, emphasis added) argues, ultimately be about securing the dominance of a particular state, but it can do so because it

> creates an order based ideologically on a broad measure of consent, functioning according to general principles that in fact ensure the continuing supremacy of the leading state or states and leading social classes *but at the same time offer some measure or prospect of satisfaction to the less powerful.*

Some of these principles would need to be universal if the idea of hegemony is to have analytical purchase: the counterintuitive idea of domination through consent would seem to be central among them. And yet what is distinctive about the American experience is that, as Ruggie (1993, emphasis added) pointed out, 'it was the fact of an *American* hegemony that was decisive after World War II, not merely American *hegemony*'. In other words, while there may be common characteristics about hegemonic rule, the particular style or content may vary by country and period. As we shall see in the next chapter, this is what makes the 'China challenge' so potentially important for the future of the international system and attempts to encourage greater cooperation and collaborative governance. The possibility that China might play a greater role in global governance has been significantly enhanced by Donald Trump's election as the 45th president of the United States.

Trump: continuity or chaos?

Donald Trump's personal qualities and the administration he notionally leads are so different from any other recent presidency that it is foolhardy to try to make definitive judgments about its long-term impact. Indeed, it is not even clear whether the Trump presidency will actually last for a full term, given the series of unprecedented problems that have plagued his first term in office from the outset (Osnos 2018). For a man who famously prides himself on his leadership qualities, his administration has been distinguished by basic failures to implement policy and a continuing, rapid turnover of senior members of the administration (Manson and Fleming 2018). It would, therefore, be unwise to try to draw too many conclusions about what Trump may mean for the United States and the international system in which it remains the most powerful actor. Consequently, I shall only offer some brief observations about what we know so far, and consider their possible consequences in subsequent chapters.

The first point to make about Trump's presidency is that it is dramatically at odds with the long-standing rhetoric about America's place as the central pillar of a 'rules-based international order' that was predicated on economic openness and political cooperation. This was always something of a caricature given the 'temptations of unilateralism' (Skidmore 2011), but Trump's electoral campaign and much of his subsequent rhetoric have worn the repudiation of liberal internationalism as a veritable badge of honor. On the contrary, Trump has relentlessly put 'America first' and claimed that the United States has actually been taken advantage of by other countries that fail to act fairly. In the trade arena, as we shall see in Chapter 7, China has been the principal offender as far as Trump is concerned.

Significantly, even within the American academic community, there are growing divisions between liberals who worry about the undermining of the institutionalized and rule-governed order they associate with American dominance. Richard Hass (2018), for example, argues that

America's decision to abandon the role it has played for more than seven decades thus marks a turning point. The liberal world order cannot survive on its own, because others lack either the interest or the means to sustain it. The result will be a world that is less free, less prosperous, and less peaceful, for Americans and others alike.

Realists such as Randall Schweller (2018), on the other hand, suggest that Trump's

realist worldview is not only legitimate but also resonates with American voters, who rightly recognize that the United States is no longer inhabiting the unipolar world it did since the end of the Cold War; instead, it is living in a more multipolar one, with greater competition. Trump is merely shedding shibboleths and seeing international politics for what it is and has always been: a highly competitive realm populated by self-interested states concerned with their own security and economic welfare. Trump's 'America first' agenda is radical only in the sense that it seeks to promote the interests of the United States above all.

Trump's protectionist, nationalist, and nativist rhetoric and agenda are therefore seen by some as entirely in keeping with the times and the actions of the rising powers considered in Chapter 5. What is different about the United States, of course, is that – rhetorically, at least – the United States has been the principal champion of 'globalization' generally, or the idea that economic integration and openness are inherently desirable and beneficial for all. Not only has the Trump administration repudiated this idea – in part because of the influence of maverick economic advisors, such as Peter Navarro (2006) – but it has allowed China to position itself as a champion of globalization in America's place (Bremmer 2018). Xi Jinping favorably impressed the world's corporate and political elites at Davos by promising to continue promoting global integration in America's absence (Wong 2017). It is testimony to just how much ideas about global governance have changed that the world's movers and shakers were apparently unfazed by the idea that a still tightly controlled 'communist' regime was promising to save a liberal version of capitalism.

The second major impact of the Trump administration has been in the area of security, as I explain in more detail in Chapter 9. The point that merits brief emphasis here is that, once again, Trump's 'transactional' approach to American foreign and security policy has undermined the foundations of the existing international order and unnerved key allies in Europe, Japan, and Australia (Beeson 2017b). While there have been efforts from Trump's inner circle to repair some of the damage and reassure America's strategic partners, it is clear that Trump himself does not regard institutions such as NATO as fundamental building blocks of the postwar international order created under the auspices of American hegemony, but as potentially redundant bargaining chips to be traded if necessary in the reassertion of American unilateralism (Erlanger 2017). When the uncertainty triggered by Trump's attitude to the existing international security is added to the growing list of possible problems and threats, especially from the equally unpredictable leader of North Korea, it is not hard to see why so many commentators and policymakers around the world think that we live in unprecedentedly challenging times as a consequence of Trump's arrival on the international stage. At the very least, he poses unprecedented dilemmas for those trying to create a more orderly, governed global environment.

Concluding remarks

The United States remains the most powerful actor in an international system it was largely responsible for creating. As we shall see, there are a number of other state and nonstate actors that are now playing an increasingly important and influential role in broadly conceived international relations, but this does not lessen the historical importance of America's role. Even though the United States may be in relative decline and its influence may not be as decisive as it once was, the future trajectory of the international system is likely to display some degree of path dependence and continuity. While there may be new or newly empowered players on the international stage, it is noteworthy that few, if any, are proposing a radically different world order. Indeed, as I shall explain in the next chapter, some of the most illuminating changes that have been proposed or enacted have occurred within the existing institutional framework that was largely established under American auspices.

Does this mean that change is impossible or that the past necessarily determines the future? While one should never rule out change, even of the revolutionary variety, for the foreseeable future it is reasonable to expect the existing array of institutions and practices to provide the core features of any 'new' world order or move toward global governance. In this context, it is possible that the current obsession with Donald Trump's disruptive, nationalistic approach to the world will come to seem less important with the passage of time. It is equally possible that the foundations of 'American hegemony' that played such an important part in defining the contemporary international system may be fatally undermined. It is important to remember that any future order will display some degree of path dependence – for better or worse. For all its undoubted shortcomings, we should acknowledge that America's dominance has coincided with – even directly driven – the greatest period of economic expansion the world has ever known and a remarkable increase in the number of states who profess some adherence to the principles, if not always the practice, of democratic rule. It is this latter achievement that currently looks most under threat, a possibility that China's reemergence as a global power may reinforce.

4

Contested Governance and the China Challenge

Legend has it that Napoleon Bonaparte said that 'China is a sleeping giant. Let her sleep, for when she wakes she will move the world.' As prescient statements go, it's hard to beat. While we may now all have become relatively accustomed to the idea that China is once again a very significant power in world affairs, the story of how it achieved this bears repetition. China's reemergence as the preeminent power in a region it has historically dominated is remarkable. What is even more important for the purposes of the present discussion, of course, is that China now seems capable of playing an international role of a sort that was simply impossible when it was at the height of its powers – and before European imperialism brought it to its knees. This chapter picks up the story of China's remarkable development where we left it in Chapter 1. The twentieth century was one characterized by truly epic fluctuations in fortune for China, the consequences of which continue to reverberate through the twenty-first. The first part of this chapter sketches some of the more important aspects of this history, before concentrating in more detail on how China's leaders managed to turn things around.

This historical background is an essential part of understanding the 'China challenge', because it is not simply China's material importance that is noteworthy and helping to transform the international order. On the contrary, part of China's significance is derived from the *way* it changed: not only was China famously a centrally planned communist regime for much of the twentieth century, but even when it did open up and become integrated into the extant global capitalist system, it did so in ways that reflected its specific historical experience (Elvin 1973; Gallagher 2002). I shall suggest in what follows that while China's experience may not provide an easily replicable developmental template for other aspiring rising powers, it has potentially major implications for global governance, not least because the current generation of leaders in China are more confident about the country's achievements and possible role in the international system.

Taking history seriously

Chinese people are not unique in taking their history seriously. But it does assume a prominence in China that is both noteworthy and understandable. After all, not only do the Chinese have more recorded history to contemplate than anyone else, but much of its recent history has also been traumatic and bloody. The so-called 'one hundred years of shame' that China experienced at the hands of European and Japanese imperialists continues to cast a long shadow over contemporary attitudes about national identity and foreign policy (Callahan 2010). Significantly, foreign policy is increasingly bound up with, and an expression of, national consciousness, with potentially major implications for the way that China acts on the international stage. The 'struggle for status' is undoubtedly one of the drivers of contemporary policy and the widespread desire to reestablish China in what is widely seen as its rightful place at the center of regional if not global affairs (Deng 2008).

The story of the end of China's dynastic rule, the descent into warlordism, civil war, and chaos has been told many times and there is no intention of trying to add to that narrative here (Elvin 1973; Hsü 1983). However, it is worth briefly highlighting a few aspects of this increasingly well-known story. First, as noted, the past and its interpretation are especially important in China. Some parts of the story of China's descent and reemergence as a major power are celebrated and replayed with remarkable and, at times, rather alarming frequency. China's relationship with Japan is the most striking illustration of this possibility (Reilly 2014; McGregor 2017). There is no doubt that the Japanese exploited China's weakness when it invaded Manchuria in 1931 and committed atrocities in Nanjing in 1937–1938, but the Chinese government plays a large part in keeping such historical memories at the forefront of national consciousness to this day (Qiu 2006; Lind 2010). The very different process of regional reconciliation that has occurred in Europe is striking and instructive. China's capacity to play a constructive role in regional, let alone global, governance is clearly constrained by its inability or unwillingness to put the past behind it (Park 2013; Rozman 2004).

Second, the intrusion of the European powers into China during the nineteenth century was not simply a deeply resented affront to national dignity and pride that reverberates to this day (French 2017), but it has also entrenched China's leaders' belief in the importance of sovereignty. As Tang notes (2018: 37), 'China remains a staunch defender of the Westphalian order in the sense that states' sovereignty comes first and everything else comes second'. Such sentiments create additional points of friction in China's case. The status of Hong Kong and, even more problematically, Taiwan is a continuing source of domestic consternation and international tension in which the practical and ideational consequences of Chinese history continue to shape contemporary policy (Bush 2016; Liu 2017).

The Peoples' Republic of China (PRC) regards Taiwan as a renegade province as it was created by the defeated nationalist forces during the bitter civil war. The discomforting reality that Taiwan now has a flourishing democracy and a growing number of independently minded citizens with few direct links to the mainland cuts little ice with the PRC or its much larger population (Huang 2018). The fact that the United States notionally guarantees Taiwan's security adds a further dangerous layer of complexity to an already knotty problem; not least because the PRC government reserves the right to use force to resolve what it sees as a domestic problem (Kastner 2016). The strategic implications of these issues are taken up in more detail in Chapter 9. Of equal importance, as far as global governance is concerned, however, are the political and economic consequences of China's historical experience.

China stands up – and cracks down

When Mao Zedong declared victory in China's bloody, drawn-out, and divisive civil war in 1949 it truly marked a turning point in Chinese history. The inauguration of communist rule not only overturned many of the fundamental suppositions of Marxist theory, but also established a political order that endures to this day, at least in name (McGregor 2010). Whether Mao would recognize, much less approve of, the current 'communist' leadership and the society over which it presides is another question (Nonini 2008). But the central reality with which China's own population and that of the rest of the world has to contend is that the CCP remains firmly in control of the state and much else, and shows little sign of relinquishing its hold on power (Cai 2008; Brown 2014). On the contrary, one of the most important consequences and goals of Xi Jinping's wide-ranging domestic reform agenda has been to reinforce the power, authority, and centrality of the CCP in every aspect of China's domestic and international affairs (Wong 2018). Whatever one may think of such policies, there is little doubt they are having a major impact.

The persistence of authoritarian rule is one of the most striking and consequential features of the Chinese experience (*The Economist* 2018a). It is also one that is a very tangible refutation of some of the most influential ideas in Western political theory. One of the theoretical and practical 'problems' of China's development is that it has failed to replicate the West's historical development pattern, at least as understood in some prominent strands of liberal economic and political theory (Chen 2002). On the one hand, China shows little sign of becoming democratic in the foreseeable future, barring some not inconceivable political upheaval, at least. Even if the CCP were to lose its 'performance legitimacy' as a result of an economic crisis, it is far from clear that this would inaugurate democratic rule. Despite the fact that China has a rapidly expanding capitalist class, it has shown little desire to push for the sort of political liberalization that accompanied the development of capitalism in Western Europe. On the contrary, China's economic elites have been incorporated into the CCP and the latter has maintained an active presence in, and control over, strategically important parts of the economy (Tsai 2007; Wright 2010).

As a result, it is hard to overstate the historical and continuing importance of the CCP. Even the architect of China's economic liberalization thought there were fundamental, nonnegotiable limits to the opening-up process: anything that threatened the continuing dominance of the Party was to be resisted – violently, if need be. The crushing of China's nascent pro-democracy movement in Tiananmen Square in 1989 was authorized by Deng Xiaoping and provided a powerful reminder of just how heavy the hand of the state could be when threatened (Vogel 2011). There is every indication that Xi Jinping takes a similarly inflexible view of possible threats to the CCP's primacy, as the recent crackdown on freedom of speech and the suppression of political opposition demonstrate (Zhixu 2018). Even the widespread use of social media has had less impact than many expected; it is often a vehicle for strident nationalists to promote their views, rather than a venue for free-wheeling political discourse, much less criticism of the state (Stockman and Gallagher 2011; Mozur 2017). The net effect is to make it difficult for the central government to back away from some of the more contentious parts of Xi's vision of national rejuvenation otherwise known as the 'China dream' (Liu 2015). The overall consequence of such moves is not simply domestic, however. On the contrary, Xi's actions are part of a general growth of 'strong man' rule and a winding back of democratic reform across much of the region and the world (Myers 2018a; Wolf 2017).

Embedded autonomy with Chinese characteristics

It is not only China's political development that remains stubbornly different from the experience of much of the West, however. Economic development in the PRC has been and remains very different to that of the so-called Anglo-American economies in particular. As has been the case across much of East Asia, China's economic development has been driven and closely controlled by the state (Beeson 2009a). While China may not have had the same sort of 'state capacity' that Japan did in the heyday of the developmental state that it pioneered, the PRC has followed in Japan's footsteps when it comes to shaping economic development (Heilmann and Shih 2013) – even if its leaders may be reluctant to admit as much. Once again, the CCP has played an important part in this process; it still does.

Perhaps we should not be surprised that the state has played a pivotal role in the economic development of a formerly centrally planned economy. What *is* surprising is the extent of the state's continuing role in the economy, even as economic activity becomes increasingly integrated with the wider international system (Szamosszegi and Kyle 2011; Hsueh 2016). China's political elites demonstrate a degree of what Peter Evans (1995) famously described as 'embedded autonomy', in which policymakers and state officials are sufficiently close to economic actors and processes to exercise significant influence, without being 'captured' by particularistic interests keen to shape policy in their favor. In China's case, this means that the CCP maintains a direct presence in the boardrooms of many notionally private companies (Hornby 2017). Indeed, according to Brødsgaard (2012: 645), the key factor that holds the Chinese system together is 'wielding personnel control', through which, he argues, 'the Party maintains the balance of power between the Party state and Chinese big business'.

In other cases, such as the financial sector, where some activities are judged to be creating unacceptably high degrees of risk, the state may directly intervene to change behavior (Wildau 2017). There is growing concern about the activities of the so-called 'shadow banking' sector (McMahon 2018), or the growing array of lending institutions outside that state-controlled banking sector. The prospect of an economic crisis is unthinkable for the CCP and Xi, whose authority is highly dependent on stability and growth. There are other, lower-profile, but equally important 'structural' constraints that limit the policy options available to China's policymaker, though. Despite expressing a desire for the yuan to play a more prominent role in the international financial system (Huang 2015), for example, there are real limits on the state's willingness to abandon capital controls and the value of the currency. As Vermeiren and Dierckx (2012: 1648) point out, it is a situation that is riddled with – possibly unsustainable – contradictions:

> the main raison d'être of the Chinese capital control regime is the consolidation of an investment-led regime of accumulation that redistributes income and wealth from Chinese workers to the Chinese corporate sector, which includes the state-owned enterprises and state banks. In other words, the dominant fractions of Chinese industrial and financial capital are the principle constituencies and beneficiaries of the capital control regime.

For some observers, the inherent tensions between the PRC's notional role as the representative of the proletariat and the growing economic divisions within the country are part of an institutionalized order that is resistant to change. Maintaining control of the economy, especially the all-important financial sector that provides funding to often-unprofitable SOEs, is crucial. Walter and Howie (2011: 78–9) argue that 'it is the Party, and not the market, that runs China and its capital-allocation process ... political imperatives make significant internationalization of the banks unlikely.' For all Xi Jinping's (2018) recent declarations about the country's commitment to further opening, therefore, the prospect that China will allow foreign financial entities or MNCs easy access remains remote. Likewise, the possibility that China's domestic economy, financial markets, or currency can play the sort of role currently provided by the United States also look equally unlikely.

The point to emphasize in this context is that the factors that limit the Chinese state's policy flexibility in the global economy – and its potential to play a leadership role – are overwhelmingly domestic. Consequently, the PRC's leaders have both the capacity and the desire to keep 'intervening' in the domestic economy and even the activities of SOEs operating overseas (Bräutigam and Tang 2014). Such policies are at odds with the notional liberal economic orthodoxy that prevails in the IFIs that have been key parts of what passes for global governance for the last fifty years or so. Despite a number of high-profile efforts to encourage further economic liberalization and market-oriented reforms (World Bank and DRCS 2012), there are clear limits to how far the PRC leadership is willing to take this process.

China's economic elites still consider themselves to be managing a 'developing economy', albeit one that will soon become the largest in the world, all other things being equal. There are clear policy advantages from being considered a developing country, not least in the expectations that other states might have about China's capacity or obligation to act in particular ways (Stone-Fish 2014). Likewise, China's desire to be recognized as a 'market economy' offers potentially major economic gains, as it would be less affected by discriminatory tariffs – which is precisely why it has been so vigorously opposed by the United States (Gao 2017a).

For all China's growing confidence and apparent desire to play an international leadership role (Bremmer 2018), therefore, it is unlikely that the broad contours of China's economic policies will undergo major change in the short term, at least. Fundamental constraints are built into the Chinese domestic political economy and this places limits on the sort of role it can play internationally. However, while the Chinese government's options may be constrained this does not mean that it is without influence or that its impact on the international system and the institutions that govern economic activity in particular will not continue to grow. To understand how, it is useful to consider the role of 'China' as a self-conscious actor in processes associated with global governance, and the possible attractions of the 'China model' as a template for other would-be developing economies.

China goes (sort of) global

While there continues to be a good deal of debate about the nature and appropriateness of state-guided economic development in general and in the PRC in particular (Lin 2012; Naughton 2015), one thing is unambiguously clear: whatever China's political and economic elites have been doing for the past thirty or forty years or so, it has plainly worked. There are two noteworthy consequences of this unprecedented historical achievement. First, and most importantly, the sheer scale of China's economic development has entirely transformed the country itself as well as the PRC's place in the international order. It is the combined increase in China's economic and latterly strategic weight that forces the rest of the world to pay attention and consider the implications that flow from the rise of a nondemocratic power to the center of international governance. Second, China's leaders are less constrained by the desire to follow Deng Xiaoping's famous dictum to 'hide its strength and bide its time' (*taoguang yanghui*). In other words, the time for meekly following the policy dictates of the West would seem to be over – if, indeed, economic liberalism was ever actually in the ascendancy in China or anywhere else in East Asia, for that matter (Beeson and Islam 2005; Cheng 2010). Significantly, the ideational impact of China's successful development experience does not even need the state to actively promote it in the way the United States did with Washington consensus.

The China model

As we have seen in earlier chapters, one of the more noteworthy features of the global economy has been the persistence of difference at the national level. Even among long-standing economically advanced and politically liberal countries major differences remain in social and organizational forms. In China's case, which was essentially a very distinctive form of primarily agrarian socialism until comparatively recently, enduring differences are even more stark. This is not to deny that there have been profound transformations in the way economic life and even private life are conducted in China; but this does not necessarily mean that 'China today is growing not by writing its own rules, but instead by internalizing the rules of the advanced industrial West', as Edward Steinfeld (2010: 18) claims. On the contrary, one of the more important potential consequences of China's rise is the possibility that the vectors of ideational influence are pointing in an entirely new direction. One important aspect of this is the emergence of the 'China model' as a possible template of economic development.

Like much else about China's rise and contemporary status, the significance and even the existence of the China model are hotly contested. For some observers, especially in China, the country's development experience and success hold important lessons for other countries. Cheng (2010: 48), for example, argues that 'the rise of the Chinese development model not only has significant long-term implications for the future of China, but also presents a distinctive model for the rest of the world, especially the developing countries, to consult in their own development endeavors'. Likewise, the former Chief Economist of the World Bank, Justin Yifu Lin (2011: 13), suggests that 'China's and other East Asian economies' experiences provide a golden opportunity for rethinking the fundamental issues of the roles of the state, market, and other institutions in a developing country's process of development and transition to catch up with the industrialized nations'.

However, whatever the merits of the China model may or may not be, Lin should have been well placed to realize that the prospects for widespread emulation faced significant ideational obstacles, not the least of which came from within the World Bank and other IFIs that have long supported market-oriented reform. During the 1990s there was a major furor around the status and possible heuristic importance of the developmental state generally and the Japanese experience in particular (Wade 1996). While the World Bank (1997) eventually came to acknowledge that the state had, indeed, played a very significant role in directing the East Asian 'miracle', the acceptance was frequently grudging and patchy, and the possible lessons were resisted. For some influential academic observers, these sorts of historical experiences and the continuing primacy and promotion of broadly neoliberal developmental policies were confirmation of the basic unfairness and unreasonableness of the 'core' group of developed economies' collective attitude to the 'peripheral' emerging economies. Ha-Joon Chang (2002) has forcefully argued that the United States and other developed states have discouraged would-be developing economies from adopting precisely the same sorts of industry policies and protection that they did themselves when they were industrializing.

The possibility that the China model may contain possible lessons that might be useful for other states keen to emulate its success is, therefore, one that deserves to be taken seriously. At this stage, however, the PRC government has been rather ambivalent about the merits of promoting a Chinese model of development, which some take to be a sign of the popularity of liberal ideas within China itself (Ferchen 2013). A more plausible explanation for the Chinese leadership's somewhat surprising bashfulness about their undoubted successes may be because of its inherent ideological contradictions. After all, success has come as a *capitalist* rather than a socialist economy. Indeed, as the late Arif Dirlik (2012: 289) observed, 'it would be intellectually self-deceptive even for the Communist Party leadership to ignore what most commentators in and out of China find attractive is not "socialism" but "capitalism with Chinese characteristics", made possible by repudiating the revolutionary socialism of the past'.

An even more fundamental problem confronting those who might wish to promote the Chinese experience, perhaps, is that it is sui generis and simply unrepeatable. As Naughton (2010: 439) pithily points out, 'nobody else is so big, possesses such a unique comparative advantage, or operates a remotely similar political system'. The size of the Chinese economy combined with an effective, highly distinctive form of state-led development may make its successes unrepeatable. For all the problems historically associated with China's form of 'fragmented authoritarianism' (Lieberthal 1992), the unambiguous reality is that it has worked remarkably effectively. According to Heilmann (2007: 22), 'the combination of decentralized experimentation with ad hoc central interference, which results in selective integration of local experiences into national policy-making, is a key to understanding how a distinctive policy process has contributed to China's economic rise'.

The complex relationship between China's central and provincial governments that has been such a distinctive part of the Chinese developmental story is complex and – like so much else – attracts very different opinions. On the one hand, there are those who see decentralization as fundamental constraint on the ability of the central government to impose its policy agenda (Mertha 2012; De Jonquieres 2014). On the other, are those who think that the central government has used its authority to drive reforms (Cai and Treisman 2006), which have been historically associated with embedding market principles across the Chinese economy (Montinola et al. 1995). It is not simply the complexity – and possibly limited relevance – of China's governance structures that makes the nature of its model questionable, however. As Shaun Breslin (2011b: 1328) points out, 'part of the problem in identifying the components of any such model is the huge diversity of developmental trajectories within China itself. To talk of a single Chinese model misses the huge variety – the different models – of economic structures within China.' Breslin further argues that the ultimate significance of the China model may be as a general exemplar of what can be achieved by addressing specific national conditions rather than universal templates.

There is one final aspect of the China model debate that deserves attention in the context of the possible relevance of Chinese modes of domestic governance for the wider world order. For some observers such as Daniel Bell, China's domestic politics contain potentially important lessons for other countries, especially nondemocratic states keen to emulate China's undoubted successes. For Bell (2015: 36),

> The meritocratic ideal – the idea that government officials are selected and promoted on the basis of ability and morality rather than political connections, wealth, and family background – is still a long way from the political reality in China. But if China continues to 'meritocratize' and avoids the bad policymaking stemming from voter ignorance in democratic countries (especially the United States, the powerful and populous country it is usually compared to), it will set a model for others.

The successful exemplar for both advocates of this argument, and for many Chinese policymakers as well, is Singapore, which has combined a distinctive form of 'semi-democracy' with impressive developmental outcomes (Ortmann and Thompson 2014). Apart from the question about whether the Singapore experience can actually be scaled up to achieve something similar in China, there is the equally important question of how well such a prospect would be received elsewhere. Not only has Singapore been the frequent target of criticism for its authoritarian approach to development and social control (Rodan 2009), but there are potentially important ramifications – even lessons – from the evolving Chinese experience, too. As Teets (2014: 176) points out, 'China, although unique in many ways, has increasingly converged with other nondemocratic regimes in developing a new relationship with civil society – one that allows autonomous civil society more participation in the policy process while creating new tools of state control'. However, government wariness about, and desire to exercise control over, civil society has increased, limiting the potentially useful and important role NGOs and other civil society actors can play in providing collective goods (Gaudreau and Cao 2015).

The Beijing consensus

Questions about the applicability of the Chinese experience would be of interest and importance at the best of times. Plainly these are not the best of times, especially for the American-led liberal order that has prevailed for the last half-century or so. This makes possible alternative models or patterns of governance of particular interest and importance. The Washington consensus has been subjected to some withering criticisms (Chang and Grabel 2005; Rodrik 2006), both in terms of its effectiveness and the possibly self-serving, inappropriate nature of some of its key policy prescriptions. Yet the surprising durability of the extant institutional order means that a major paradigm shift in policy ideas has *not* occurred in the international system thus far (Babb 2012; Beeson and Li 2015). However, the actions of the current American administration led by Donald Trump make the search for leadership and even new ideas a more plausible possibility than it has been for decades (Stephens 2018).

Significantly, there are many observers keen to champion the possible lessons of the Chinese experience and/or of the merits of the closely associated 'Beijing consensus', and not just in China either. Martin Jacques, for example, has famously argued that it is only a question of time until 'China rules the world'. In the meantime, 'China's success suggests that the Chinese model of the state is destined to exercise a powerful global influence, especially in the developing world, and thereby transform the terms of the future economic debate' (Jacques 2009: 185). At this stage, the possible basis of this influence revolves around the 'Beijing consensus', which some are equally convinced will sweep the world, its authoritarian basis notwithstanding (Halper 2010).

It is important to remember, however, that when Joshua Ramo came up with the idea of the Beijing consensus in 2004 it was short on specifics and more concerned with highlighting the dramatic shift in the way China was coming to be seen as an international actor. Indeed, in some ways, the Beijing consensus looked rather familiar when conceived of as 'a ruthless willingness to innovate and experiment, by a lively defence of national borders and interests, and by the increasingly thoughtful accumulation of tools of asymmetric power projection' (Ramo 2004: 4). This privileging of pragmatism and the national interest looks a decidedly nonrevolutionary, not to say an unlikely basis, for global collective action. It is for such reasons that Ramo's conception has been taken to task by a number of 'China experts', such as Kennedy (2010: 462), who claims 'it not only gets the empirical facts wrong about China, it also disregards the similarities and differences China's experience shares with other countries, and it distorts China's place in international politics'. Other more sympathetic observers think that the key is to refine rather than abandon the basic insight about China's different approach to development (Li et al. 2009).

Perhaps the salient point to emphasize from this inconclusive discussion is that it is the very *idea* that China might present an alternative to the increasingly discredited neoliberal, Washington consensus orthodoxy that is so striking. After all, only thirty or forty years ago, the PRC was noteworthy primarily for its export of revolutionary ideology (Van Ness 1970), rather than as an exemplar of the effective management of an essentially capitalist economy. It is precisely this sense that China's political and economic elites might have some useful ideas about international economic management that is leading many to call for the PRC to play a greater role in global governance (Liu 2016). Before we consider what such a role might look like, however, it is important to acknowledge that there are some rather large flies in the proverbial ointment of Chinese-style governance, which may place the credibility, even the durability, of the China model and the Beijing consensus in question.

Minxin Pei has been one of the more outspoken critics of China's developmental model, arguing that 'the political logic and institutional determinants of autocracy … are more likely to create a predatory state than a developmental one' (Pei 2006: 207). He has also drawn attention to the perverse and destructive effects of endemic corruption in the Chinese bureaucracy, claiming that 'elites in control of unconstrained power cannot resist using it to loot the wealth generated by economic growth' (Pei 2016: 261). Such views may not be terribly popular in China, but their implications are taken increasingly seriously, nevertheless. Xi Jinping's seemingly genuine, if selectively implemented (Wong 2016; Buckley 2016), anti-corruption drive may be laudable, but it is generating some unintended and unwanted consequences in the process. Many bureaucrats appear reluctant to act lest they attract unfavorable attention (Bell 2017), and the entire process may have created some powerful enemies for Xi as a consequence (Bradsher and Myers 2018). In the event of a domestic economic crisis that undermines his authority and popularity, Xi's position may be less secure than it currently seems (Special Correspondent 2017).

Indeed, one of the distinguishing features of authoritarian regimes, especially where power is increasingly concentrated, is that they are brittle and may be swept away rapidly and unexpectedly (Brownlee 2007). Regimes that derive legitimation for the 'authoritarian bargain' as a consequence of their ability to generate economic growth, rents, and patronage, are especially vulnerable in this context (Desai et al. 2009). This may help to explain the otherwise puzzling increase in spending on domestic security, which actually outstrips the much more widely noted external variety (Tan 2018). This extended commentary on China's domestic politics and governance structures is merited because it is seen by some as an alternative to the prevailing, notionally liberal, order. Whether China's leaders actually have the capacity to put their ideas into international practice is, however, another question. Whether China's elites are revisionists, much less revolutionaries, is also debatable. The answers to both questions are potentially important in determining the future of the international system of governance.

China and global governance

One big, rather clichéd, point about China that merits endless repetition relates to the speed of its development, and not just economically. Chinese diplomacy has also been transformed. Many in the United States may think it is still not the sort of 'responsible stakeholder' that former World Bank president Robert Zoellick (2005) famously urged it ought to become, but its position in the international system has changed profoundly, nevertheless. At one level, this can be seen most clearly in the number of international organizations in which the PRC is a member. However, some observers in China emphasize that the PRC is very wary of the obligations this may entail (Dai and Renn 2016). Such reservations may help to explain why China is also beginning to establish its own. Before looking at China's role in these IOs in any detail, however, it is important to say something about the capacity of extant organizations to socialize their members into 'appropriate' behavior. One of the key roles of any social institution, after all, is to encourage members to internalize the norms and beliefs that they embody, and in the case of IOs actively attempt to promote. The key question in China's case is how far has this process of socialization gone, and is it becoming a two-way street? In other words, are the former rule takers becoming rule makers?

Changing 'China'?

One preliminary observation to make is that when we talk about socialization we need to carefully differentiate who we are actually talking about. For some observers, one important focus for analysis is the entire society. Edward Steinfeld (2010: 45), for example, argues that 'communist' China no longer exists and that 'Communism as an ideology is dead in China. Claims to legitimacy on the basis of past revolutionary glories are virtually inoperative. The government rules today on the basis of its ability to deliver a version of modernity defined by the advanced industrial democracies.' He has a point: 'China' is a very different country today than it was even twenty years ago, especially in the wealthy Eastern seaboard where individualistic, consumerist lifestyles prevail and a younger generation has little interest in 'socialism' (Guo 2012). As we have seen, however, the CCP remains firmly in command, and the structures and connections that distinguish China's domestic and even international economic relations remain very different from those found in the United States.

At another, elite level, things are also transformed, but perhaps not as much as we might think. True, the relative handful of policymakers and officials who represent and rule China are also very different from their socialist forebears. But there are limits to this socialization process, too. While China's diplomats may be increasingly comfortable and confident about their ability to operate in the institutions of global governance (Foot 2014), this does not mean that they necessarily accept all of the norms and practices of the extant system. As one might expect with such a complex and comparatively new process, there is a range of sometimes conflicting opinion about the extent and nature of the ideational and normative change that has been exerted on China's leaders and people.

Noted China watcher David Shambaugh (2013: 7, emphasis in original), for example, argues that China remains a 'partial power', that is '*in* the community of nations but is in many ways not really *part* of that community; it is formally involved, but it is not normatively integrated.' And yet it is clear that the views of China's leaders have changed profoundly from the relatively recent past, when the PRC was seen primarily as a source of destabilizing revolutionary ideology (Van Ness 1970). Some things have clearly changed; the question is what and how much. Another prominent analyst of China's international relations, Iain Alastair Johnston (2008: xiv), suggests that 'there is considerable, if subtle, evidence of the socialization of Chinese diplomats, strategists, and analysts in certain counter-realpolitik norms and practices as a result of participation in these institutions'.

One of the seminal moments in this socialization process was China's admission to the WTO, a drawn-out process that culminated in the PRC having to agree very stringent entry requirements (Lardy 2002), which ultimately had major domestic and international consequences. The international consequences are most visible and have led to the rather paradoxical situation in which the PRC has arguably been one of the principal beneficiaries of the hegemonic order that the United States created – an outcome that may have precipitated and/or accelerated a process of hegemonic transition. Internally, the initial changes were rather more subtle: WTO accession effectively snuffed out any lingering domestic opposition by 'conservatives' concerned about going down the capitalist road (Breslin 2007: 83). In retrospect, however, it is also important to recognize that a degree of socialization into Western ways must already have occurred in China for its leaders to have been even thinking about joining such an IO in the first place.

One of the distinctive features of China's integration into the WTO in particular and into other IOs more generally has been a desire to retain the primacy of the CCP and the state in domestic affairs. As Hsueh (2011: 3) notes, China

> employs a bifurcated strategy to meet its twin goals of complying with WTO commitments and retaining state control. In strategic sectors – those important to national security and the promotion of economic and technological development – the government centralizes control of industry, and strictly manages the level and direction of FDI. In less strategic sectors, the Chinese government relinquishes control over industry, decentralizes decision making to local authorities, and encourages private investment and FDI.

While this may represent a form of 'globalization with Chinese characteristics' in some ways, it also reflects China's continuing commitment to a very Westphalian sense of sovereignty and the continuing importance of a distinctive sense of the national interest and domestically driven policies. Indeed, Scott Kennedy argues that China's approach to global governance is conservative, not revisionist and that this inhibits needed reforms at the domestic and international levels: 'My fear … is not that China has been or will be an anti-status quo power, but that it won't be, that it is so wedded to the status quo that China will forestall important reforms that are desperately needed' (Kennedy 2012: 11).

Although the belief that China is a status quo rather than a revisionist or revolutionary force in global governance is widely shared, this does not mean that China's leaders are entirely satisfied with the existing system or China's role within it. The fact that China continues to push for forms of representation that more clearly reflect its growing power and contribution to specific organizations such as the UN, the World Bank, and the IMF is one important indication of this possibility. An even more unambiguous indication of China's possible dissatisfaction with the extant order, though, can be seen in China's development of entirely new IOs. The key question in this context is whether such institutional innovations are complementary or competing. Nothing better illustrates the possible tensions and contradictions than the creation of the Asian Infrastructure Investment Bank (AIIB).

A new global order?

The inauguration of the AIIB, especially in tandem with the closely associated Belt and Road Initiative (BRI), is one of the clearest indicators of the scale of China's ambitions. The AIIB is designed to provided much-needed lending for infrastructure development in a region which badly needs it. The BRI is a monumental project designed to provide precisely that and link Southeast, Southern, and Central Asia more closely to China in the process. Both the BRI and the AIIB are illustrations of the possible importance of China's growing 'geoeconomic' leverage (Beeson 2018a). The potential significance of geoeconomic power was first identified by Edward Luttwak (1990), who recognized that the end of the Cold War had profoundly changed the geopolitical environment within which states interacted and *competed*. Significantly, in an era where direct military conflict between states was becoming very rare, the principal manifestation of such competition was economic. In Luttwak's (1993) view it was a competition that the United States was losing to countries that had a more sophisticated grasp of the new economic realities and which were employing industry policies to assist the development of 'national champions'.

It is no coincidence that Luttwak's ideas have enjoyed a renewed prominence in the wake of China's rise and the growing economic competition between China and the United States. For a new generation of observers such as Blackwill and Harris (2016: 8), geoeconomics means 'applying economic instruments to advance geopolitical ends'. The organization of economic activity in China, in which the state continues to play a major 'interventionist' role, is reminiscent of the Japanese developmental model (Beeson 2009a). It is generating similar tensions with the United States, where policymakers consider they are 'losing' the economic competition with China because of the latter's 'unfair' practices (Page et al. 2017). The merits of these claims and the subsequent 'trade war' they have recently generated is taken up in more detail in Chapter 7. What matters at this stage is that China's state-centric development model is potentially a direct challenge to the long-standing liberal order and for the prospects of agreement on global economic governance.

There is some irony in all this. After all, when the United States became the hegemonic power of the era, it employed similar sorts of policies to those of China now. The Marshall Plan, for example, bears a striking similarity to China's nascent BRI, and not just in the provision of much needed infrastructure development (Shen 2016). On the contrary, as we saw in Chapter 3, American aid was intended to help reconstruct the war-ravaged economies of Europe and Japan, and the creation of the Bretton Woods institutions was an integral part of the process. American geoeconomic power was institutionalized and complemented its geopolitical goals. What is different in the contemporary period is the absence of similar geopolitical pressures. China's goals may be less ideological as a consequence, but they are no less ambitious. On the contrary, Tom Miller (2017: 18) argues that 'the goal of China's economic diplomacy is to create a modern tribute system, with all roads literally leading to Beijing'.

In this context, the AIIB is at one level simply the means with which to facilitate the realization of the BRI. At another level, however, the AIIB is an expression of Beijing's unhappiness with the prevailing global order, which it sees as still dominated by the United States and its allies, despite the more prominent role China has played in major IOs of late (Beeson and Xu forthcoming). That there is a need for major infrastructure investment in much of Asia is not in doubt. One might have thought that any new initiative that promised to fill a genuine need would be welcomed, therefore. One would be wrong. The United States mounted what many – including some Trump advisors (Zhuang et al. 2016) – regarded as a misguided campaign to dissuade close allies from joining China's initiative. The Obama administration clearly feared a diminution of its influence in a region that China has historically dominated. Yet American efforts looked like an anachronistic throwback to the Cold War era, especially in Chinese eyes (Nagy 2016; Wilson forthcoming). They also looked overblown: the reality is that to ensure the participation of Europeans and other Western states, China's policymakers had to agree to adopt many of the principles of the existing international economic order (Hanlon 2017).

So, while there may be limits to China's ability or even willingness to try and change the rules that govern economic activity, the impact of the BRI may be another thing altogether. The sheer scale of the BRI, which is intended to link Europe with Asia and incorporate strategically important but occasionally problematic neighbors such as Central and Southeast Asia, as well as relative outliers such as Pakistan, is what sets this project apart (Clarke 2017; Sender and Stacey 2017). The BRI also promises to help resolve two pressing domestic problems as well. On the one hand, the BRI fits in with China's 'march westwards', helping to further integrate the restive province of Xinjiang, as well as expanding the reach of China's geopolitical influence in Central Asia (Wang 2012). In this context, it is important to note that China has already established itself as the region's preeminent diplomatic power through the successful inauguration of the Shanghai Cooperation Organization (SCO) (Cheng 2011). On the other hand, the BRI may help to resolve some potentially serious domestic economic problems, if that is the way to describe the remarkable expansion of China's building industry (Beeson 2018c). However we describe this formidable capacity to deliver infrastructure projects domestically, though, it bodes well for China's ability to do the same thing internationally. It also stands in sharp contrast with the record of the United States (Browne 2018).

Concluding remarks

There is little doubt that China is attempting to give very tangible expression to its geoeconomic and geopolitical ambitions. For many strategic analysts in the United States and allied states, there is growing concern that China is skillfully combining the two: economic assistance is locking poorer, strategically important states into its geopolitical orbit, expanding China's strategic footprint in the process (Zumbrun and Emont 2018). Whether it is also attempting to reconfigure or compete with the existing international order in which such plans will be realized is less clear. For some observers, it is only a question of time until China attempts to establish its own norms and principles as the foundation of global governance (Chan et al. 2012: 39). For others – the majority at this stage, perhaps – China is not attempting to change things, especially where this helps to reinforce rather than undermine sovereignty (Chin and Thakur 2010; Harpaz 2016). In this context, at least, Kahler (2010: 189) argues that China is but the most prominent and important exemplar of a more generalized Asian attitude to global governance:

> Asian governments have expanded their influence in global governance and key global economic institutions. At times, they have challenged prevailing economic orthodoxies, but those challenges have been incorporated in a constantly evolving policy consensus rather than overturning that consensus. As major stakeholders in the existing international order, Asian governments, including China, are unlikely candidates for revolutionary change.

While Kahler may be right to suggest that change is unlikely to be revolutionary, even incremental change may ultimately prove transformative – especially in an environment where the traditional defender of liberalism and democracy appears to be uninterested at best, positively sympathetic to illiberal norms and authoritarian modes of governance at worst (Haas 2018; Sit 2018). In such a context, the durability of existing democracies may be in question; its once-predicted inexorable spread looks like a pipedream (Fukuyama 1992). As Cooley (2015: 51) observes, China, rather than the United States, may be at the leading edge of a historical wave that may entrench illiberal forms of rule and ultimately international governance:

> Appeals to 'civilizational diversity' and the principle of noninterference in the domestic affairs of sovereign states form another class of emerging counternorms. The People's Republic of China is the leading supporter of this manner of critiquing liberal democracy's universalism as well as the political conditionality that international institutions adopt to further universal democratic norms.

One of the reasons that the United States was – and to some extent, still is – the most influential state in the period following the Second World War is because it combined geoeconomic and geopolitical power and influence, even if we didn't always describe them in quite that way (Beeson 2018a). China is developing the capacity to do the same. Although China's policymakers may be uncertain about precisely what it is they wish to do with this growing power, or what ideas and norms they wish to promote, there is less doubt about the rapidity with which China's place in the international system has been transformed.

Politicians across the world are prone to indulging in soaring rhetoric, and Xi Jinping is clearly not immune to the temptation. Xi's address to the UN scaled new heights in this regard:

> let us unite ever more closely to create a new mutually beneficial partnership and community of shared future for mankind. Let the vision of a world free of war and enjoying lasting peace take root in our hearts. Let the aspirations of development, prosperity, fairness and justice spread across the world! (cited in Gao 2017b)

Noble sentiments, indeed, the question is does he actually mean what he says and are these ideas actually in keeping with China's recent foreign and even domestic policies? The answer would seem to be unambiguously 'no'. Xi appears just as enthusiastic about 'putting China first' as Trump does about America. Realizing unambiguously *national* interests appears to be inextricably linked to domestic political reform and the centralization of power around Xi and the CCP, on the one hand, and an increasingly 'assertive' approach to foreign policy, on the other (Callick 2018). As we have seen, China has displayed a willingness to buy off or bully some of its less powerful Southeast Asian neighbors into either going along with Beijing's wishes or, at least, not actively opposing them (Beeson 2015). China's long-term vision may, indeed, be good for the 'development and prosperity' components of his vision, but they seem a bit deficient when it comes to the 'fairness and justice' elements. Unfortunately, such views are not confined to China.

5

The Rise of the Rest?

The rise of China may have attracted the most attention among policymakers and scholars of late, but it is not an isolated phenomenon. As we have seen, China's position is not so much a 'rise' as a reemergence. Equally importantly, China is not the only state moving up the international hierarchy of states – now or in earlier periods. On the contrary, other powers have also 'emerged' at various times in recent history. What distinguishes the current moment in some observers' opinion, however, is a more broadly based process: the 'rise of the rest' (Amsden 2001). This formulation is a convenient shorthand for the growing prominence of a number of states, especially the so-called BRICS (Brazil, Russia, India, and China), as well as a range of other 'middle powers', which are attempting to influence regional and even global governance processes. The concomitant rise of a new array of IOs in addition to the BWIs discussed in Chapter 3 is another important part of this story and expression of the evolving international order.

The key question, as ever, when considering these new patterns of international interaction is deciding quite how significant they actually are. Have any of the rising powers other than China actually been able to make a discernible, much less a decisive, impact on the extant modes of governance, especially in the economic and political spheres? As we shall see in Chapter 9, there is an argument to be made that some of the rising (or reemerging) powers – especially Russia – have, indeed, made an impact in the security arena, but this has generally been destabilizing and antithetical to the prospects for collective governance. The rather tarnished reputation of the United States' economic model and the existence of potentially viable alternatives have opened up the possibility that new modes of economic governance and thinking may be feasible – in theory at least (Beeson 2017a).

It may not surprise the reader to learn by this stage that things are often rather more demanding in practice, and not simply because of the technical difficulty of addressing complex questions of international coordination. Equally unsurprisingly, perhaps, there are significant agential and structural obstacles facing would-be reformers of the international system. It is one thing to establish new more inclusive organizations such as the G20, for example; it is quite another to enable it to reflect new ideas, modes of governance, or centers of power. In order to assess how much impact 'the rest' are actually likely to have on the extant international system, it is important – once again – to provide a little historical context. Following this, I consider some of the specific states and institutional innovations that have attracted so much recent commentary.

Early risers

One of the problems that scholars and policymakers from the West face is that most of us have no experience of anything other than a world shaped and dominated by American power. As we have seen, even China has been profoundly influenced by its recent integration into a global capitalist system that is ubiquitous, even if there are important variations in the way its component political and economic parts are organized at the national level. Even when China was unambiguously a communist power and enthusiastically trying to encourage its neighbors to adopt a similar paradigm, it was acting in response to the supposed inequities and shortcomings of an evil capitalist system. It is one of the great ironies of history that 'communist China' is one of the most important sources of growth in the global economy and on track to become the largest economy in the world in the near future (O'Brien 2017).

This is not without historical precedent. As recently as the nineteenth century, China was the largest center of economic activity in the world. In 1820, China's economy was larger than Western Europe's and the United States' combined. India's economy was nearly ten times the size of America's (Maddison 2007: 174). The subsequent transformation in America's position during the latter half of the nineteenth century was remarkable and strikingly similar to China's today. It is precisely because of the importance of economic development that some scholars argue that 'the rise and decline of leading sectors in the global economy are coordinate with the rise and decline of world powers' (Modelski and Thompson 1996: 3). It is also why a failure of economic development is such a potentially critical determinant of a state's position in the hierarchy of nations and its concomitant ability to influence the way the international system is governed. Little wonder that the perceived economic and political inequities that are seen to result from the structure and operation of the international economic system are such a source of unhappiness and resentment.

The new international economic order

A growing sense that the international economy may not simply have been unequal, but actually responsible for keeping some states in a subordinate, dependent position culminated in demands for a more equitable international order. The perception that the world was divided between the 'developed' and – what was, and sometimes still is, rather patronizingly known as – the 'developing' world became part of the discourse of international diplomacy. Two aspects of this process are especially noteworthy. First, predominantly Western ideas about the nature of economic development and the necessity for countries to 'modernize', if they wanted to enjoy similar living standards to those of Europe and North America, became highly influential, not least within the IFIs that were responsible for dispensing aid (Latham 2010). Such ideas would culminate in policies designed to encourage 'good governance' and major reform of what were seen as 'backward' and inefficient patterns of political and economic organization across what came to be known as the 'Third World' (Berger 2006).

The possibility that some economic ideas and policies were inherently better than others was not simply a 'technical' question, however. Especially during the 1960s, development policy became associated with the Cold War struggle against communism. It is no coincidence that Walt Rostow's (1960) highly influential prescription for developmental success, *The Stages of Economic Growth*, was imbued with the suppositions of modernization theory and subtitled *A Non-Communist Manifesto*. Indeed, the normative principles and ideological implications of development theory often seemed as important as their pragmatic consequences. Yet other prominent voices in the theoretical struggle against communism that gripped the United States during the 1960s recognized that 'the most important political distinction among countries concerns not their form of government but their degree of government' (Huntington 1968: 1). In other words, developing the sort of state capacity discussed in Chapter 1 could be decisive, especially in the context of an ideological struggle with an attractive alternative paradigm.

This was the second consequence of the new discourse of development and international relations: a striking feature of the first few decades of American hegemony was a growing consciousness on the part of the world's disadvantaged nations and peoples that 'the system' was unfair and something ought to be done about it. Not only was the world an unequal place, but it was also one from which the rich world was seen to benefit at the expense of the poor (Amin 1978). Nowadays it is considered more appropriate to talk about a north–south divide that bears a rough resemblance to the geographic division between the world's rich and poor countries. But whatever broad-brush labels we apply to the structural divide between states in the international system, there was a sense that it was unfair and that the institutions established under the auspices of American hegemony were part of the problem rather than the solution. A major response to this sense of structural inequality and the systematic neglect of voices from the South was the formation of the Group of 77 (G77) and the concomitant call for the creation of a New International Economic Order (NIEO) (Toye 2014).

The G77 was composed of the developing countries that existed when the UN Conference on Trade and Development (UNCTAD) was established in 1962. UNCTAD itself was an expression of the need to include a wider range of economic perspectives when trying to explain, let alone do something about, inequality and the persistence of poverty. UNCTAD's first head, Raúl Prebisch (1962), was an Argentinian economist and leading proponent of dependency theory. His ideas represented a major critique of the prevailing liberal logic of comparative advantage theory, favoring instead something akin to the interventionist industry policies that were such a key part of the 'Asian miracle'. The agenda of NIEO reflected some of these ideas and argued that developing countries should have the right to regulate powerful MNCs; the right to nationalize economic activities, even if foreign owned; the chance to establish primary producer associations of agricultural producers; and the opportunity to utilize discriminatory tariffs and technology transfer to speed development (Biel 2000).

Despite the fact that precisely the same sorts of discriminatory, 'interventionist' policies had underpinned the earlier rise of key Western states such as Britain, Germany, and even the United States itself (Chang 2002), there was predictably little enthusiasm among the established powers about transforming a system from which they benefited. In retrospect, therefore, what is significant about the period is that it reminds us that there have been significant attempts to transform the basis of global governance from time to time, largely because it was seen to be inequitable and dysfunctional, as least as far as the increasingly dissatisfied and prominent developing states were concerned. The formation of groupings like the G77 and the earlier Bandung conference in 1955, which brought together Asian and African states, at least marked an important moment of consciousness-raising, even if such initiatives were unable to make much impression on the prevailing order. Indeed, 'revolutionary' China's principal contribution to the Bandung conference was to lay out a blueprint for protecting Westphalian-style national sovereignty (Zhao 2016).

Late developers

Given the clear links between economic development and increased political influence that the rise of Britain, the United States, and most recently China illustrate, one of the more surprising features of the international system over the last few decades has been the relatively limited impact of the 'newly industrializing countries' (NICs) of Northeast Asia in particular. All other things being equal, we might have expected that the so-called Asian miracle, which saw a number of East Asian states achieve in decades levels of economic development that had taken centuries in the West, would have allowed those states to have had a much bigger impact than they have. 'Normally' rising powers are supposed to assert themselves and present a challenge to the existing order, as they seek to reshape the international system to reflect their interests and growing importance (Gilpin 1981). And yet one of the most striking features of South Korea's, Taiwan's, Singapore's, and especially Japan's rise as major centers of regional economic activity is that they have had relatively little impact – even on the way we think about the causes of unambiguously successful economic policies (Klein and Cukier 2009; Kahler 2010).

Given that inequality and developmental failure remain prominent and potentially destabilizing parts of the international system, this is a noteworthy anomaly that takes some explaining. After all, all other things being equal, we might expect that successful models of development would be applauded and widely emulated. But in the much-invoked 'real world' things are generally not always equal, and that is a fundamental part of the problem, according to critics of the international order created under American auspices (Pieterse 2004). As we have seen, the capacity to normalize – even impose – particular ideas about 'good governance' and supposedly optimal economic policies is not only a reflection of the sort of productive power discussed in Chapter 2, but may also help to achieve specific economic and even strategic advantages for states powerful enough to exercise such influence.

Many of these possible forms of power and influence have characterized relations between the United States and Japan, and they merit brief consideration because they help us to understand what is similar and different about China's challenge to the existing order.

Japan: Still abnormal?

Japan was the quintessential rising power in the late nineteenth and early twentieth centuries. The first Asian state to successfully industrialize, it provided a profound shock to a rather complacent European-dominated international system, not least by defeating one of the existing great powers – Russia – in a short, but decisive war. The other noteworthy feature of Japan's rise was that it subscribed to a decidedly 'Western standard of civilisation' (Gong 1984), which provided something of a template for international behavior. Not only did Japan assiduously borrow from Europe when embarking on a major process of national 'modernization' of its political, economically, and military institutions, but it also did what any self-respecting European great power did: it tried to acquire an empire (Beeson 2014a).

As we shall see in Chapter 6, Japan's 'Co-prosperity sphere' was an interesting experiment in coercive region-building that ultimately ended in failure and catastrophic conflict. While the story of Japan's suicidal embrace of militarism and territorial expansion is well known (Dower 1986), less widely recognized are the long-term consequences and lessons that flow from Japan's defeat at the hands of the Americans. Perhaps the most striking feature of Japan's postwar experience was the paradoxically limited impact of America's occupation and efforts to remake Japan in its own image. While there were certainly a number of high-profile initiatives, such as the imposition of a new 'Peace constitution' and the restoration of democratic government, American efforts to reform Japanese business–government relations along liberal lines were far less successful. On the contrary, major features of Japan's distinctive corporate networks and their close ties to the state remained intact, and provided the basis of the highly effective developmental state that directed the course of national reconstruction (Johnson 1982).

So successful were the efforts of the Japanese state in guiding the postwar process of economic reconstruction, in fact, that by the 1980s many informed observers thought that Japan was on track to become 'No 1' (Vogel 1979) and destined to overtake the United States as the world's largest economy. Equally importantly, it was widely believed that the United States was not only in relative decline when compared to Japan, but that this was an indictment of the comparative limitations of American capitalism. Many of the debates that currently characterize the increasingly fraught relationship between China and the United States were prefigured here. Americans complained about Japan's 'unfair' protectionist, neo-mercantilist approach to international trade, and demanded that something should be done to restore what was seen as the natural order of things (Lincoln 1990). There was, however, one very significant difference between America's relationship with Japan and the contemporary contest with China: Japan was an ally of the United States and this had very significant consequences for America's ability to achieve national objectives and its views about the merits of a liberal international order.

Because Japan had effectively outsourced responsibility for its strategic and foreign policy to the United States in the postwar period, it was especially susceptible to American pressure (Katzenstein and Tsujinaka 1995). Consequently, the United States was able to compel the reluctant Japanese to revalue their currency in a misguided attempt to fix its politically sensitive trade surplus with America. Not only did this do little to address the trade 'problem', but it also helped trigger a major economic crisis in Japan, which finally put paid to any prospect of becoming the world's biggest economy (Katz 1998). There was one other important ideational consequence of this period that merits mention, however. Despite Japan's efforts to champion its own developmental experience and the merits of the advantages of an interventionist state, and to play a leadership role in responding to the Asian financial crisis (AFC) of the late 1990s, the United States was effectively able to nullify both initiatives (Amyx 2004; Wade 1996). Japan's strategic subordination to the United States meant that the prospects for alternative ideas about economic governance being taken seriously were dramatically reduced.

The significance of this brief historical sketch is that it illustrates how potentially important the overarching historical context is in shaping the dynamics of key bilateral relationships. Although most attention focused on the economic aspects of US–Japan relations, in the absence of their unique historical relationship and America's long-term determination to 'restrain' Japan and keep it strategically subordinate (Pyle 2007: 349), things might have evolved very differently and Japan's rise might have had altogether different historical consequences. None of the rising powers that are currently attracting such attention – and this applies especially to China – have any such contingent historical constraints or sense of obligation to the United States. Their capacity collectively or independently to influence the nature of governance practices at a moment of historical uncertainty and flux is, we might suppose, much higher as a consequence. The reality is more complicated, and it helps to make sense of the currently complex nature of global governance.

The BRICS

In retrospect, one of the most consequential contributions of the BRICS (Brazil, Russia, India, China, and subsequently South Africa) may have been to give tangible expression to the more generalized notions of 'rising powers' and 'emerging markets'. Indeed, it is important to remember that when Goldman Sachs analyst Jim O'Neil coined the acronym in 2001, no such grouping existed. Remarkably enough, what began life as a convenient way of thinking about a collection of countries with few connections and little in common became a reality as the states involved took up the idea and gave it institutional expression. At the very least, the history of the BRICS demonstrates how an idea that seems to capture the zeitgeist can provide a basis for real action in the material world.

Given the BRICS' unlikely origins, any achievements might be considered noteworthy and slightly surprising, perhaps. Yet given that they seemed to collectively represent, and give expression to, a historical turning point as power drained from the United States and the West to a new range of actors, expectations about their capacity to represent and enact different ways of thinking about governance issues were understandably high (Stephen 2014). After all, one of the central critiques of the old order was that it failed to recognize how much was apparently changing in the world, and how the key institutions that sought to manage international relations ought to recognize this evolving reality in their ideas, practices, and memberships. The possibility that the existing IFIs were unrepresentative, non-inclusive, and susceptible to the influence of the United States in particular was firmly held in many parts of the global South, and helps to explain China's efforts to develop an alternative institutional order.

Establishing new and different institutions has proved difficult enough for China acting on its own where it only has to consider one state's conception of the 'national interest'. Trying to arrive at a common policy position among a group of states with radically different histories, goals, and identities always looked like it was going to be problematic, and so it has proved to be. As Shaun Breslin (2013: 629) observes, 'while the BRICS states might agree on what they don't like and what they are dissatisfied with, there doesn't seem to be a shared vision of what a radically different world order might look like. Rather, the agenda seems to focus primarily on the redistribution of power within the existing order.' Other than a common sense of being unjustly marginalized by a US-centric, unrepresentative international order, the BRICS have few issues on which they can find common cause or that might provide the basis for an alternative international order. Indeed, it is possible to argue that China may actually have more in common with the United States than it does with its fellow BRICS (Bergsten 2008), and this may be one of the principal reasons that BRICS have found it difficult to develop a common sense of purpose.

Rising power or rising hegemon?

As we saw in the previous chapter, China presents a challenge to the United States and the extant international order like no other in history. The scale of China's growth, development, and ambitions are potentially an even greater problem for its fellow BRICS, however, which are even more overshadowed by their colossal partner. There is consequently a potentially irreconcilable tension at the heart of this accidental grouping: China is far bigger than all of the other BRICS combined, and has a capacity to influence – and pay for – any initiatives the BRICS might endorse in a way the others cannot match (Pant 2013). This was an issue even before the recent downturn in the prices of resources in the global economy, which has further diminished the relative importance of South Africa, Brazil, and Russia; it is doubly so now. Russia has found it especially difficult to come to terms with its neighbor's dramatic rise and its own comparatively diminished status on the world stage. There are indications that Russia has made a long-term geopolitical shift eastwards, however, in which its 'pivot to Asia is a reality [and] in all likelihood, irreversible' (Lukin 2018: 182). Either way, Vladimir Putin's goal of restoring Russia's former greatness, and his willingness to take major strategic risks to do so, only highlights the continuing importance of potentially incompatible *national* goals within a grouping whose members otherwise have little in common other than a predilection for 'strong man' leadership, perhaps (Lucas 2014).

Given the cyclical nature of the global economy, it is entirely possible and even likely that at some stage a new 'resource boom' will restore the relative standing and fortunes of Russia, Brazil, and South Africa. It is also important to note that this may well entrench authoritarian rule and make any transition to democratic governance, of a sort favored by the United States and the IFIs, even more difficult: the perverse impact of the 'resource curse' and its potential to encourage patronage politics and corruption in states reliant on a limited number of commodities has long been recognized (Ross 1999). Equally importantly, price volatility for natural resources high-lights both the vulnerability of some BRICS economies to forces over which they have little control and the very different positions of India and China, which actually stand to benefit from cheaper energy imports. The fact that

China's economy has become more diversified and its leadership has a demonstrated capacity – thus far, at least – to deal with major economic shocks suggests that underlying structural constraints may continue to determine the relative fortunes of the BRICS in ways that could prove divisive rather than the basis for cooperative behavior. In many ways, the BRICS internal contradictions and differences illustrate some of the most enduring obstacles to collective action and the prospects for global governance (Beeson and Zeng 2018).

This is not to say that the BRICS have no points of convergence or common interest, however. Unfortunately for the BRICS, though, this is not necessarily a good thing. Indeed, some of the things that do distinguish the BRICS as potential new forces of international cooperation represent potential threats to the existing order and may not provide the basis for a viable alternative. One of the most widely noted features of a number of the more prominent rising powers is that they are often illiberal and authoritarian (Gat 2007). Even India, which is frequently praised by Western commentators as an example of a large, long-standing Asian democracy, is currently led by someone – Narendra Modi – who is considered to be a populist and a Hindu nationalist, and who is intent on creating a personality cult around himself (Coll 2017). While Modi may have that much in common with Xi Jinping in this regard, this is unlikely to make their sometimes fractious relationship any easier. Not only are there unresolved territorial issues between the two Asian giants, but India is being assiduously wooed by the United States, Australia, and Japan to become part of the The Quadrilateral Security Dialogue (QSD) that is widely seen as a direct response to the possible strategic implications of China's rise (Grigg 2017).

Strategic issues are taken up in more detail in Chapter 9, but they are not the only possible obstacle to cooperation among the BRICS or the creation of an alternative international order. The most tangible manifestation of the BRICS' potential thus far has been the creation of the BRICS Development Bank (BDB), now rebadged as the New Development Bank (NDB). Established at the 4th BRICS summit in 2012, the NDB was intended to encourage private sector investment in and the development of infrastructure projects, with a particular focus on renewable energy. However, its performance has been somewhat underwhelming thus far, and it embodies some of the BRICS' difficulties. Not only is the NDB heavily reliant on China to provide the lion's share of its funding, but, as we have seen, China has set up an alternative institution in the shape of the AIIB, which is better funded and which looks destined to play a more central role in *China's* grand strategic vision. Even the NDB, though, Greg Chin (2014: 370) argues, is largely about pursuing national objectives as far as China is concerned: 'China sees the NDB as a way to redistribute some of its massive surpluses to reduce the heat from the major deficit countries, build stronger ties with other developing countries and secure resources.' In this context, China's policies reflect a long-term pattern of using its growing economic leverage to further its own engagement with the world and pursue its own national developmental goals (Bräutigam and Tang 2012).

There *are* common problems and concerns that the BRICS might tackle, but they are unlikely to prove attractive. Corruption, for example, is an endemic and growing problem across the BRICS (Bremmer 2017a). But while there are a few encouraging signs – the belated removal of Zuma in South Africa and Xi's crackdown in China – there is little appetite or capacity for the sort of large-scale reform that might be required to address the problem seriously. Even in China, where the process has gone furthest and the reform efforts seem genuine, the close ties between political and economic actors make reform inherently difficult and potentially threatening to key institutions of governance (Pei 2016). In Russia, patterns of corruption are even more ingrained and central to the very operation of the state: 'The Kremlin's top priority then is not purging corrupt elites, but nationalizing them. Russian elites have the right to be corrupt, but only if they have proved their loyalty' (Krastev 2016). Patronage politics, in other words, is endemic and encouraged by the sorts of inequality that have become synonymous with Brazil (Acemoglu and Robinson 2006; Felter and Labrador 2018).

Of course, corruption and compromised governance are hardly a problem that is unique to the BRICS. On the contrary, 'regulatory capture', income inequality, and close relations between political and economic elites were seemingly inescapable parts of the American political economy long before Donald Trump's ascension seemed to personally embody so many of these pathologies (Baker 2010; Piketty 2014), as we saw in the discussion of the GFC. And yet – in principle, at least – the United States continued to champion a broadly liberal policy agenda in which 'transparency' and 'good governance' featured prominently. The significance of the Trump administration in this context is that it no longer appears to find it necessary or ideologically useful to even pay lip service to the central tenets of the liberal order American power did so much to construct (Rachman 2018b). One might expect that such circumstances would provide an unparalleled opportunity for China and institutions such as the BRICS to put forward alternative ideas about how the world might be ordered. The supposedly unrepresentative nature of the extant institutional order has, after all, been one of the constant criticisms of non-Western states. The actual record of new institutions suggests that translating potential into actual influence may be difficult.

A new institutional order?

One of the issues that has united and galvanized the BRICS is the sense that the extant system does not represent them, their views, or their interests. In this context, they are far from alone. Some of the most powerful institutions in the world are seen as emblematic of an earlier period of history in which Western dominance was overwhelming. The classic example of this possibility was the UN Security Council (UNSC), which remains primarily constituted by the major powers that prevailed during the Second World War. The specific problems of the UNSC and other forms of security governance are taken up in Chapter 9. The focus of attention here is on some of the other existing governance forums that have the potential, at least, to play a more prominent part in both addressing problems and giving expression to a new distribution of institutionalized influence. Few recent initiatives are invested with greater hope and expectations than the G20. Its evolution tells us much about the prospects for reform and the development of more representative forms of global governance.

The G20

The G20 was established in 1999. Significantly, however, it was initially restricted to a meeting of finance ministers, something that reflected its origins as a response to a series of economic crises that had affected East Asia and Latin America. While its rationale may have been crisis-driven and technocratic, it had long been apparent that the existing G7/8 groupings were composed of essentially Western powers – the United States, Britain, Germany, Japan, Italy, Canada, Russia, and the EU – and unrepresentative of new geopolitical realities or of the normative case for greater inclusiveness and representation in international bodies. Even Russia's inclusion was largely as a consequence of its status as the Soviet Union, a UNSC member and an unambiguously great power. Japan may have been noteworthy as the only Asian nation, but its close strategic ties to the United States and its undoubted economic importance gave it particular claims for representation. When the G8 was founded in 1975, China was still a poor, primarily agrarian economy with little international impact, other than as a source of radical, anti-capitalist ideology.

It is not just China's rise that has led to calls for more representative institutions, however. The perception that most states in the world were effectively rule takers rather than rule makers was increasingly evident and difficult to justify on normative or pragmatic grounds (Hurrell 2005).

As Woods (2010: 52) points out, the G7 countries 'were beginning to sound shrill and unauthoritative as they collectively implored other countries to abide by their pronouncements'. In the aftermath of the East Asian financial crisis in particular, a growing chorus of critics were making the point that not only were neoliberal policies of a sort promoted by the IFIs not necessarily part of the solution to the region's problems, but they were actually part of the problem (Stiglitz 2002). Equally importantly, if global responses to crises were actually to be developed, as seemed increasingly necessary, then it made sense that more countries were involved in the development and implementation of crisis-management policies. The potential utility of new, more inclusive IOs such as the G20 was put to an early test when the so-called global financial crisis erupted in 2008.

The G20 grouping is significant in its own right and because it is illustrative of potentially significant changes in the nascent institutional architecture of global governance. Indeed, some observers take the G20 and its associated B20 (business) and T20 (think tanks) forums to epitomize new forms of networked governance that bring together states and nonstate actors. In this regard, the G20 builds on practices established by the G7/8, 'in which knowledge, information and other scarce resources are transferred from one actor to another' (Eccleston et al. 2015: 303). What is significant about the G20 in this context is, first, the more inclusive nature of its membership and, second, its capacity to respond to and reflect a rapidly changing international environment. When the GFC erupted in 2008, the G20 looked like an organization that was in the right place at the right time and an implicit vindication of the merits of a more broadly based membership.

Perhaps the single most important transformation in the G20's role and status was its upgrading to become a Leaders' Summit, rather than just a meeting of finance ministers. It is worth noting in this context that former Canadian prime minister Paul Martin (2005) played a prominent role as a 'policy entrepreneur' and 'ideas broker' of the sort that some hoped would be a feature of new, more inclusive and receptive, international forums (Eccleston et al. 2015). The possibility that the leader of a so-called 'middle power' such as Canada might play a prominent role in reshaping the institutions of global governance was itself considered to be emblematic of a new, post-ideological order in which the best policy ideas would succeed, no matter where they came from (Cooper 2010). This was precisely the sort of thinking and policy activism that was championed by another prominent policy entrepreneur – Australia's Kevin Rudd (Beeson 2011a). As we shall see in Chapter 8, however, good ideas and intentions have not been enough to bring about significant change in environmental outcomes.

Even at this stage, though, it is important to consider how important the nature of the issue is in driving cooperation and increasing the potential importance of the organization in question. The environment is a comparatively drawn-out crisis; policymakers may not reap the political dividends that accrue from doing something to address climate change, for example. Economic crises, on the other hand, have an immediacy that can make policymakers quite desperate to find possible solutions to problems. Moreover, the fact that policymakers are often judged first and foremost by their ability to manage economic issues is also an important factor when trying to explain policy priorities. It is also important to recognize that the structural power and support of business, especially in democracies, provides another important source of support for particular policy ideas (Culpepper and Reinke 2014; Fuchs 2007). Such factors help to explain why some ideas about environmental management, for example, may be much harder to implement (Baker 2014; Beeson and Stone 2013a).

Business support for a rapid response to the crisis was understandable given that the GFC affected the 'real' economy of goods and services production, as well as the more volatile financial sector. There is no intention of trying to provide a detailed analysis of the crisis itself here as many good summaries already exist (Bell and Hindmoor 2015; Crotty 2009). The most important features of the crisis for the purposes of the current discussion were that it, first, exposed the lack of effective regulation at both the transnational and – especially in America's case – the national levels and, second, illustrated the manner in which affected states rapidly moved to develop mechanisms that could provide crisis management. The key innovation in this context was the establishment of the Financial Stability Board (FSB), which was charged with strengthening international prudential regulation – put simply, trying to ensure that similar crises did not occur in the future by ensuring that risks and vulnerabilities of the financial sector were more effectively managed (Helleiner 2010).

The limits of inclusion

Like the G20 of which it was a part, the FSB highlighted the evolving nature of transnational cooperation and governance efforts. The membership of the Financial Stability Forum, out of which the FSB developed, included not only the finance ministers of the G20 countries, but also representatives of other IOs and agencies, such as the IMF, the World Bank, the Bank for International Settlements (BIS), and the Organisation for Economic Cooperation and Development (OECD), among others. In short, it was an important example of the sort of networked governance that many feel is such a distinctive, effective, and necessary part of the evolving international order. And yet, once the crisis had abated and the apparent need for emergency measures seemed to have receded, both business interests and individual governments moved to recover their autonomy and freedom of action. This was especially noteworthy in the United States where 'Wall Street' is an especially powerful force and source of financial support for individual politicians (Baker 2010); the ideological commitment to liberalism and market forces reinforced an innate suspicion of government 'intervention' that is such a feature of American politics. As Helleiner and Pagliari (2011: 182) point out, in another revealing and rather ironic development,

> The very feature of the networks that had been their strength before the crisis – their carefully cultivated autonomy – now became the subject of criticism from politicians who held the unelected international committees of technocratic officials at least partially responsible for the crisis … Increasingly strong and public disagreements among financial officials from the leading powers eroded the cohesion, and thus the influence, of transgovernmental expert networks.

Even before Donald Trump became president, it was evident that the capacity of new actors to influence the actual policy recommendations of the G20, much less their actual implementation at the national level, was limited. The United States continued to exercise an outsize influence over internal deliberations and processes within the G20, in much the same way as it had exercised a decisive influence over the IMF (Beeson and Bell 2009). With the arrival of the Trump administration and a significant number of high-profile appointees drawn from Wall Street generally and Goldman Sachs in particular, even the modest reforms of the Obama era were overturned (Jopson 2017).

For the purposes of this discussion, what is significant about this period and the reduced influence of the G20 and the FSB is not that it threatens to create the preconditions for yet another crisis – although that is, of course, tremendously important and likely to further damage the reputation of the 'American model' of capitalism (Kirshner 2014) – but the continuing role of great power influence and politics. Far from marking the arrival of a new era of networked politics in which an array of new actors dispenses apolitical advice to solve technical problems and provide collective goods, the Trump administration is single-mindedly attempting to reassert national autonomy and an agenda that reflects narrow, sectoral interests (Fleming et al. 2018). The possibility that this agenda, along with the equally nationalistic trade agenda, is an inappropriate, unsustainable throwback to an earlier era is less important in the context of the current discussion than is the fact that powerful states continue to pursue national interests when it suits them.

Even in an era supposedly characterized by global forces and problems, one might be forgiven for thinking that the old adage about all politics being local continues to apply. As Drezner (2007: 210) points out, 'state preferences on regulatory issues have their origins in the domestic political economy'. In other words, the decisions of policymakers continue to be profoundly affected by powerful domestic interests, and not just the more obvious economic variety either. The rise of populist politics is both an expression of the growing importance of domestic social forces and popular opinion and a potential constraint on the options of policymakers (Luce 2018). In this context, it is significant that the Trump administration has chosen to act on more visible trade 'problems', discussed in Chapter 7, while the intangible realm of finance and banking remains largely unreformed and as great a threat to the international system as ever. Given the increasingly aggressive pursuit of unambiguously 'national interests' – no matter how conceptually impoverished and discursively contingent such conceptions may be in reality – things are unlikely to change.

The key question about the policies of rising powers is whether they are subscribing to the extant international order dominated by the United States because they think it is optimally superior to possible alternatives or because they have no choice. In this context, it is important that the Trump administration, like other American governments before it, still has some powerful geoeconomic tools at its disposal, some of which are barely known to the general public. The Society for Worldwide Interbank Financial Communication (SWIFT) has become an indispensable part of the global financial messaging system, without which individual national banking systems may struggle to function. The threat by the United States and the EU to cut off Russia from this system placed enormous pressure on Putin to modify his aggressive foreign policies – although not enough to bring about a radical change of direction (Katada et al. 2017: 418). Other countries may not have the political will, domestic backing, or resilience to resist such pressures, however.

The limits to change?

As we saw in Chapter 4, one of the principal reasons that China looms so large in contemporary discussion of global governance is because it represents a profound challenge to the extant system of global governance.

Implicitly and explicitly, whether by intentional design or simply because of its sheer material weight, the PRC epitomizes very different ideas about the possible organization of domestic political practices and modes of economic relations, and one that may ultimately eclipse the American model (Bremmer 2017b). This is predictably not a view that is especially popular with American policymakers or, more interestingly perhaps, scholars either (Kruathammer 2009).

The possibility that American policymakers might find it difficult to recognize or accept that rising powers generally and China in particular might pose something of a challenge to the existing order is understandable, perhaps. After all, what Layne (2017: 264) describes as the 'foreign policy establishment' in the United States is a 'subset of the corporate and financial elite'. The consequence of this is that

> The core components of the foreign policy establishment's world view are: the primacy of national security, the imperative of American leadership, the importance of an open international economy, and the need to export America's liberal political ideas. (Layne 2017: 267)

While this may go a long way to explaining the core components of America's distinctive form of liberal hegemony, or 'leadership', as most American analysts and policymakers prefer to describe it, the reality is that American scholars such as Layne are very much the exception rather than the rule. The key question in the face of the challenge posed by the rising powers is whether the international order created under the auspices of American hegemony is durable, with or without the Trump administration and its skepticism about its benefits.

To judge by some of the most prominent supporters of liberal hegemony, the answer is clearly 'yes'. Kahler (2013: 712) argues that the rising powers are 'less likely to be radical reformers than conservative' because 'their domestic political and economic dilemmas induce an aversion to risk'. John Ikenberry is possibly the most influential exponent of the idea that the US-led international liberal, rules-based order will not only endure, but socialize the likes of China, Brazil, and India into the norms and practices from which they have been major beneficiaries. While Ikenberry recognizes that the rising powers represent a challenge and may have an impact, he argues that in the longer term the liberal order will endure because

> as this hegemonic organization of the liberal international order starts to change, the hierarchical aspects are fading while the liberal aspects

persist. So even as China and other rising states try to contest U.S. leadership – and there is indeed a struggle over the rights, privileges, and responsibilities of the leading states within the system – the deeper international order remains intact. (Ikenberry 2011: 61)

There is plainly something in this argument. As we saw in Chapter 4, some of China's policy initiatives, especially the AIIB, are at least as noteworthy for what they are not as for what they are: yes, they represent an alternative institutional order in which China can expect to exert a greater influence, but – at this stage, at least – the norms and principles that the AIIB subscribes to are not that different from those of similar 'Western' institutions (Ikenberry and Lim 2017). The key question in this context is about the relative importance of strategic dominance and power in underpinning a specific order. While many of the scholars who reject the American decline thesis emphasize the factors that they believe underpin continuing primacy (Krauthammer 2009; Brooks and Wohlforth 2016), the fact remains that the United States is confronted by profound problems of agency and structure that look likely to inevitably undercut the foundations of its postwar primacy. The only question would seem to be how quickly this is likely to occur and what implications this may have for global governance as a consequence.

Concluding remarks

There is no doubt that there have been important 'structural' changes in the economic and strategic order with which we have been familiar for more than half a century. There are a number of rising or reemerging powers that are exerting an influence on the international system. The question is, how much? Measuring influence is notoriously difficult, although this has not stopped people from trying, of course. Once we get past crude material measures of economic weight, population, or military potential, however, it becomes more difficult to gauge the impact of the rising powers collectively or individually. China is the exception that proves this rule: its size and power are of a different order of magnitude across a variety of measures. While this may reinforce the idea that the old order is being upended, it is not clear that the rising powers other than China are likely to play a major role in shaping what comes next – unless they intentionally or accidentally trigger a major international conflict, of course.

One thing that does seem clear is that the impact of the BRICS as a unified collective force in international affairs has been limited thus far. There are simply too many internal contradictions, potential rivalries, and tensions to permit them to develop a common agenda, much less act to replace the hegemonic power of the era. This is not to say that there are no examples of effective action or cooperation in the international system. The European Union is the quintessential example of this possibility. It also suggests that there may be important *regional* constraints on effective action, which may help to explain why the BRICS, the G20, and the G77 have struggled to gain real traction or transform the existing international order. Consequently, some scholars argue that the end of the old order is not necessarily going to produce a new global hegemon to underpin global governance – or not yet, at least. On the contrary, Amitav Acharya (2014: 81) argues that American decline will encourage the emergence of 'regional worlds', which may appear 'without hegemonic organization or even resistance'. It is an intriguing and potentially important claim, and one to which we now turn.

6
Regionalism in a Global Era

One of the most striking features of the contemporary international system is the continuing prominence of, and interest in, regional organizations and even identities. Despite all the problems that are currently afflicting the European Union (EU), the increasingly nationalist tone of much political rhetoric around the world, and a general decline in confidence about the prospects for effective transnational cooperation, regions remain important. Many geographers, political scientists, and policymakers continue to believe that regions matter and are potentially part of any possible solution to many of the world's problems (Fawn 2009; Acharya 2014; Jones and Passi 2017). Indeed, former European Commissioner for Trade and Director-General of the WTO Pascal Lamy (2012: 727) argues that 'regional integration represents the essential intermediate step between the national and the global governance level'.

This chapter explores the role of regions in this context and considers whether they are or have the potential to become an integral part of the development of effective institutions of global governance. It is not hard to see why Lamy might continue to believe that regions remain important: we have all too few examples of effective transnational cooperation at any level of governance. The fact that we have *any* effective examples at all is, perhaps, the remarkable and potentially optimism-inducing idea that emerges from a consideration of regional projects. After all, according to some of the most influential theories of international relations considered in Chapter 2, the sort of institutionalized patterns of cooperation that some regions have developed are supposed to be unlikely if not impossible. For some influential observers, they still are (Mearsheimer 1994/95).

At a time when transnational cooperation looks increasingly difficult, and even some of the most established elements of global governance look

fragile and incapable of addressing unprecedented challenges such as climate change, the realists look to have a point. And yet it is also clear
that there have been some equally unprecedented changes in the way at
least some states interact and are prepared to sacrifice a degree of national
autonomy to achieve goals that would otherwise be unrealizable. Peace
and security are plainly the most important of such possible benefits; the
historical experience of the EU in this regard – as in so many others – is
instructive and still rather inspiring. Consequently, quite a bit of the subsequent discussion is taken up with a consideration of the EU case, which
pioneered regional integration and which has gone further than any other
part of the world. In many ways the EU remains something of a benchmark
for judging the 'progress' and efficacy of regional projects, even if it is
rather controversial and methodologically – even politically – incorrect to
say so (Acharya 2012). Before examining the success and failures of the
EU and a number of other regional initiatives, however, I provide a few
brief remarks about the nature of regions, their capacity to act, and the
forces that have driven (or obstructed) their rise in different parts of the
world.

Regions: Good in theory?

When thinking about regions it is important to make an initial distinction
between regions as convenient ways of describing brute material reality and
regions as purposive, political projects, which are the product of human
agency. One of the advantages of this distinction is that it alerts us to the
fact that the sorts of regions that have become important parts of the international system are, in fact, the creation of actors intent on achieving particular
goals. Having said that, it is also apparent that some regions are more likely
and 'natural' than others. North and South America, as well as Africa, have
a geographical distinctiveness and separateness that seem to lend themselves more easily to the creation of regional identities. The 'Asia-Pacific',
by contrast, which includes East Asia and much of north and south America,
looks altogether more improbable and artificial, not least because of its size
and the highly diverse nature of its membership (Buzan 2012: 23). It is
unsurprising, perhaps, that it has proved to be one of the less successful
regional projects as a consequence (Beeson 2006). As Paasi (2003: 478) has
pointed out, one of the prerequisites for regions actually becoming vehicles
for political, economic, and perhaps even strategic action is their ability to

create a sense of identity or consciousness of the region being something distinctive and important:

> 'Regional identity' is, in a way, an interpretation of the process through which a region becomes institutionalized, a process consisting of the production of territorial boundaries, symbolism and institutions ... it is useful to distinguish analytically between the identity of a region and the regional identity (or regional consciousness) of the people living in it or outside of it.

There is, of course, currently a major debate about quite how resilient and consequential such regional identities actually are in a world that is increasingly riven by conflict of one sort or another (Oliver 2016). There is also an important question about the extent to which the process of institutionalization has taken place in different parts of the world, as I shall explain. Before doing that, however, it is important to make one other distinction that is routinely made when thinking about regions and their emergence as potentially significant elements of global governance processes: that is between region*alism* and regional*ization* (Breslin and Higgott 2000). Regionalism refers to the self-conscious, intentional efforts of state-based policymakers to encourage cooperation and create specific regional organizations to institutionalize and facilitate such processes. Regionalization, on the other hand, refers to the less focused or coherent activities of private sector actors, primarily in the economic sphere. Regional economic integration, of the sort that has been driven by the evolution of the transnational production processes described in Chapter 1, has been one of the big drivers of regional development.

As a result, the lines between regionalism and regionalization are often blurred. This is not surprising given that one of the primary goals of national policymakers has been to encourage precisely the sorts of valuable, job-creating activities that potentially footloose MNCs increasingly undertake (Yeung 2009). Creating a 'business friendly' investment climate has generally been one of the principal goals of regional agreements, especially for some of the 'emerging markets' that have been reliant on foreign direct investment (FDI). It is not the only one, however. Even more importantly, especially in the case of the EU and some of its more significant counterparts in Asia, geopolitical considerations have also been a major factor encouraging regional cooperation and, it is claimed, something that accounts for the surprisingly durable peace of East Asia (Kivimäki 2014). The possible significance of regional 'security communities' is taken up in more detail in the next chapter. However, it is important to say something about the historical connection between regional development and great power politics as it helps to explain the promise and potential pitfalls of regional cooperation.

Regional history

The links and interactions between globalization and regionalization extend beyond politics and economics. It is important to recognize that it was only possible to begin thinking of the world as composed of regions in relatively recent times. When China dominated its 'region' for hundreds, if not thousands, of years there was no sense of what we now think of as East Asia as being one region among others. On the contrary, China's imperial rulers considered themselves to be at the center of a world that was composed of itself, a small group of adjacent subordinate states, and a vaguely understood, distant world of barbarians, about which generations of Chinese leaders took remarkably little interest (Fairbank 1968). The tribute system over which China presided for so many years had no 'other' to be distinguished in opposition to. While China's world may have been a stable, remarkably durable hierarchical system with political, economic, military, and cultural dimensions (Kang 2010), it was not a 'region' in the contemporary sense because it had no significant external relations. One of the defining qualities of regions in the modern period is that 'insiders' may not only enjoy specific benefits from membership, but are defined in part by those that are excluded.

Recent interest in theories of regional development have been divided into two distinct waves: a first wave during the Cold War that focused primarily on the experiences of the EU, and a second wave that was spurred by the Cold War's ending and the geopolitical changes and possibilities that emerged in its wake (Fawcett 2017). Before considering the implications and utility of some of these perspectives, however, it is important to say something about the precise historical conditions in which regional projects have emerged. The two regions considered in most detail here – Europe, the first self-consciously created region, and East Asia, the region that contains China – were both profoundly affected by the dynamics of the Cold War, albeit in strikingly different ways.

This is why Eurocentric analyses can be a problem: not only does Eurocentrism downplay the enormous contribution that East Asia generally and China in particular have made to world history (Hobson 2012), but it obscures the very different impact that broadly similar processes can have in different parts of the world. This possibility is nowhere clearer than when we consider the way regional processes evolved – or in East Asia's case, did not evolve – as a consequence of the impact of America's hegemonic influence and grand strategic objectives. In Europe, the geopolitics of the Cold War period had the effect of encouraging greater European integration; in East Asia, they had precisely the opposite effect. In Europe, American power was applied to encourage potentially like-minded, broadly liberal, capitalist powers to band together to stop the possible threat of communist expansion (Milward 1984).

In East Asia, by contrast, while the ultimate goal might have been the same, the way this was achieved was very different from the integrative dynamics associated with the EU and NATO. On the contrary, the series of so-called 'hub-and-spokes' bilateral security relationships which were centered on Washington rather than Asia were established with the likes of Japan, Korea, Taiwan, Thailand, and the Philippines, and effectively entrenched the divisions of the Cold War. America's dominant position made any region-wide collaboration or institutionalization impossible until the Cold War ended (Beeson 2005; Hemmer and Katzenstein 2002). Indeed, Victor Cha (2016: 4) argues that the security relationships established by the United States in the aftermath of the Second World War amounted to an 'informal empire', in which it exercised near-total control over the foreign and domestic affairs of its allies, and created 'an asymmetry of power that rendered inconceivable counterbalancing by these smaller countries, on their own or in concert with others'.

Regions everywhere are embedded in a wider global and geopolitical context that is shaped in large part by the great powers of the era. The relationship between regional and global levels is not sharply drawn, but fluid, open-ended, and dialectical. Andrew Hurrell (2010: 17) captures its essence when he suggests that

> regional powers cannot be understood unless they are viewed within a global context. This does not imply systemic determinism, nor a rigid idea of historical path dependence. It is precisely the shifting relationship between the one world of the global system and the many regional worlds that helps us to make sense of the ideas, the interests and the resources available to regional powers as well as the scope, domain and character of their regional playgrounds.

The precise importance of economic, political, or, indeed, geopolitical issues will vary at particular moments in history, in part because of concomitant shifts in the relative importance these issues have in the minds of policymakers and other actors with the capacity to influence regional outcomes. This possibility helps to explain why and how political and economic dynamics, as well as overarching geopolitical structures, have played themselves out quite differently in East Asia and Western Europe.

Conceptualizing regions

The possible importance of different 'levels of analysis' assumes particular significance in the context of theoretical debates about what drives or constrains regional cooperation. It is evident that no single paradigm can explain the complex array of factors that influence regional political, economic, and strategic outcomes. At different times, some forces may be more powerful than others (Ripsman 2005), and it is therefore necessary to place such influences in a historical context that allows us to more clearly assess the variable impact of strategic constraints or economic incentives, for example. Plainly economic interdependence has had an impact on interstate relations and behavior in Europe, but it has also done so in East Asia, too – as the emergence of 'greater China' which includes both Taiwan and the PRC reminds us (Chan 2009). While realists may be right to emphasize the importance of interests and grand strategy in determining economic outcomes (Grieco 1999), it is still evident that economic imperatives have the power to shape policy priorities where other circumstances are conducive.

It is also clear that a new range of actors, of the sort described in earlier chapters, have become important factors in both global and regional governance. In an effort to more clearly identify the forces that have influenced regional development at different times, it became commonplace to make a distinction between 'old' and 'new' forms of regional development.

The 'old' regionalism was overwhelmingly focused on the experience of the EU, which was essentially the only example of significant cross-border cooperation. As a result, the first theories of regionalism were preoccupied with federalism, functionalism (and neofunctionalism), and the particular features that distinguished the EU and its historical evolution (Söderbaum 2012). Great attention was given to the distinctive internal political and administrative architecture of the EU and its capacity to provide collective goods of a sort members could not provide on their own. It is partly as a consequence of the dominance of the EU in this period of regionalism studies that many scholars have complained about the inherent eurocentrism of much of the literature and the need to include other, possibly different, forms of regional development. Hettne (1999: 7) suggested that new forms of regionalism might be distinguished by: their post-Cold War origins; emerging 'from below' rather than being imposed 'top down' (as in the EU); being 'open' economically; and including nonstate actors.

More recent theories of regionalism consider the role of institutional development and design. One of way of attempting to make sense of an evolving and complex set of processes has been to adopt an explicitly comparative approach (Sbragia 2008; Börzel and Risse 2016). One of the more important contributions to this still rather limited literature was provided by Acharya and Johnston (2007: 259), who pointed out that in all the regions they considered, domestic politics was 'the most important factor shaping institutional design'. Furthermore, they suggested that the more insecure regimes were, 'the less intrusive their regional institutions' (Acharya and Johnston 2007: 262). In other words, one reason that the EU has generated such distinctive, powerful, sovereignty-pooling, and ultimately *effective* institutions is because the states that make up the EU have generally been comparatively stable and confident about domestic security. Indeed, the EU, as I shall explain, has benefited from something akin to a virtuous circle in that the economic development and international security have been mutually reinforcing. It is precisely this happy state of affairs that is currently under strain and raising questions about the precise circumstances in which regional, let alone global, governance can flourish and endure.

One way of distinguishing between the EU and other regions is to make a distinction between 'soft' and 'structured' regionalism and between formal informal processes (Acharya 1997; Zhao 1998). While the reality may be rather more blurred than these labels suggest, one of the most important differences between the EU and regions such as East Asia, is the former's reliance on legal mechanisms to reinforce or even compel compliance with agreements and policies. In East Asia, by contrast, where states – including China – are fiercely protective of their sovereignty and wary of possible 'interference' from external actors in domestic affairs, there is little enthusiasm about legally binding agreements (Kahler 2000). The consequent preference for informality and consensus-based policymaking that is so distinctive of the 'ASEAN Way', has made effective policy implementation inherently problematic. It has also made it difficult for organizations such as the Asia Pacific Economic Cooperation (APEC) grouping, which includes Anglo-American and Asian states, to bridge cultural divides and develop an effective modus operandi (Bisley 2012).

To put these differences in more theoretical language, the sort of sovereignty 'pooling' employed by the EU is the exception rather than the rule. Most regions, including East Asia, prefer to 'delegate' authority. The reasons are not difficult to discern and revolve primarily around the fact that pooling involves a shared process of decision-making and a process of qualified majority rule. Delegation, by contrast, involves a conditional grant of authority from principal to agent, which can be revoked. In reality, Lenz and Marks (2016: 514) argue that agents may retain a degree of autonomy and a capacity to pursue their own agendas. There is, however, one other major distinction that sets the EU apart from other regions such as East Asia and that is the existence of a 'thick' layer of independent institutions and actors outside of the state, which may be included in the process of governance and the implementation of policy (Beeson 2001). As we shall see, this enables the EU to act in ways that their counterparts elsewhere simply cannot, even if they actually wanted to delegate authority for decision-making and/or policy implementation to other actors.

To explain these differential outcomes, it is important to recognize – and no coincidence – that preferences about policymaking processes and the collective obligations they might imply closely map onto the differing 'political rationalities' that are found in Europe and Asia (Beeson and Jayasuriya 1998). The very different approaches to policymaking and the potential willingness to pool rather than protect sovereignty reflect a major and enduring difference between liberal and illiberal political regimes in the two regions. Although this broad-brush distinction contains some important exceptions and anomalies, it also provides a useful heuristic for thinking about major regional variations in the policymaking process. Indeed, it is also no coincidence that the rise of populism and illiberalism within Europe is one of the most important factors in undermining the European project and raising doubts about the continuing efficacy of its distinctive approach to policymaking (Barber 2017).

Nevertheless, as we saw in Chapter 2, some scholars argue that there is something inevitable about the decline or – more accurately, perhaps – the transformation of the state as a consequence of globalization, the growth of networked-based forms of governance, and the emergence of new actors and centers of power in the international system. The basic argument, it will be recalled, is that the state is simply not capable of addressing certain problems without cooperating with a range of other actors. As a consequence, it has been suggested, there is a process or 'rescaling' taking place across the world, in which different problems are addressed at different levels or scales as states grapple with new challenges that defy national solutions (Brenner 2004). Indeed, new forms of 'regulatory regionalism' are emerging as a consequence, it is claimed, in which the internal institutional architecture of the state itself is being transformed. While such processes are clearly discernible in Europe, as I shall explain, Kanishka Jayasuriya argues that similar processes are beginning to occur in East Asia, with potentially significant implications for the region and China in particular:

> the rise of China, rather than leading to an emerging Sino-centric regional order, represents a new form of production that is not necessarily bound to a national territorial space. Therefore, the regional transformation catalysed by China's economic and social transformation is more appropriately conceptualized as a symptom of a new system of regionalized economic governance transcending national territorial boundaries. (Jayasuriya 2009: 338)

Given what we have already seen in China's approach to policymaking, the desire of the CCP to retain control over political and economic activity, and the growth of a popularly supported nationalist discourse, claims about the leadership of the PRC being willing to share governance on a regional basis look inherently implausible. At the very least China's regional policies merit closer examination as they have the potential to reveal pressures on states to change and adapt, as well as their respective capacities to resist or manage such pressures. Before doing so, however, it is important to consider how the EU has developed and responded to such pressures. The EU may not be the only or even the best model of regional development, but it remains the most illuminating point of comparison for the others, and a telling illustration of the problems of transnational governance more generally.

The EU: First and foremost?

In the aftermath of the global financial crisis (GFC) in 2008, the immigration crisis that erupted in 2015, a general rise in populism, and Brexit, it is increasingly common – and realistic – to ask whether the EU can actually survive – or survive in anything like the form it assumed at the height of its powers, at least (Barber 2017). Many of the apparent certainties about the course of European development are much less assured than they once were (Webber 2014). This is not only Europe's problem: for anyone interested in the possibility of global governance the EU has assumed a talismanic status. If Europe with all its experience and capabilities can't manage transnational governance on a regional scale, the prospects for the global variety look bleak.

Given the loss of confidence so many Europeans apparently feel in the EU and its leadership (de Vries 2018), it is worth considering how much leadership actually matters in determining the effectiveness of governance more generally. As we saw in the consideration of the more general features of the new global environment in Chapter 1, one of the striking features of contemporary patterns of international and national governance is the increased numbers of actors involved in such processes, and the potentially competing sources of authority in various issue areas. It is no coincidence that Walter Mattli's (1999: 64) influential analysis of regional integration, which focused primarily on the European experience, argued that the gains from, and feasibility of, regional projects are significantly reduced in the absence of an 'undisputed leader'. True, Mattli was referring primarily to the possibility that a single country might provide a leadership role to drive integration and cooperation, but this only serves to highlight the possible importance of leadership more generally.

A key question in this context is whether the current generation of European leaders is particularly inept, or whether the problems they face and the complexity of governance arrangements they attempt to utilize and control simply do not lend themselves to the exercise of effective leadership at either the individual or the national level. Once again, historical comparison helps to illuminate some of these issues.

In the beginning ...

Perhaps the most distinctive feature of the formation of the EU was that much of the leadership was provided at a distance by the United States (Beeson 2008). The United States had emerged as the hegemonic power of the era and was keen to shore up the position of the damaged and discredited capitalist economies that had been ravaged by years of war and economic crisis. In the context of a rapidly intensifying confrontation with the Soviet Union, America's leaders were concerned to ensure that 'potential adversaries must never again be allowed to gain control of the resources of Eurasia through autarkical economic practices, political subversion, and/or military aggression' (Leffler 1992: 23). One way of trying to ensure that this did not happen in the face of a Soviet ideological challenge that seemed credible – especially given the continuing economic crisis in the immediate postwar period (Milward 1984) – was to offer direct economic support via the Marshall Plan. European reconstruction was to be the bedrock of the emerging 'containment' strategy that was designed to stop what seemed the inexorable spread of global communism.

Such fears may look somewhat overblown in retrospect, but this should not blind us to the significance of the Marshall Plan at the time, or its place in America's evolving grand strategy. American policy was designed not only to stabilize the still fragile economies of Western Europe (and Japan), but to prepare the way for what Lundestad (1986) famously described as an 'empire by invitation'. American policy was designed to overcome any lingering ideological opposition to its role within Europe, and to remake the region along liberal lines. Having said that, it is also important to recognize that the Europeans were not the passive recipients of American aid or policy direction. On the contrary, the British were instrumental in laying the groundwork for the creation of NATO (Folly 1984), and the French played an important part in creating the European Coal and Steel Community (Lovett 1996), which provided the foundations for the subsequent development of the EU itself. Crucially, the overall intention of these initiatives was to provide the basis of a political framework with which to reconcile and unite former foes (Trachtenberg 1999). In this regard, there is little doubt that it succeeded far beyond the expectations of its original architects.

The key question to ask in retrospect is how decisive leadership was in determining the course of immediate postwar history. Clearly, American power and purpose were pivotal, but how important were Europe's leaders? The likes of Jean Monnet and Robert Schumann are generally depicted as visionary statesmen who were effectively the 'founding fathers' of the European project. There is evidently also something in this idea, but in some ways, they were also aided by the times: not only was American aid and encouragement a major factor in achieving their goals, but so too was the support of the European people (Maier 1981). As was also the case in Japan (Tabb 1995), it proved easier to mobilize a war-weary population desperate for stability and economic development than it might have been at other times. How would some of these leaders have coped with the fallout from the GFC, Russian mischief-making in the Ukraine, the migrant crisis, or the general loss of confidence in the current generation of leaders?

Before trying to answer that question, we need to remind ourselves of how the European project developed from inauspicious beginnings to become the most important example of successful, institutionalized cooperation across national borders that the world has ever seen. Unsurprisingly, perhaps, this raises yet another difficult question: how much credit should the early generation of European leaders – in the collective sense – be given for what the French refer to as *Les Trente Glorieuses*, or the period from 1945 to 1975 when economic development recovered dramatically, welfare states were established, peace prevailed, and all boats seemed to be rising (Glyn et al. 1990). As with the successful establishment of the European project itself, were these leaders simply in the right place at the right time and had merely to allow pent-up demand and market forces to work their magic? One point that merits emphasis, and which may explain subsequent problems such as Brexit, is that significant differences in the way capitalism was organized persisted in

Britain and much of the rest of 'continental' Europe (Albert 1993), something that may help to explain Britain's belated admission to the EU.

The evolution of the EU

The EU's development has been long, complex, and marked by some unique institutional innovations and agreements. Until recently, this story, which can only be sketched here in broad outline (see Wallace et al. 2000), looked to be heading inexorably and rather triumphantly in one direction. There was an inescapable element of eurocentrism about this story and its implications, no doubt, but there was also a degree of self-satisfaction and complacency, too. The failure to listen to the concerns of many European citizens about a growing democratic deficit, and the presumption that 'Europe' was still exercising a benign and beneficial influence on less enlightened parts of the world, contributed to and reflected a certain self-satisfaction that seemingly left the EU apparently unprepared to meet the challenges of a rapidly changing international order (Peterson 2017). It was not always thus, however, and its history tells us much about the prospects for, and obstacles to, global governance.

The first major milestone in the European project was the creation of the European Economic Community (EEC) in 1957, which contained only France, Italy, Belgium, Luxembourg, the Netherlands, and what was then West Germany. The subsequent years saw continuing 'widening' (more members) and 'deepening' (ever greater union and institutionalized integration). Neither of these processes has been problem-free and both highlight the challenges of expanding the EU's principles and practices to other states that might not be either enthusiastic about or ready to adopt them (Börzel et al. 2017). Britain has long been an example of states that joined subsequently and which were examples of the former, but it is also important to recognize that it was instrumental in bringing the Single European Act (SEA) into being (Moravcsik 1991). The SEA promoted internal economic liberalization and the consolidation of a single market – itself a major attraction for other would-be members in an East European region suddenly freed from Soviet domination. The SEA also introduced the principle of Qualified Majority Voting, however, an idea that proved contentious, not least because it threatened national sovereignty.

One of the most striking features of the EU's development, and one that has been driven by, and a response to, increasingly ambitious transnational governance objectives, has been the depth and complexity of its unprecedented institutional architecture (Wallace 1996). Not only is there an array of powerful agencies at the heart of EU decision-making and policy implementation, but they have also effectively taken responsibility for many of the roles that were formerly the exclusive preserve of states. It is also important to note that the one of the underlying rationales for creating agencies such as the European Commission (an executive cabinet of public officials), the European Central Bank (ECB), and the European Court of Auditors was in part, at least, a technocratic pursuit of efficiency (Radaelli 2017). In some ways, this mirrored the sort of generalized changes described in Chapter 1, in which experts and specialist agencies have assumed greater responsibility for policy development and implementation because they are judged to have the requisite expertise to do so.

Other aspects of EU development mimic the sorts of separation of powers that distinguish the American federal system, and can be seen in the European Council (which provides general policy direction from heads of government), the Council of the European Union (an 'upper house' where member states' ministers review policy), the EU Court of Justice, and, of course, the European Parliament. This latter body has proved somewhat controversial, a reality that is reflected in the strikingly low participation rates in European elections. Nevertheless, the power of the Parliament relative to other governance agencies was substantially increased by the Lisbon Treaty of 2009, which gave it greater influence over the budget and the authority to appoint the Commission president. However, its capacity to actually make policy remains limited and remains dependent on the support of the Commission (Kreppel 2006). It is precisely these sorts of tradeoffs between possible gains in organizational efficiency and democratic legitimacy that have been at the center of criticisms about a supposedly overweening, unrepresentative bureaucracy in Brussels (Kröger 2007).

The EU's overall development continues to reflect the wider geopolitical context of which it is a part, and provides a powerful reminder of the importance of contingent events and history in shaping governance outcomes. The end of the Cold War, for example, not only provided the opportunity to expand the EU's – and NATO's – influence eastwards, but also saw a reunited Germany emerge as the most powerful force in Europe (Crawford 2007). The enduring legacy of, and sensitivity about, Germany's war-time role has meant that it has not played the sort of role that it 'ought' to have done from a simple realist-style calculus of material power (Beddoes 2013). While this may have compounded the EU's leadership problems and ability to play a foreign policy role commensurate with its collective importance (Smith 2013), it stands in marked contrast to the East Asian experience, nevertheless. East Asia's remarkable inability to come to terms with its traumatic twentieth-century history remains a major obstacle to the possibility of regional cooperation and highlights the competing claims to internal and external leadership that continue to undermine effective collective action (Beeson 2017c).

Yet if East Asia cannot collectively put the past behind it, the citizens of the EU are in danger of forgetting theirs. Generations that have grown up without the specter of potential conflict looming over their heads – in what has historically been one of the most blood-soaked regions of the world, of course – may take the EU's achievements for granted, without recognizing quite what an achievement peace, security, and confidence in the future behavior of former foes actually is (Down and Wilson 2013). As I explain in Chapter 9, the creation of an effective and enduring 'security community' in Western Europe is a remarkable and unprecedented historical achievement and one that laid the ground work within which many of its other achievements have been realized. The creation of the Schengen Agreement, which moved to eliminate internal borders among participating states and allow the free movement of people, is emblematic of the EU's overall vision and a core part of its operating principles. It is also one which traditional defenders of national sovereignty have had difficulty accepting (Medrano 2010), and which looks increasingly unlikely to survive.

No country has had greater domestic problems as a consequence of the clash between national and transnational goals than Britain. Although most commentators were surprised by the British people's narrow decision to leave the EU, perhaps they should not have been. After all, there has been long-standing, well-organized opposition in Britain to issues such as the Common Agricultural Policy, European law, 'creeping federalism', and anything else that seemed likely to undercut British sovereignty (Startin 2015). While Brexit may be the most dramatic manifestation of the fundamental clash between national and transnational goals, the British experience is an especially illuminating symptom of underlying and possibly irresolvable tensions as some of the EU's newer, Eastern European members also seek to reassert sovereign control (Witte and Birnbaum 2018). The unexpected immigration crisis has heightened tensions between members, fueled popular concerns about the loss of control over national borders, and generally undermined confidence in the EU's capacity to deal with major transnational challenges (Dinan et al. 2017).

The EU's reputation had already been in decline as a consequence of its inability to successfully manage what has hitherto been its strong suit: its capacity to manage economic development and deliver rising living standards. The creation of a common currency initially looked like the sort of development that would provide a structural underpinning for greater integration, both economic *and* political. And yet the subsequent crisis in Greece, which famously failed to meet the so-called 'convergence criteria' for euro membership, was cited by critics as an example of political idealism getting ahead of economic reality (Beeson and Bell 2017). There was plainly something in such charges. More importantly in the long run, perhaps, the seemingly unending series of economic, social, and political crises that has gripped the EU since the GFC have damaged its credibility, and not just in the minds of Europeans. On the contrary, the EU's experience has had a negative impact on other parts of the world as they come to see the EU as a model to avoid, rather than to emulate (Beeson and Stone 2013b). The EU's place as the region that has gone furthest toward the increasingly remote goal of global cooperation makes its now diminished position all the more significant. An examination of East Asia suggests that it is unlikely to seize the ideational or inspirational baton.

The Asian alternative

There is a major and revealing paradox at the heart of East Asian patterns of regional cooperation: despite the growing number of regional institutions, the effectiveness of such initiatives actually seems to be declining (Beeson 2016). In part this may be because the sheer number of competing proposals creates duplication and uncertainty about which organization – if any – has authority in a particular issue area. More fundamentally, perhaps, the limited impact of East Asia's superficially impressive-looking institutional architecture reflects an underlying lack of enthusiasm and nervousness about giving greater power to external organizations and actors. In short, for reasons that reflect the region's troubled history and a continuing preoccupation with protecting rather than pooling sovereignty, the potential for effective, institutionalized forms of cooperation remains limited. That is precisely the way most of the region's political elites would like it to remain.

Paths of dependence

While China's tribute system may have been one of the first and most enduring experiments in 'regional' cooperation, it was not the only one. Japan's abortive efforts to develop coercively a 'Co-prosperity sphere' during the Second World War serves as a reminder of how not to do regional cooperation (Beeson 2009b). It also highlights the continuing importance to the contemporary region of various historical traumas that have proved enduring and seemingly immovable obstacles to regional cooperation, especially in the other parts of East Asia. Indeed, the very identity of the region in question is more uncertain and *contested* than it is in Western Europe. There are a variety of possible ways of thinking about the region – East Asia, Southeast Asia, the Asia-Pacific, and the newly fashionable Indo-Pacific – that present an initial problem for any aspiring regional grouping. Who does it claim to represent and, equally importantly, who is excluded?

The EU demonstrates just how important exclusion and inclusion can be, so it is little wonder that questions of membership have played an important role in the various initiatives that have been attempted in the broadly conceived Asia-Pacific region. It is no coincidence in this regard that the Association of Southeast Asian Nations (ASEAN) is the most enduring organization of its sort in the so-called developing world because its membership was initially limited and defined by geography. Even in this comparatively successful case of institutional development, however, it is important to note that, first, the designation 'Southeast Asia' was externally imposed during the Second World War as a consequence of Britain's conflict with the Japanese in Burma/Myanmar (Emmerson 1984) and, second, geopolitics continued to play a profoundly important role in shaping the subsequent evolution of Southeast Asia as a collective actor.

When ASEAN was founded in 1967 at the height of the Cold War, ASEAN was – lofty rhetoric about the importance of promoting intra-regional understanding, notwithstanding – essentially a response to the uncertain strategic position of the ASEAN states. In this context, two considerations are pivotal. First, the original members of ASEAN – Indonesia, Malaysia, Singapore, Thailand, and the Philippines – were all still quite new independent states and as such still extremely concerned about protecting their recently acquired independent sovereignty. Threats to sovereignty at this time were both internal and external. Southeast Asian states were faced with the multiple challenges of spurring economic development while trying to reinforce a sense of national identity where one had often not existed before. Indonesia is the definitive example of a state that had to create a new nation and sense of identity out of the disparate parts bequeathed by Dutch colonialism. This was still (and arguably remains) a work in progress at the time of ASEAN's founding (Acharya 2001).

Adding to these difficulties in the 1960s was the fact that the Cold War was becoming increasingly hot (McMahon 1999). The Vietnam War was in full swing and some expected the rest of Southeast Asia to fall to the temptations or predations of communism like so many dominoes. Nor were such concerns entirely without foundation: 'communist insurgencies' could be found across the region, and the PRC remained a source of revolutionary ideology within a region with a large Chinese diaspora (Van Ness 1970). Even if we now think that some of these fears look overblown, rather paranoid, and remarkably undifferentiated in hindsight, they capture something important about the febrile mood of the times and help to explain why cooperation among similarly positioned states looked increasingly attractive. It is also important to remember that it was not only the superpowers that threatened to undermine the security environment in Southeast Asia. On the contrary, the 'Confrontation' between Indonesia and Malaysia was only the most dramatic and potentially consequential of a number of intra-regional disputes that threatened to get out of hand (Glassman 2005).

There were, then, many reasons for the strategically weak, economically small, and potentially fragile states of the region to consider seeking strength in numbers. There was also some geographical basis and idea of 'Southeast Asia' upon which to build, even if it was largely one that was inherited from the former colonial powers. Cooperation seemed one way of not only trying to deal with internal disputes, but also providing 'the region' with a more powerful presence on the international stage. The ASEAN grouping's celebrated (or reviled) modus operandi – the so-called 'ASEAN way' – also becomes easier to understand in such circumstances. The attractions of consensus, consultation, and face-saving may be traceable to common cultural practices in the region (Haacke 2003), but they also have more prosaic and contemporary attractions, too: nonbinding, voluntaristic diplomacy is not only easier to achieve among states unfamiliar with cooperation or even formulating foreign policy, but it is also not threatening to national autonomy either. One of ASEAN's key goals – even if not explicitly articulated as such – has been to reinforce domestic sovereignty, a critical consideration for states that were generally nondemocratic if not unambiguously authoritarian (Narine 2002).

Although it may have attracted a good deal of opprobrium over the years, the propensity for authoritarian rule in the region is understandable if not excusable. The emergence of 'strong man' leaders such as Sukarno and Suharto in Indonesia, Mahathir in Malaysia, Marcos in the Philippines, and Lee Kuan Yew in Singapore was in part a response to the unforgiving geopolitical context and the limited pressure for reform from the United States in particular. Tolerating, if not actively propping up, ideologically sympathetic or acceptable authoritarian leaders was the default policy position for the United States in East Asia (Root 2009). Given the prominent role played by the military in underwriting independence and maintaining domestic order across Southeast Asia, it is hardly surprising that authoritarian rule flourished and endured. It is equally unsurprising that the diplomatic style of Southeast Asia's first attempt at regional cooperation should have reflected domestic political realities and priorities (Beeson 2013b). Critics who bemoan ASEAN's lack of achievements or 'progress' consequently rather miss the point (Jones and Smith 2007): ASEAN's principal goal has always been to maintain stability, especially domestically. In this regard, the organization has arguably been a resounding success. What is more surprising, perhaps, is the impact that the ASEAN way has had on subsequent regional organizational development.

ASEAN's offshoots

The APEC grouping that emerged around twenty years after ASEAN reflects a different set of dynamics and drivers. Significantly, APEC's foundation in 1989 occurred at the same time that the Cold War ended. Although interest in developing some sort of regional grouping to promote cooperation had been around for some time (Woods 1993), a number of factors conspired to make APEC seem like an idea whose time had come. On the one hand, states around the world had become increasingly conscious of the impact of the EU. The EU highlighted both the potential benefits of establishing a large internal market and the possible dangers of being locked out of the sorts of regional trade blocs which looked set to become a larger part of the international institutional architecture (Hurrell 1995). On the other hand, economic issues generally were becoming increasingly important parts of national policy agendas and geopolitics became a less prominent influence on public policy.

Despite its potential, APEC developed the sort of distinctive regional identity and underlying historical connections that ASEAN had. As Barry Buzan (2012: 23) notes, 'a region that spans oceans and contains half of the world stretches the concept beyond breaking point'. APEC contained a highly diverse group of countries with without either the common history or the compelling geopolitical constraints to encourage unity. Despite the efforts of an 'epistemic community' of liberal economists to promote free trade, in APEC's Asian membership powerful vested interests with close connections to national governments frequently resisted an agenda of domestic economic liberalization (Beeson and Islam 2005). Crucially, APEC lacked the sort of institutional firepower and capacity that enabled the WTO to actually coerce members to go along with its trade liberalization agenda (Ravenhill 2000). Indeed, the parallel existence of the WTO begged the question of precisely what value APEC actually added to international efforts to promote trade liberalization and cooperation.

Significantly, the 'critical juncture' – which some consider an essential element of institutional reform (Capoccia and Kelemen 2007) – provided by the AFC in 1997/8 did far more than APEC to promote reform, especially when reinforced by the interventions of the IMF at America's behest (Stiglitz 2002). It is equally important to note that the Asian crisis had precisely the *opposite* effect that the GFC had in Europe, in that it actually encouraged regional cooperation (Beeson 2011b). Indeed, the earlier financial crisis marked a turning point in the region's development at a number of levels. First, the crisis punctured the idea that Asia was immune to the sorts of problems that have afflicted other parts of the world from time to time. This is not to understate the very real achievements that have occurred before or after the Asian crisis, but it did profoundly change the way that the region was viewed and not only by the controllers of mobile capital. On the contrary, the way regional elites thought about the region changed profoundly, too (Grimes 2009).

The second major lesson to emerge from the region, and the one with the most immediate impact on thinking about regionalism in particular, was the recognition that the region had little indigenous capacity to manage crises or defense mechanisms with which to ward them off (Beeson 2014a). An interest in developing 'monetary regionalism' was one of the most important consequences of this belated recognition of the paucity of regional crisis management mechanisms (Dieter 2008). It was also painfully apparent just how exposed the region was to the interventions and preferences of those agencies that *were* in a position to offer crisis management and advice. The role of the IMF in particular, and its close links to the United States, which was keen to seize the opportunity of encouraging – if not imposing reform on the region – was widely resented in the most badly affected countries (Higgott 1998).

The crisis spurred interest in developing new forms of monetary cooperation and raised the profile and potential importance of the ASEAN Plus Three (APT) grouping (Henning 2002), which included China, Kapan, and South Korea in addition to the ASEAN states. The idea of developing something like the APT had been around for some time, and the grouping was taking on an increasingly substantial looking presence on the margins of various ASEAN Summits. However, it required the sort of catalytic impact that a crisis has the potential to impart to really trigger action. In this context, the APT was in the right place at the right time and provided a potential vehicle through which all the members of the badly affected East Asian region could coalesce. The fact that the APT not only had a specific role to play, but also enjoyed the strong support of China, East Asia's rapidly rising superpower, seemed likely to ensure its preeminence. But yet again, East Asia continues to surprise and throw up important comparative lessons that we should not ignore. In this case, the lesson of the APT would seem to be that functional necessity can only take regional processes so far. In the face of growing geopolitical obstacles and tensions, such initiatives may flounder. This is precisely what seems to have happened.

By contrast, if there was one organization that seemed likely to suffer from a lack of support, purpose, and specificity it ought to have been the East Asia Summit (EAS). The EAS itself seemed almost entirely redundant given the existence of the APT, and it is striking that Chinese officials initially did not see the EAS as a threat to their preferred regional option, the APT. Indeed, the inclusion of not only Australia and New Zealand, but also India and eventually the United States was seen by some observers as suiting Chinese interests as the entire grouping was becoming increasingly incoherent and lacking in focus and purpose (Camroux 2012). The lack of an effective champion that might give it real influence and the initial indifference of the United States to the organization seemed likely to consign the EAS to the institutional wilderness.

Recently, however, the EAS's prospects have dramatically improved. Two interconnected geopolitical events have seen the EAS assume an unexpected prominence among the region's competing and overlapping institutions. On the one hand, the continuing 'rise of China', especially when coupled with an increasingly assertive foreign and strategic policy, has unnerved many of its neighbors and made the cultivation of strategic ties with the United States a much greater policy priority. However, even if the so-called 'Pivot' to the region inaugurated by Obama is not supported by Trump, the EAS provides a ready-made, if hitherto neglected, vehicle with which the United States can institutionally reengage with the region. Until recently, at least, the US government regarded the EAS as the region's premier forum for Asia-Pacific leaders to discuss pressing political and strategic issues (White House 2012). Not only is the United States a member, but so too are critical regional allies such as Australia and even India, with which the United States is attempting to develop closer strategic ties. However, there is yet another regional vision on offer in the shape of the 'Indo-Pacific', which its advocates hope will provide the basis for a new regional security relationship. The signs are that the Trump administration may see the Indo-Pacific idea as the best way to engage with the region. The implications of the rise of the Indo-Pacific and America's rapidly evolving attitude toward the region are taken up in Chapter 9.

As far as the hitherto promising-looking EAS is concerned, China's misgivings about US policy generally and the EAS in particular make it difficult to imagine it making much progress. Indeed, at this juncture, it is hard to see *any* of the region's growing number of regional initiatives making much of a difference to the way that national rather than regional priorities are decided. As far as both the United States and China are concerned, such an outcome may not be disastrous: for the United States, the EAS and the pivot mean that China is unlikely to play a dominant role in regional affairs. For China, a weak institution that lacks identity and purpose at least has the merit of allowing China to participate in regional multilateral institutions without necessarily being constrained by them too severely. Such an outcome may be unsatisfactory as far as those who view institutions as potentially vital parts of regional problem-solving, but they would be entirely in keeping with the region's history – be it the East Asian or the Asia-Pacific variant.

Concluding remarks

Space – and authorial limitations – precludes a detailed exploration of Latin American, African, or other possible regional configurations, but some general points may be drawn from the preceding discussion. First, the EU is in many ways sui generis and it is difficult to infer what will happen in other regions on the basis of its unique and possibly unrepeatable experience; it is also impossible to be certain, at this stage, what will happen to the EU itself. It is an open question whether 'more Europe' is the solution to some of the EU's current problems, but one possibility that cannot be dismissed is that Brexit may make other states recognize the difficulty and folly of leaving. Second, the rise of China and the relative decline of the United States are undoubtedly having a major impact on the international system and regional economic, political, and strategic relations. Again, it is impossible to know how this structural transformation will play itself out, but it is not fanciful or unreasonable to assume that China's influence over East Asia will continue to grow. Given that China appears entirely comfortable with the sort of undemanding regionalism that has evolved in its neighborhood, *East Asian* institutions may actually prosper if they provide a veneer of cooperation without threatening national sovereignty or curbing China's pursuit of its ambitions. Third, and following the previous point, the East Asian experience suggests that it is far from clear that regionalism will provide an alternative or a substitute for any governance deficit at the global level.

This is not to say that regions will not be significant, however, even if the form they assume looks rather more reminiscent of the nineteenth century rather than the twentieth or what we expected from the twenty-first. It is becoming increasingly common to suggest that we may see the emergence of regionally based 'spheres of influence' in which great powers exert a growing influence over 'their' regions (Buranelli forthcoming). In such a world, the possibility of global governance may become less likely, not least because the prospects for requisite leadership of a sort formerly provided by the United States are constrained by structural and agential factors (Waever 2017). The idea that the United States might not be capable of providing leadership was a well-established possibility even before the advent of the Trump presidency (Kupchan and Trubowitz 2007; Bremmer 2012). Subsequent events and the increasingly nationalistic policies of the Trump regime have done nothing to overturn such predictions. Trump's approach to the North American Free Trade Agreement (NAFTA) is indicative of his disdain for multilateralism, not to mention the impact of his policy preferences on his neighbors (Flannery 2018). The consequences of such policies and the absence of American leadership are becoming increasingly apparent. The next three chapters illustrate just how damaging this may be in several critically important issue areas.

7

Governing the Global Economy

The 'global economy' occupies an ambiguous place in the international system. Not only are there continuing doubts about just how global it actually is, but there are also growing differences of opinion about the way international economic activity could and should be managed. Such doubts have grown in the aftermath of the GFC of 2008. China has been an increasingly outspoken critic of the liberal form of 'light touch' regulation that was promoted by the United States and Britain in particular, but doubts about economic management predate the GFC. 'Critical' scholars of international political economy have long argued that the management of the international economic system is generally poorly done, in large part because it reflects the particularistic interests of privileged global elites, especially in the financial sector (Mügge 2011). The frequent outbreak of crises that have their origins in the financial sector would seem to confirm such claims.

This chapter considers some of these debates and the changes in the international economic order that have sparked them. It does so by building on the observations made about globalization and American hegemony developed in Chapters 1 and 3 respectively. Once again, the focus is primarily on the United States and China, not simply because they are the two largest economies in the world, but because their complex interdependent relationship highlights both the nature of contemporary economic relations and the competition to shape the international economic order as well as the norms and rules that seek to govern it.

In this context, it is important to stress that there is more at stake than the possible 'technical' merits of one possible economic paradigm or another, although such debates can be revealing and politically consequential. The real question for those interested in global governance is whether the global capitalist economy can actually be managed effectively at all. Many observers on 'the left' – if such labels are actually meaningful in a world where 'communist China' has one of the most successful capitalist economies in the world – still consider that capitalism is riddled with unsustainable 'contradictions'. Such contradictions explain the seemingly inescapable recurrence of crises and may, the argument goes, lead to the demise of capitalism itself, not least because of its environmental consequences (Harvey 2010; Kovel 2007).

While these sorts of questions are impossible to resolve, they are pertinent in any discussion of global governance. If the international economic system is seen as chronically unstable, unable to overcome structurally embedded patterns of inequality, and primarily working for the interests of a privileged minority, then the prospects for global governance are not bright, to say the least. There is, after all, good evidence about the social unrest that economic inequality and lack of opportunity can cause at the national and the international level (Li et al. 2013; Piketty 2014). High levels of unemployment among young men in the Middle East are plainly a contributing factor to that region's manifold problems (Zahid 2010). For global governance to amount to anything more than a slogan or collective wishful thinking, it has to be able to deal with the most difficult regions and incorporate them and their populations into some wider, optimism-inducing process of economic development, social inclusion, and increased opportunity.

Conceptualizing the evolving economic order

Discussions of the 'global economy' face even greater initial conceptual hurdles than some other aspects of possible global governance. First and foremost, perhaps, is the question of whether it actually makes sense to talk about a *global* economy in the first place. As we have seen in earlier chapters, one of the striking features of contemporary patterns of economic development and integration is their unevenness: some parts of the world are far more deeply interconnected than others. Indeed, one of the possible explanations of the relative failure of some regions in the world to achieve similar levels of economic growth and expansion is that they are not as deeply linked to international flows of trade and investment as they could be, and this goes a long way to explaining their marginal or unfavorable positions in cross-border economic relationships (Ravalliona 2008).

Somewhat paradoxically, therefore, one question to ask about a global *capitalist* economy is about the degree to which it can be governed successfully without dampening the 'animal spirits' that provide its underlying dynamics. While there may be no doubt about which system triumphed in the epic confrontation between market-based and centrally planned economies, questions about the degree and nature of state 'intervention' in market processes remain unresolved and contentious. Even more uncertain are questions about the extent and the very possibility of international collaboration to address issues of inequality, uneven development, exploitation, and, as we shall in the next chapter, climate change. Indeed, a central concern for some prominent critics of unfettered capitalist development is about its impact on politics generally and on democracy in particular. As Wolfgang Streeck (2014: 159) puts it, 'in the early twenty-first century, capital is confident of being able to organize itself as it pleases in a deregulated finance industry. The only thing it expects of politics is its capitulation to the market by eliminating social democracy as an economic force.' Robert Kuttner (2018: 257) makes a similar point even more forcefully when he argues that,

> Today, it is not communists, but capitalists, who are seeking to impose a single economic on the globe. On balance, the institutions of global governance tend to reflect and reinforce rather than challenge that dominance. Globalism has been great at advancing the interests of capital and feeble at defending or enlarging the domain of human rights. The home of democracy – or antidemocracy – continues to be the national polity.

Assessing these important claims is made more difficult by the evolving nature of economic activity itself. It has long been customary to make a broad distinction between the 'real' economy which is based on the production of 'things you can drop on your foot', as *The Economist* (2013) memorably put it, and the service sector, which produces less tangible commodities, such as transport, wholesaling, retailing, and – most importantly for the purposes of the current discussion – the financial sector. As we saw in Chapter 1, the rise of MNCs has transformed, disaggregated, and redistributed the production process, meaning that 'trade' frequently occurs within an individual firm or its network of suppliers and service providers.

Not only do such developments raise major questions about the way we measure economic activity, but there are also important consequences for states and their ability to tax the activities of firms that can choose where to realize profits and losses through transfer pricing strategies (Sikka and Willmott 2010). Wealthy MNCs are able to employ the most talented tax 'minimization' specialists, too, meaning that the balance of power between states and companies is increasingly shifting in the latter's favor (Khanna 2016). All of this makes it difficult both to neatly conceptualize the contemporary international economy and for policymakers – and private sector actors, for that matter – to 'govern' complex, interconnected economic activities that may include integrated manufacturing and service sector activities that are distributed across national borders. As Richard Baldwin (2016: 6) points out, 'the contours of industrial competitiveness are increasingly defined by the outlines of international production networks rather than the boundaries of nations'.

Governing global production networks

Global production networks (GPNs) have rapidly become one of the defining features of the contemporary international order. The 'value chains' embedded in GPNs are an increasingly important and prominent part of economic analysis, although one that is often radically at odds with traditional conceptions of discrete national economies competing with one another at arm's-length. As we shall see, this underlying structural reality makes some of the policy initiatives of the Trump administration potentially inappropriate and unrealizable. It also makes it increasingly difficult – and arguably counterproductive – to wind back the way production is organized and return to some sort of golden age of trade relations in which 'the United States' can emerge triumphant. Private sector companies are by definition responsible primarily to their shareholders not to 'their' national governments – unless the state continues to exercise a degree of ownership and/or control as they do in China, of course. In such circumstances, it is difficult to see how the Trump administration could 'win' a trade war with China, or what such a victory would actually look like, given that 'American' firms such as Apple are responsible for many of 'China's' exports (Strauss 2018), and that exports from the United States to China support nearly 1 million jobs in the United States (OUSTR 2018).

Value chain analysis and the activities of GPNs provide one way of thinking about the way economic processes, especially in the 'real' economy, are currently organized – even if they do not always generate obvious or politically palatable policy options. In their influential conceptualization of contemporary production structures, Gereffi and colleagues (2005: 98) suggest that

the structure of global value chains depends critically upon three variables: the complexity of transactions, the ability to codify transactions, and the capabilities in the supply-base. These variables are sometimes determined by the technological characteristics of products and processes (some transactions are inherently more complex and difficult to codify than others, for example) and they often depend on the effectiveness of industry actors and the social processes surrounding the development, dissemination, and adoption of standards and other codification schemes. It is the latter set of determinants, in particular, that opens the door for policy interventions and corporate strategy.

The broadly conceived electronics industries are some of the quintessential examples of this complex processes in practice (Dicken 2011). It is now possible to source parts of the production process in places where considerations of comparative advantage – especially as they apply to labor costs – may be crucial determinants influencing the 'lead firm's' decisions about investment and location. Even in more liberal market economies, governments may well try to persuade potentially footloose MNCs to invest in their countries, with subsidies, tariffs, and tax holidays (Berger 2005). This is where the significance of the varieties of capitalism discussed in Chapter 1 can become potentially important. MNCs may be attracted to invest in states that can provide educated workforces, social stability, and economic security.

Although the analysis of GPNs and value chains represents a major step forward in our understanding of the way that firms respond to the various regulatory frameworks created by states, as Gereffi (2005: 170) notes, it is an approach that 'tends to focus on the strategies and behavior of the players (firms), while the rules of the game (regulatory institutions) are taken as an exogenous variable'. But as we have seen, the relationship between actors and regulatory frameworks is interactive and invariably mutually constitutive; it is also one that varies from region to region and even state to state. Governance happens at a number of different levels giving different actors the chance to shape the regulatory outcomes they prefer (Jayasuriya 2008). Not only can this work to the advantage of more powerful actors, be they states or other entities, but it can also disadvantage the less powerful, too. As we have seen in earlier chapters, concerns about continuing asymmetries of influence and power remain a major obstacle to developing the sorts of common approaches and ideas that might constitute a part of any global governance regime.

Indeed, the relationship between states and MNCs is not unidirectional. Specific forms of national regulation and control continue to have an important role in influencing corporate decision-making. Gourevitch (2005: 57) argues that 'the struggle for power inside the firm is settled by the struggle for power outside the firm, in the political system that determines the rules'. This is especially the case in China, where the state continues to play an interventionist role, and not just in the decision-making processes of indigenous companies. True, China is arguably sui generis in terms of its market size and strategic importance, but as Coe and colleagues (2008: 283) note, 'whereas in many cases, TNCs are able to play off one country against another to achieve the best deal, in the Chinese case it is the state whose unique bargaining position has enabled it to play off one TNC against another'. China's status as the world's largest market for cars, for example, has given the Chinese government significant influence over the activities of foreign MNCs, restricting equity stakes to 50 percent and actively promoting indigenous firms through its 'Made in China 2025' initiative (*The Economist* Intelligence Unit 2017; Hopewell 2018).

The continuing importance of industry policies in China and state-led efforts to influence the course of domestic development and the nature of external integration is highlighted in the BRI. Although the governance of global value chains is largely the preserve of large firms from the private sector (Gibbon et al. 2008), as we have seen, in China's case the extent of the privatization process is often constrained and the state's influence remains significant, especially in 'strategic' industries. One of the consequences of China's rapid development has been to establish the PRC as a key part of regionally based production networks (Athukorala 2009). The BRI promises to entrench this position *and* the potential for the PRC to exert an influence over the development and governance of regionally based production processes more generally. Even if Yeung (2016: 15) is correct to suggest that 'the developmental state approach is becoming increasingly obsolescent in the post-1990 context of the dynamic articulation of East Asian economies into the global economy', the scope and scale of the BRI has the potential to transform the context within which the private sector operates. It will also influence the sorts of strategic decisions that even genuinely independent firms make about investment decisions and their mode of integration into what may prove to be the defining development project of the era. Even more contentiously, the BRI has a demonstrated potential to influence to policy agenda of states that accept loan packages from the Chinese government as part of their incorporation into the increasingly expansive and ambitious project (Beeson 2018c; Kehoe 2018).

At a time when the Trump administration is actively trying to 'bring home' supposedly 'American' companies, China's industry policies and its associated grand strategy are likely to generate increased friction and come under ever greater scrutiny. Significantly, while the Trump administration has tried to encourage such developments through tax incentives, the PRC has been investing in specific developmental projects that are having direct impacts on the ground (Browne 2018). Trump's tax policies, by contrast, are actually providing further incentives for firms to offshore their production and to take advantage of tax havens overseas (Miller 2018). Two points are worth highlighting about such contrasting Chinese and American strategies and approaches to governing the real economy. First, the PRC leadership's understanding of contemporary economic development actually seems a more accurate basis for effective policies than the Trump administration's, especially when considered from the perspective of the elusive 'national interest'. Second, as the tax minimization strategies of MNCs remind us, activities in the service sector and/or the knowledge economy present even greater governance challenges for individual governments. These developments raise fundamental questions about the durability, capacity, and role of the foundational institutions created under the auspices of American hegemony discussed in Chapter 3.

Significantly, divisions between 'North' and 'South' not only continue in such circumstances, but are integral to the rapid growth in preferential trade agreements (PTAs) that both reflect and drive greater economic integration. As Manger (2012) points out, vertical specialization not only allows for greater 'efficiencies' in the production process, but also helps to create political coalitions within developing countries that support trade liberalization. While this may confirm the idea that GPNs and the trade relations that facilitate them are here to stay, such developments are potentially very significant for the East Asian region in particular, where interventionist developmental states have traditionally played a prominent role in actually *shaping* comparative advantage through specific industry policies. The implication, according to Yeung (2013: 74), is that 'inter-firm dynamics in global production networks tend to trump state-led initiatives as one of the most critical conditions for economic development'.

Trade has a materiality and visibility that gives it a talismanic status in international economic disputes. In an era of strongman leadership, this makes the resolution of differences and the fulfillment of promised national reconstruction all the more problematic. Trade disputes in particular highlight the apparent continuing importance of national interests, geographically demarcated spheres of economic activity, and the potentially decisive actions of nationally based policymakers. The reality, as we have seen, is rather different. Not only is 'trade' a far more complex, transnational process than the pronouncements of populists like Trump would have us believe, but many of the most consequential decisions that are made about economic governance are not made by the traditional political class – whether it was democratically elected or not.

Some of the most important developments in governance and transnational coordination are happening in other economic issue areas, and may actually prove to be more significant despite their comparatively lower profile. They also raise fundamental questions about the evolution of, and prospects for, economic governance in more technically challenging policy domains. For some observers, economic governance is still inexorably shifting from states to nonstate actors in the way many of the early analysts of globalization predicted. The reason for this long-term structural transformation is straightforward: policymakers from individual nation states acting alone simply cannot provide the requisite regulatory and institutional infrastructure necessary to allow complex economic processes and relationships to occur across national borders. As a result, Koppel (2010: 7) argues, 'the triumph of functional governance comes into better focus every day'.

In support of this claim, Koppel cites the growing importance and authority of what he calls 'global governance organizations' (GGOs), which do much of the heavy-lifting when it comes to providing an environment in which international commerce in particular can occur. GGOs are 'organizations engaged in substantive arenas with straightforward public policy significance', and include familiar entities such as the WTO and the IMF as well as less familiar bodies such as the Basel Committee on Banking Supervision (BCBS), the International Accounting Standards Board (IASB), the World Intellectual Property Organization (WIPO), and many others (Koppel 2010: 80). Despite the fact that many of these GGOs are specialist entities and largely unknown to the general public, they are key parts of the contemporary governance arena without which the international economy in particular could not function. GGOs such as the IASB, the WIPO, and the International Organization for Standardization are especially important examples of the largely invisible, but vital nongovernment agencies. The key point that many observers make about the growth in the sheer number and importance of GGOs and the increased cooperation between private sector actors in providing elements of governance is that this has led to a concomitant increase in their authority (Cutler et al. 1999).

The possible transformation in the relative importance of nongovernment actors and states is also highlighted in Braithwaite and Drahos's (2000) magisterial survey of global business regulation. However, they also point to the role and continuing importance of state power – even coercion – in entrenching particular norms and practices at the center of various regulatory regimes in different economic sectors. As they point out, 'US corporations exert more power in the world system than corporations of other states because they can enroll the support of the most powerful state in the world' (Braithwaite and Drahos 2000: 490). The political influence of American-based pharmaceutical companies is a good, if contentious, example of this possibility, and helps to explain the concern with intellectual property rights that has become such a prominent feature of trade negotiations and disputes (Stiglitz 2007: 105). One of the many paradoxes and puzzles of the Trump regime's approach to trade results is that the TPP actually promised to advance the interests of American-based corporations by tackling 'behind the border' regulatory issues and protecting the lucrative intellectual property of 'Big Pharma' (Gleeson 2015).

The erosion of the old order

The difficulty of reconciling a populist discourse about the national economic interest with complexities of contemporary economic reality is even more evident in financial sector regulation, despite the United States also enjoying major 'structural' advantages other states cannot match. The most obvious manifestation of this possibility, as noted earlier, is the continuing dominance and centrality of the American dollar in the world's financial and trade relations. This situation is likely to continue despite the United States' role in the GFC and what Kirshner (2013: 41) describes as the 'completely unbound … disreputable' model of American finance. As Stokes (2014: 1085) points out, there is 'a path dependency to US hegemony, with both states' and private actors' interests mutually bound into the relative health of the US dollar and the American economy.' These entrenched advantages and the reliance of other states and actors on the American economy help to explain the continuing importance of key institutions such as the Federal Reserve, too.

'The Fed' is emblematic of both the novelty of some aspects of economic governance and some surprising elements of continuity. On the one hand, central banks have become an increasingly important and influential part of governing the financial sector (Solomon 1995), especially in the wake of the transformation that Richard Nixon was instrumental in unleashing in the 1970s, and which triggered the demise of the old system of fixed or managed exchange rates. It is important to remember that states generally and the United States in particular were responsible for overseeing a transfer of responsibility from governments to markets when they abandoned the old order and set the stage for the remarkable growth in the size and influence of global financial markets (Helleiner 1994; Cerny 1996). For all the subsequent problems this transfer of power has caused at times, the Trump administration seems committed to reinforcing rather than reforming the power of the financial markets.

By definition, hegemonic powers can do things that other, lesser powers cannot. There is, however, a fundamental, and potentially irreconcilable tension between the pursuit of narrowly conceived 'national interests' and the provision of the sorts of collective goods that Charles Kindleberger (1973) thought were prerequisites of a stable international economy (Beeson and Broome 2010). What Skidmore (2011) calls the 'unilateralist temptation' proved irresistible to the administration of Richard Nixon when it unilaterally 'closed the gold window' and abruptly ended the notional relationship between the value of the American dollar and the value of gold (Gowa 1983). While this may have been inevitable given the imbalances that were building up in the international economy, it represented a seismic shock that effectively undermined the old order, nevertheless. There were two pivotally important consequences of this period that illustrate the unpredictable and mutually constitutive relationship between states and markets.

First, the creation of a system of market-determined exchange rates effectively ended the old order of embedded liberalism (Ruggie 1982). States were suddenly involved in the sort of 'beauty contest' that Keynes (1958: 156) had spoken of so scathingly in connection with equity markets. Market forces or, more accurately, newly empowered actors in the rapidly expanding international money markets, were increasingly able to pass judgment on the actions and policies of individual states. Governments that failed to subscribe to the fiscal orthodoxy of the day could be punished by having their now freely floating currencies sold off. Subsequently, new institutions and actors would be established to manage – and take advantage of – the new economic order in ways that few had predicted, which marked a long-term transfer of power and authority from states to markets (Sinclair 2005). The potential impact of greater market power, increased liquidity, and herd-like behavior was vividly demonstrated in the highly destructive crisis that unfolded with such rapidity in Asia in the late 1990s (Wade and Veneroso 1998).

Second, the role of one of the principal IOs that had provided the regulatory infrastructure of the old order was completely overturned. From being primarily responsible for managing a system of fixed exchange rates, the IMF suddenly found itself having to adapt to an entirely different and unanticipated role. Now the IMF was to oversee a market-based system that would prove to be far more crisis-prone than its tightly regulated predecessor. As Louis Pauly (1997: 116) points out, 'the Fund's capacity to provide surveillance developed, quite by accident, into an incipient capacity to manage systemic crises in a world of expanding capital markets'.

There is a good deal of debate and controversy about how and why the IMF acted as it did at moments of crisis in the case of the Asian crisis (Stiglitz 2007), for example. The IMF policy response was widely condemned as doctrinaire and inappropriate – advocating the sorts of austerity policies that have also been judged to have failed in the more recent crisis in Greece, and elsewhere (Blyth 2013). Stiglitz (2002: 89) argues that this was especially unforgivable as the Asian economies were in generally good shape before the crisis, and their problems emerged because the IMF encouraged them to pursue 'excessively rapid financial and capital market liberalization [that] was probably the single most important cause of the crisis'. The point to emphasize here, though, is that the Asian crisis highlighted how IMF personnel had rapidly embraced their new role and become major parts of the dissemination of broadly neoliberal ideas about public policy in ways that had not been originally intended or foreseen (Babb 2007; Chwieroth 2007).

Whatever the merits of the Fund's policy prescriptions, however, the key consequence of this period from the 1970s onward was to transform the role of the IMF and ultimately the conventional wisdom about the conduct of economic policy across the Anglo-American economies in particular. Ironically, the Fund in particular and the other IFIs more generally were instrumental in entrenching an economic and political order that helped establish the preconditions for new crises that would have similarly transformative impacts in later years. The rapid increase in the scale of capital flows and the growing influence of financial markets gave capital an enduring 'structural' power that would place significant constraints on the actions of the very states that were instrumental in creating the regulatory environment that allowed them to flourish (Andrews 1994; Helleiner 1994).

While central banks and intergovernmental institutions like the Bank for International Settlements (BIS), which is a forum of the world's major central banks and devoted fostering international monetary and financial cooperation, would come to play a prominent and increasingly influential role in managing the global economy, they were far from alone (Germain 2004). On the contrary, in keeping with the ruling ideational orthodoxy, and as a result of the state's unwillingness or inability to address some of the more 'technical' complexities of managing international economic interaction, the private sector assumed an ever-larger role in governing the global economy – or the 'global economy' as it operated in the developed Western economies that had hitherto dominated an increasingly interdependent international order, at least. While the supposed expertise and independence of central bankers and institutions such as credit ratings agencies has been a distinctive feature of contemporary patterns of governance in the financial sector, they have not necessarily been politically neutral or capable of dispassionate judgment.

American support for the BIS has been important in both underwriting the BIS's authority and allowing the United States to promote its preferred policy agenda (Porter 2002). From the perspective of nascent forms of global governance and inclusivity, the BIS faces some key challenges because of its implicit normative commitment to limited government intervention and a prominent role for the same financial institutions it seeks to regulate. As Ozgercin (2012: 99) notes,

> the most powerful idea that shaped the BIS's original institutional design in 1930, and has guided its institutional culture ever since, is that central bankers and to a lesser, albeit significant, extent prominent international commercial bankers – not 'politically controlled' finance ministers – should be responsible for governing finance. That is, state regulation of financial markets should be minimal, and insofar as states do intervene, intervention should take the form of independent central bank action, conceived and implemented in collaboration with leading private banks in each financial centre.

Significantly, the BIS's view of its role and the optimal management of the international banking sector is potentially radically at odds with China's and other state-dominated economies. As Bell and Feng (2013: 5) point out, 'the rise of the People's Bank of China (PBC) has been based on a relationship of growing mutual dependence with the party leadership'. In other words, rather than being a notionally independent agency distinguished primarily for the expertise of its personnel, the PBC is a central component of the state's continuing influence over economic activity in China. The point to emphasize once more is that even in issue areas that are apparently quintessentially 'global', distinctive national approaches continue and are institutionalized in differently constituted organizations that seem to serve the same purposes. Such differences pose major obstacles to cooperation as a result.

Indeed, it is important to note that even where institutions such as central banks have been given more authority and independence, this has not stopped their actions from becoming highly politicized or guaranteed that their policy prescriptions will either work or be well received. On the contrary, the inauguration and subsequent management of a common European currency are generally considered to have been badly handled at best, fundamentally ill-conceived, and unworkable at worst (Beeson and Bell 2017). The European Central Bank (ECB) does, indeed, have a remarkable amount of autonomy and policy discretion (Menon 2008: 101), but this has only made it the focus of controversy and if not outright resentment. It has also highlighted potentially irreconcilable policy, economic, and political divisions between different parts of the EU (Stevis and Thomas 2015). If the EU and its key institutions cannot resolve differences between broadly similar states within a relatively limited geographical space, it is not unreasonable to be skeptical about the prospects for effective economic governance and cooperation at the global scale.

There is something paradoxical and ironic in all this that is especially relevant in any discussion of economic policy. After all, one of the criticisms of 'neoliberal' forms of governance is that it has become all pervasive and inappropriate for developing economies in particular. Even more nuanced critiques revolve around the idea that neoliberal orthodoxies restrict the development or utilization of local knowledge, or even the sorts of policies that the early industrializers themselves employed at a similar stage (Chang 2002). As Block and Evans (2005: 508) argue 'by definition, all of these efforts to construct global governance regimes are efforts at institutional innovation. But they come into direct conflict with the logic of global neoliberalism that imposes a kind of "institutional monocropping" that severely constrains the possibilities for innovation both within and across societies.' Put differently, ideational hegemony on the part of Western states limits the sorts of theoretical and policy approaches that are deemed feasible when formulating policy.

At one level, Block and Evans clearly have a point: the remarkable dominance of theoretical notions such as the 'efficient markets hypothesis' (EFH) in the run-up to the GFC clearly helps to explain why some approaches to economic management came to dominate thinking in the Anglo-American economies in particular, and why the regulation of the financial sector was so inadequate as a consequence. Simply put, the EFH suggested that asset prices fully reflect all available information, allowing rational investors to make informed decisions in their best interests. It is a theoretical picture that Adam Smith might have recognized, in which the combined effects of market forces and utility maximizing individuals lead to the best of all possible worlds. At the very least, the EFH should have made the formation of stock market bubbles (and the subsequent crashes they caused) unlikely if not impossible. And yet the reality has been that 'irrational exuberance', as former Chair of the Federal Reserve Alan Greenspan famously described it, has been an increasingly prominent feature of international capitalism over the last few decades. In such circumstances the growing interest in radical scholars, such as Hyman Minsky (1986), becomes more explicable, even if their actual influence on the policy process remains limited.

The conceptual case against the EFH is long-standing (Haugen 1995) and vindicated by the actual evolution of the GFC – even if many of the lessons remain unlearned (Quiggin 2012). And yet, the rise to prominence of neoliberal ideas themselves also serves as a reminder that 'ideas do not float freely': without political support, even the best ideas will not have the capacity to influence policy debates (Risse-Kappen 1994). After all, Friedrich Hayek's ideas about the supposed benefits of free markets had been around for a long time before they were championed by Margaret Thatcher and a well-organized network of think tanks and policy networks in Britain (Cockett 1994). Much has been written about the shortcomings of neoliberalism generally and of the regulatory failures in the international financial sector in particular (Harvey 2007; Crotty 2009; Bell and Hindmoor 2015), but it is worth highlighting a few general points about GFC and its aftermath as they illustrate many of the problems confronting advocates of global governance in this area.

The GFC and its aftermath

The first point to make about the GFC from the perspective of the existing international order is that it was unambiguously made in America. Indeed, despite its name the 'global' financial crisis was largely confined to the United States itself and Western Europe. China and much of the rest of East Asia emerged relatively unscathed, largely as a consequence of China's rather orthodox, Keynesian-inspired policy response to an external shock, which stabilized not only its own economy but also those of the rest of the region as well (Yang 2015). The damage to the reputation of the United States, its policymakers, and an economic community that had previously seen itself as the fount of policy wisdom was significant (Colander 2011), although far from terminal. On the contrary, despite a number of detailed analyses of the crisis laying the blame squarely at the feet of a poorly regulated financial sector driven by greed and a misplaced faith in poorly understood innovations, Wall Street has regained much of its former prominence and appears to have learned nothing from this earlier episode. Global economic governance, in other words, continues to be dominated by many of the same ideas, institutions, and practices that were responsible for the GFC (Wolf 2018). Even more importantly, key elements of the financial sector are once again exerting a major influence over the Trump administration, despite Trump's promises to 'drain the swamp' of vested interests and insiders (McLannahan 2017).

Unsurprisingly in such circumstances, the Trump administration has not absorbed the lessons of the GFC, either. Given Trump's disdain for any sort of regulation this outcome may be entirely predictable, perhaps. As a result, his administration is working assiduously to dismantle the regulatory reforms the Obama administration enacted in the wake of the GFC. What *is* surprising is that Democrats are apparently complicit in these efforts, suggesting that the influence of the financial sector and its army of lobbyists is as powerful as ever (Konczal 2018). Such apparent groupthink and 'institutional monocropping' looks especially dangerous when historically literate observers consider that many of the preconditions are in place for yet another crisis (Ferguson 2017). This apparent inability to learn lessons from financial history is not something that is confined to a famously ill-informed president, however. On the contrary, one of the pervasive features of financial crises is the recurring belief that 'this time it's different' (Reinhart and Rogoff 2009) and the normal rules do not apply to the new masters of the economic universe (Bell and Hindmoor 2015).

Having said that, every crisis has its own distinctive drivers and dynamics. In the case of the GFC it was the failure to understand, much less regulate, the way in which the financial sector was operating, combined with a blithe disregard of what the possible consequences of such practices might be. One of the most distinctive and destructive features of the GFC was not only the failure to regulate the financial sector, but the manner in which the 'financialization' of every aspect of social life had drawn in all sectors of the population and generated new risks – and sources of profit – in the process (Montgomerie and Williams 2009). The fact that the origins of the GFC were in the 'subprime' market for real estate loans is a telling indicator of the extent of the penetration of the financial sector and the difficulty of regulating it as a consequence (Blackburn 2008). A key part of the dynamics of recent crises is that the US economy is not simply an unfortunate example of 'bad' policy driven by particular vested interests that stand to benefit from particular regulatory frameworks. Part of the problem and difficulty of reforming the domestic *and* international economy revolves around the way the US economy is integrated into, and benefits from, its place in the global economy.

One of the striking features of both the GFC and the earlier AFC is the pernicious role played by the American economy. During the AFC the US dollar's role as the world's reserve currency and the fact that its value was not tied to gold meant that the US government was able to finance persistent and growing external deficits though the issuance of government bonds (Wade 2000). Somewhat ironically, the surpluses that have been generated by emerging markets in the aftermath of the AFC have allowed the United States to continue its reliance on recycling capital from its trade partners around the world, heightening the underlying structural symbiosis and the persistence of potential structural vulnerabilities (Vasudevan 2009). The key macroeconomic consequence of this US-drive codependence, Vermeiren (2013: 247) argues, is that

> the main function of US structural monetary power was to consolidate finance-led growth in the US economy at the same time as inducing East Asian countries to pursue export-led growth. The dynamics of US monetary hegemony thus crystallized a symbiotic relationship between the US and East Asian growth regimes in a way that supported US macroeconomic autonomy at the cost of escalating global current account imbalances.

There are a number of implications of these claims that remain contentious but are worth highlighting as they present potentially implacable obstacles to cooperation between the United States and other key actors such as China, especially under the nationalistic Trump administration. The first point to emphasize is that despite China's unhappiness with the United States' continuing primacy in global financial markets and the role of the dollar as the world's reserve currency (Wildau and Mitchell 2016), such advantages are unlikely to disappear in the short term and are likely to be exploited by the Trump administration where possible. The reality is that the United States can behave in ways that other countries cannot despite a policy regime 'that would, anywhere else, elicit a withering "disciplinary" response from international financial markets' (Kirshner 2008: 424). Running persistent trade and fiscal deficits in ways that contribute to politically problematic imbalances looks likely to be a continuing and contentious feature of the international political economy and a fundamental obstacle to cooperation.

Such an outcome is, perhaps, more surprising than it might seem. For some observers, there is evidence of the emergence of transnational class interests discussed in Chapter 2. Hung Ho-fung, for example, suggests that China's export-oriented industries have become so economically and politically important that they are transforming the basis of the bilateral relationship with the United States.

This dominant faction of China's elite, as exporters and creditors to the world economy, has established a symbiotic relation with the American ruling class, which has striven to maintain its domestic hegemony by securing the living standards of US citizens, as consumers and debtors to the world. Despite occasional squabbles, the two elite groups on either side of the Pacific share an interest in perpetuating their respective domestic status quos, as well as the current imbalance in the global economy. (Hung 2009: 24–25)

Even if Hung is correct in identifying potential synergies between economic elites on both sides of the Pacific, this does not mean that they will be able to influence the policy debate in either country sufficiently to avoid a trade war. On the contrary, not only do some of Trump's key advisors have a nationalistic, zero-sum view of trade relations (Navarro 2006, 2018; Ball 2018), but the inability of the Trump administration to develop a consistent, coherent position on bilateral economic relations with China – or anything else, for that matter – means that the United States may blunder into economic conflict whether it wants one or not. Even if the Chinese government was willing to accede to American demands – and given the possible loss of face this would involve for Xi and the CCP this seems unlikely (Myers 2018b) – it is not clear they could easily fix the deficit even if they wanted to. The underlying reality is that 'the United States exports only $130 billion in goods a year to China. Finding more goods to buy to reduce China's trade surplus by $200 billion would be extremely difficult, except if China cut its own exports to the United States' (Bradsher 2018).

The specifics of any trade deal with China may prove less important in the long run than the damage that the Trump administration may inflict on the international economic system and any hopes for a collective system of governance to manage economic problems and development. Significantly, Trump abandoned the painstakingly negotiated Trans Pacific Partnership (TPP), despite the pleas and protests of key allies such as Australia and Japan (Hodge 2017). While the other members of the TPP grouping have pressed on with the agreement without the United States, the absence of America's customary leadership on trade promotion has dealt a further blow to an international trade regime that was already under severe strain. As we saw in Chapter 6, regional trade agreements have had a patchy record in the Asia Pacific at the best of times.

More broadly, the continuing inability of the WTO to reach or enforce comprehensive trade agreements has further undermined the authority of transnational regulatory institutions. In the WTO's case, this problem has been exacerbated by the actions of the Trump administration, which claims that American participation in the WTO was a 'mistake' (Donnan 2018). More directly, the United States has refused to appoint or reappoint any member of the WTO Appellate Body, meaning that the WTO's ability to judge trade disputes may actually break down. Equally importantly, the fact that the United States is attempting to negotiate directly with China, rather than using multilateral auspices to resolve disputes, is a further blow to the credibility of the WTO and the principle of universal reciprocity. In such circumstances, some commentators are looking to the PRC to 'save' the WTO and the fabled 'rules-based international order' of which it has been a prominent part for so long (Brewster 2018). If China does act to preserve the WTO and the international rules from which it has benefited it could be seen as rather paradoxical and ironic evidence of the 'socializing' capacity of international institutions. And yet it is entirely possible that China may seek to put its imprint on not only the WTO, but also the broader array of institutions of which it is a part.

Concluding remarks

This volume has focused much attention on relations between the United States and China, not simply because they are the world's two largest economies, but because they represent very different regimes with potentially incompatible goals. As we saw in Chapter 2, liberal interdependence theorists are clearly right when they point to the transformative effects that greater economic integration can have on the way that policymakers think about their relationship with the rest of the world. China's remarkable transformation over the last twenty or thirty years is the most tangible and important manifestation of this possibility. And yet the current economic dispute with the United States and the seemingly incompatible nature of both countries' economic and political goals provide a sobering reminder of the persistence of national priorities and the difficulties of achieving agreement – even in a bilateral context. How much more difficult to achieve meaningful agreement at a broader international level when many of the most important multilateral institutions that might be expected to manage this are suffering crises of legitimacy and relevance? The growth of bilateralism in trade negotiations in particular is a telling, not terribly productive consequence and illustration of this phenomenon (Dent 2010; Stokes and Waterman 2017).

Sino-US relations continue to highlight many of the most fundamental, seemingly nonnegotiable obstacles to greater economic cooperation, and not just because of the unpredictability and inconsistency of the current incumbent of the White House (Rodrik 2018). A key constraint on China's ability to strike deals is that its ruling elites are wary of seeming to give in to American bullying (Myers 2018b). As we have seen in other chapters, the incorporation of China into the existing global order presents a particular challenge because of its unique – and troubled – relationship with the West. The idea that the United States in particular and the West more generally might be – once again – conspiring to inhibit its development is especially sensitive, and a fundamental threat to its East Asian-style development strategy. But the structurally embedded advantages that the United States continues to enjoy in terms of its possession of sophisticated technology and especially the importance of its financial sector limit China's options. China is heavily dependent on American semi-conductors for many of its electronics products, for example. As *The Economist* (2018b) points out, of even greater concern to China's leaders is the possibility 'that America can weaponise its financial system. By denying banks access to its market, it can freeze them out of international transactions.'

While there is no doubt that the scale of China's ambitions has grown in line with its economic development, as we saw in Chapter 4, there are still major constraints on its ability to realize them. Despite the fact that many of America's traditional allies in places like Europe are deeply concerned about the negative impact the Trump administration is having on the existing international order, it is difficult to imagine many of the United States' traditional partners giving up on America and looking to China for leadership. This is not to deny that China's influence and economic weight have grown enormously, even in Europe, but this is unlikely to provide the basis for the sort of close ties that have existed among NATO's members. On the contrary, precisely the same sorts of concerns have emerged about China's potentially pernicious political influence and about the possible negative consequences of its economic model (Benner et al. 2018; Braw 2018).

Anxiety about the wider possible impact of China's rise in the United States and elsewhere is a reminder that economic development and possible governance occurs in a specific historical context, and one that is inevitably overlaid with distinctive, possibly unique, geopolitical characteristics. The inauguration of American hegemony was the quintessential example of this possibility and helps to account both for the particular form that economic governance took in much of the world and for its durability. As China is discovering, it is not easy to establish a new international order or transform an existing one. It is not even clear whether the sort of role the United States played as a system stabilizer is either possible or necessary in the contemporary era: while states are undoubtedly still the most important actors in the international system, there are limits to what even the most powerful of them can do, especially without the support of their most influential peers.

This would be the case no matter who was in the White House. The fact that it is currently occupied by someone who takes an entirely instrumental attitude to international cooperation and demonstrates a disdain for multilateralism may be aggravating rather than creating a problem. However, it is worth remembering that key IOs such as the WTO and the IMF were showing signs of strain even under Barack Obama, a committed internationalist, but one who is now seen by some as subscribing to 'a sincere but fundamentally mistaken and unrealistic theory of international relations' (Dueck 2015: 106). Apparent divisions between Emmanuel Macron and Angela Merkel over reforms in the eurozone, especially when combined with unresolved Brexit problems and an unpredictable, indebted Italian government, mean that the EU is likely to remain preoccupied with its own problems and be incapable of offering effective regional leadership, let alone the global variety (Crook 2018).

It is possible that China and the United States may make a deal over trade given how much they both have to lose if they don't. It is even possible that a new crisis will galvanize institutions such as the G20 into action once again, but the problems outlined in Chapter 5 illustrate how difficult it can be to address major crises and – equally importantly – to maintain the momentum for needed reforms. The Trump administration's moves to wind back even the limited reforms undertaken in the wake of the GFC suggest that important lessons remain unlearned and agreement about policy within countries, let alone between them, remains as elusive as ever. Without the support of states and the authority that confers, IOs will find it even more difficult to play the sort of functional role many consider a vital part of effective economic governance. Significantly, this is not the only area in which cooperation is conspicuous by its absence. It may not be the most important either.

8

Governing the Global Environment

If there is one issue area that epitomizes both the necessity of and impediments to global governance it is managing the manifold consequences of climate change. At best, climate change is going to compel demanding forms of adaptation as the world's environment changes as a consequence of global warming. At worst, it is increasingly recognized even by 'traditional' security specialists that climate change is likely to emerge as a growing source of insecurity and exacerbate many of the problems that are already destabilizing some of the poorest parts of the planet (Campbell et al. 2007). It is equally apparent that such problems can no longer be compartmentalized into zones of peace and conflict or affluence and poverty, as some imagined (Singer and Wildavsky 1993). On the contrary, as the recent influx of illegal migrants from sub-Saharan Africa demonstrates, when the very circumstances that support life – or a life worth living, at least – are thrown into doubt, people will vote with their feet, making conflict all the more likely (Parenti 2011). Consequently, the formerly privileged and insulated societies of Western Europe, North America, and the Antipodes may find themselves directly affected by the impact of environmental degradation.

The good news, such as it is, is that there is a growing recognition that climate change is a problem that affects the entire planet and it is something that demands a suitably global response if anything is to be done about it – especially in the forbidding time frames that climate specialists think are available to take effective action (Garnaut 2011). The scale of the problem is unprecedented and the 'solutions' are formidably challenging – even if there was complete agreement on what should be done, who should do it, or even of the necessity of acting in the first place. Unfortunately, one of the reasons that addressing climate change is such a 'wicked' problem is that some politically influential, well-resourced individuals and vested interests believe – or profess to believe – either that climate change is a hoax or that the scientific evidence is insufficiently compelling to merit taking drastic action (Oreskes and Conway 2010). In the meantime, of course, the planet continues to heat up and the problems intensify (Gills and Schwartz 2017).

In many ways, therefore, the challenge of environmental management and sustainability make climate change the quintessential governance problem. Even 'normal' security questions are at least familiar, if intractable, problems of a sort human beings have been dealing with for thousands of years. Climate change, by contrast, is a novel problem, not least because it involves the entire planet in a way that even the 'world' wars of the twentieth century did not. If humanity can actually do something about developing sustainable environmental practices then it would, indeed, be an epochal change for the ages. As might be expected about such an unprecedented challenge, however, it is possible to find evidence to support a number of possibilities, not all of them apocalyptic. At the outset, however, it has to be acknowledged that the skeptics have some compelling arguments about the difficulty of achieving change (Hamilton 2010). And yet China's response offers some surprising, albeit very qualified, grounds for optimism. Before considering what some of the other major powers and nonstate actors have tried to do and why, we need to briefly state a few of the facts about the nature of climate change and the particular challenges that it poses.

The inconvenient truth

Al Gore (2013) famously made the idea of climate change part of popular discourse. However, his 'inconvenient truth' was not universally accepted precisely because it was potentially unsettling for many people with a vested interest in the status quo. In some cases, the reasons for casting doubt on what might otherwise have been seen as incontrovertible scientific evidence were patently clear and revolved around short-term self-interest. The coal lobby, for example, is a highly effective, well-funded advocacy group that represents an industry that stands to be negatively affected by any serious effort to phase out coal production (Dunlap and McRight 2011). Coal is, of course, one of the main contributors to the carbon dioxide emissions that are central components of the so-called greenhouse gases that are causing global warming. The fact that Donald Trump has appointed a former coal industry lobbyist and climate change denier to be head of the Environmental

Protection Agency (EPA) is emblematic of the problems facing those wanting to address global warming (Davenport 2018).

That powerful actors might pursue their own interests at the expense of the collective good is not, perhaps, that surprising. What is surprising is that the arguments that they muster in support of their position are designed to cast doubt on the evidence and even the very basis of the scientific methodology that has been such a central part of the Western tradition and the accumulation and production of knowledge (Wynne 2010).

In this regard, there is a noteworthy difference between the behavior and rhetoric of authoritarian China and the democratic leader of the 'free world', the United States. Al Gore (2013: 120) argues that 'US self-government is now almost completely dysfunctional, incapable of making important decisions necessary to reclaim control, of its destiny'. China, by contrast, is trying – albeit not without complete success – to shift from a carbon-intensive economy to one based on renewables and less polluting energy sources. In the United States, the Trump regime has made a virtue of 'freeing' the coal industry from regulations designed to curb its negative environmental impacts and economic importance (Volcovici and Mason 2017; Ip 2018). Equally importantly in the long run, perhaps, the coal industry and key members of the Trump administration have been guilty of producing or regurgitating misinformation about the nature of climate change and coal's role in causing it that is designed to create uncertainty in the minds of the voting public. Scott Pruitt, the former head of the EPA and a recipient of fossil fuel campaign funding, famously suggested that global warming is not necessarily a 'bad thing' (Embury-Dennis 2018).

While Pruitt and his successor Andrew Wheeler have occupied a uniquely powerful position to frustrate efforts by the United States to respond domestically and internationally to climate change, they are emblematic of a more generalized effort to cast doubt on the overwhelming scientific consensus about the nature of climate change, its impacts, and causes (Harvey 2016). The possible consequences of such developments are not confined to specific issue areas, however, even if climate change is the most politically divisive, visible, and consequential. One of the more significant achievements of 'Western civilization' was the creation of the scientific method of discovery and the verification of what counted as credible knowledge. Indeed, the foundation of the West's economic success and technological innovation was bound up with an increasingly specialized and complex division of labor in which technology, critical thinking, and scientific experimentation were produced by a specific cultural environment (Mokyr 2017). Expertise, of a sort possessed by climate scientists, played a prominent role in such processes. There is an intellectual division of labor that mirrors and builds on the more familiar occupational variety, but which is an essential part of the idea that collective 'progress' is theoretically and practically achievable. It is not altogether fanciful to suggest that this basic feature of the scientific paradigm underpinned modern civilization, economic development, and much else.

Plainly the coal lobby is not responsible for the end of Western civilization as we know it, but is symptomatic of a broader malaise in which there has been a widespread loss of confidence in 'experts', 'unaccountable elites', and a growing belief in the validity of what the Trump administration has described as 'alternative facts' (Sinderbard 2017). The leadership provided by the Trump administration is significant in this context, if only because it is making agreement within, let alone between, different political jurisdictions increasingly difficult. If there is no basic agreement on the nature of the problems that humanity collective faces, then there is little possibility of mobilizing an effective response. These observations provide a rather sobering but essential backdrop for the following discussion: without common agreement on the necessity for action any global efforts to address climate change look doomed to failure. An obvious point, perhaps, but one that is too often neglected in some of the more Utopian ideas about what should or could be done. It is equally important to note another frequently overlooked possibility: that there is something fundamentally incompatible between 'modernization', capitalism, and billions of people living consumerist lifestyles.

The arrival of the Anthropocene

It has become increasingly commonplace to talk about the dawn of the Anthropocene, or the idea that the impact of human beings has become so great that it is now the biggest influence on the natural environment and its development (Zalasiewicz et al. 2010). So great has the collective impact of humanity been, in fact, that it is literally transforming the planet as basic resources such as water, soil, and air are used up, transformed, and transported. For the other inhabitants of the planet, human domination, reproduction, and the gradual colonization of every part of the Earth have also led to massive species loss and declining biodiversity (Leakey and Lewin 1995). Apart from the possible moral questions raised by humanity's less than outstanding stewardship of the natural environment, there is the more fundamental question about the long-term sustainability of our collective actions, especially in a context where market-oriented capitalist development is the principal mechanism for determining economic and, by extension, environmental outcomes.

Unsurprisingly, perhaps, scholars working in a broadly Marxist tradition have been at the forefront of drawing out the possible tensions between a capitalist mode of production and sustainable environment. Kovel (2007: 159), for example, argues that 'it is either capital or our future. If we value the latter, capitalism must be brought down and replaced with an ecologically worthy society.' Given the appalling environmental record of the Soviet Union and – even more pertinently for the purposes of the current discussion – China under Mao Zedong (Shapiro 2001), the critique of capitalism looks somewhat overblown. Indeed, one of the most widely held ideas is that there is an 'environmental Kuznets curve' that actually encourages a greater concern about environmental issues as living standards rise (Dinda 2004). There are also potentially plausible sounding ideas about developing a 'Green New Deal', in which economic development is maintained while simultaneously switching to a more environmentally sustainable mode of production (Barbier 2010).

Such ideas are potentially encouraging evidence of more thoughtful and innovative responses to environmental problems and the challenge of collectively taking meaningful action. Peter Newell, for example, argues that we need to recognize the structural power of business and the reality that it needs to be encouraged to behave in a sustainable fashion: 'the governance of globalization, such as it exists, is much stronger, more effective, more wide-reaching and more aggressively enforced when it takes the form of regulation *for* business rather than regulation *of* business' (Newell 2012: 147, emphasis in original). Likewise, Keohane and Victor (2011: 7) argue that the nature of the international economic and political order militates against the creation of an integrated regime, and we must instead develop what they call 'regime complexes', of loosely coupled regimes. These could, they believe, provide 'more focused and decentralized activities [that] will have a bigger impact. In settings of high uncertainty and policy flux, regime complexes are not just politically more realistic but they also offer some significant advantages such as flexibility and adaptability.'

Nevertheless, radical scholars continue to argue that there is something fundamentally inimical to environmental sustainability in an economic system that is predicated on increased economic growth and the consumption patterns that go with it (Foster et al. 2010: 377). While it may be difficult to resolve such questions unambiguously, it is clear that the same sorts of enduring patterns of inequality and disadvantage that make international cooperation inherently difficult in economic issues also affect environmental cooperation. One of the arguments that has been used by would-be developing countries is that the developed economies of the West not only enjoy first mover advantages and considerable structural power, but achieved their dominant positions by exploiting their own (and others') natural environments and resources in ways that they are trying to stop others emulating. Precisely the same sorts of arguments have been made about the economic development process more generally, as we saw in earlier chapters. Significantly, critical scholars and policymakers from developing countries claim that a similar process of 'unequal exchange' helps to explain the relative positions of various countries, only in this case it is uneven ecological exchange.

This is a complex idea, the reality of which appears to depend on the 'intensity, volume and trend' of the economic and ecological exchange in question (Moran et al. 2013: 185). What we can say though is that there is a pattern of ecological exploitation and degradation between the 'North' and 'South' that mirrors the overall economic relationship, and which exacerbates environmental problems in the developing world. Significantly, China has been involved in these processes, too:

> Developed regions, such as North America, the EU and East Asia including Japan, South Korea, Taiwan, Hong Kong etc,. externalize environmental degradation through importing goods and services produced in other, mainly lower-income countries such as China. By contrast, less developed regions, such as Southeast Asia, South Asia and Africa, export large quantities of goods and services to China and generate much SO_2 and CO_2 emissions and consume water and land resources domestically, but only gain relatively small shares of economic values in exchange. This uneven ecological exchange dynamic reveals the disproportionate consumption of natural resources by developed regions at the expense of less developed countries. (Yu et al. 2014: 161)

Japan's relationship with Southeast Asia and the Pacific is one of the clearest regional illustrations of this process. Japanese MNCs have ruthlessly exploited Japan's poorer neighbors for timber and other resources, which has allowed Japan itself to actually significantly improve its own domestic environmental outcomes (Dauvergne 1997). Of even greater significance from the perspective of prospective global efforts to govern environmental problems is the connection between ecological degradation and insecurity.

There is a growing body of evidence that highlights the connection between environmental problems and a decrease in overall security

(Campbell et al. 2007). So-called climate wars, in which either food insecurity or declining access to water cause conflict, are predicted to increase as populations continue to grow, especially in parts of the world where environmental problems are already acute (Dyer 2010). Environmental refugees are already becoming a major problem, and one that is no longer confined to the poorer continents, but which can spill over into the rich world. It is also argued that the origins of the seemingly irresolvable conflict in Syria may be found in the droughts that forced people off the land and into cities where old social tensions and conflicts reemerged (Gleick 2014). Although these claims have proved controversial, they build on a long-standing and increasingly credible body of work that suggests that environmental degradation and conflict are linked and likely to become more significant as the world heats up (Homer-Dixon 1999). Indeed, without wanting to unduly labor the point, if global warming continues unchecked, some of the predicted consequences are truly apocalyptic (Lynas 2008), rendering debates about prospects of global governance and much else irrelevant.

The politics of climate change

Despite – or because of – the unprecedented nature and difficulty of the challenge posed by global warming in particular, a large number of initiatives, actors, and processes have emerged in response. Two of the more encouraging features of the international response to climate change are that, first, it is just that, i.e., international. Second, there is general agreement on the nature of the problem, not least because of the work of transnational organizations such as the International Panel on Climate Change (IPCC 2007). At the outset, however, it must be recognized that even this apparently important evidence of international expert cooperation in action has been undermined by a sustained attack on the credibility of the IPCC in general, and by the policies of the Trump administration in particular (Hein and Jenkins 2017). The United States may currently be something of an aberrant outlier in this context, but it is a hugely significant one; without the cooperation of the United States not much of substance is likely to be achieved.

As with other issue areas considered in earlier chapters, efforts to address environmental issues generally and global warming in particular have grown increasingly complex, involve more actors, and occur at different levels or scales of governance activity. Significantly, attention to the possible importance of environmental problems was largely brought to our collective attention by the efforts of individuals such as Rachel Carson (2002 [1962]), and by a growing number of nonstate actors in civil society, such as the Club of Rome, which produced a landmark report on the possible *Limits to Growth* (Meadows et al. 1974). More recently, broadly based international pressure groups such as Friends of the Earth and Greenpeace have built on these pioneering efforts (Zelko 2013).

As a consequence of such high-profile and influential interventions on the part new actors and voices, great hopes and expectations were held about the emergence and impact of 'global civil society' as a new force in international affairs (Lipschutz 2005; Keane 2003). While there is no doubt that the environment has assumed a transnational presence as part of a broadly based social movement, the impact of such processes is difficult to gauge. One of the most prominent analysts of such phenomena, John Dryzek (1997: 20), argues that the impact of environmental discourses and ideas can be seen in their impact on government policies and the emergence of new intergovernmental bodies. While there is no doubt that environmental rhetoric and consciousness has expanded dramatically over the last few decades, its actual impact on policy implementation and mitigation is far less certain.

Rhetoric and reality

Environmental issues dramatically highlight many of the contradictions and complexities confronting the very possibility of global governance. On the one hand, there is no more 'global' issue than the possible future of humanity's collective relationship with the planet. Yet the unambiguously material nature of the problem means that there are necessarily limits to the sorts of possible responses and future options that can be undertaken. As has frequently been pointed out, the planet has finite resources and an ultimately limited carrying capacity that represents a nonnegotiable limit to the sorts of policies, processes, and even populations that are possible as a consequence (Cohen 1995). On the other hand, however, the potential range of ideational, theoretical, and normative responses to the problem of climate change is open-ended. Successfully navigating a path between planetary 'structural' constraints and our collective ability to exercise 'agency' looks like the defining challenge of the twenty-first century. There is no doubt that human beings will have no choice other than to respond to climate change; the big question is whether it is a coolly calculated, technically optimal response, or one generated by a Darwinian struggle for survival in increasingly challenging circumstances.

Such sobering realities merit repetition because some of the intellectual responses to environmental problems, especially in the West, seem strikingly at odds with the political and social realities they seek to influence. Once again, such developments highlight and build on a more generalized distinction between broadly Western ideas about governance, political order, and the trajectory of development. Influential thinkers such as Jürgen Habermas epitomize a long-standing tradition of post-Enlightenment thinking that is predicated on the underlying assumption that human progress is not only possible, but may be achieved by adhering to certain processes of knowledge production and rational debate. Habermas's (1985) vision of the 'ideal speech community' is perhaps the best-known example of this idea, and it is one that has provided a foundation for similar ideas about the deliberative democracy and its capacity to produce rational and effective responses to collective action problems.

The debate about the possible relationship between democratic deliberation and environmental mitigation merits brief consideration for three reasons. First, it illustrates the very demanding circumstances in which deliberative democracy can actually be realized (Bohman 1998). Even without the actions of powerful vested interests noted above, the existence of an informed, normatively motivated citizenry actually taking part in such processes looks inherently improbable, especially at a time when confidence in democracy itself is at a low ebb. As Arias-Maldonado (2007: 248) points out, 'the belief that citizens in a deliberative context will spontaneously acquire ecological enlightenment, and will push for greener decisions, relies too much on an optimistic, naive view of human nature, so frequently found in utopian political movements'. Second, despite the fact that even sympathetic observers recognize that the conditions that might facilitate deliberative democratic practices are not in place (Eckersley 2004; 2000), such ideas and assumptions about the possibility of rational policymaking underpin some of the more important proposals for institutionalized collective action (Hilde 2012). The third reason for thinking about the possible significance of deliberative democracy is that some observers believe that a form of authoritarian deliberation may be at work in China, and may even lead to better policy outcomes (He and Warren 2011).

Whatever the merits of claims about experimentalist governance at the local level in China, as we have already seen, the reality at the national level and in China's foreign policies is of continuing efforts to centralize rather than diffuse power. Somewhat surprisingly, however, from an environmental perspective the Chinese approach may actually have some potential advantages. Before considering what any possible Chinese alternative to the prevailing Western order and ideational assumptions may be, though, it is important to consider how international cooperation on environmental problems has actually developed so far. Significantly, it is not only Marxists that highlight the importance of economic relations and capitalist development as a potentially significant constraint on the possible responses to ecological problems (Newell 2012). As Christoff and Eckersley (2013: 163) point out, the spread of a distinctively neoliberal form of globalization has 'made it easier for more powerful social agents and social institutions to avoid or evade taking responsibility for the consequences of their decisions and actions'. The question this raises is whether China's approach, in which the state retains a much closer control over the market, offers a viable approach to that of the United States and other liberal economies.

Governing the environment

As with other issue areas considered in this book, environmental governance involves a growing array of actors operating at various levels, including state and nonstate actors. If progress in environmental management was measured simply by the number of multilateral agreements reached, there would be ample grounds for optimism (O'Neill 2017). The question, as ever, is whether the creation of specific environmental regimes, even those with binding embedded agreements between the participants, is actually sufficient to ensure compliance and implementation.

Despite the attention that has been given to the new actors and processes in environmental management, the UN has been at the center of efforts to promote understanding of the problems and coordinate state-based responses. From the 1970s onward, the UN has established various bodies to further this process, culminating with the first report of the IPCC in 1990 and the subsequent 'Earth Summit in Rio de Janeiro, organized by the UN Framework Convention on Climate Change (UNFCCC) in 1992. The noble aim of the Rio meeting, which generated great hopes and expectations, was that greenhouse gas emissions might be stabilized at 1990 levels by the year 2000. In pursuit of this goal, more than 150 countries signed the 'Kyoto Protocol', which committed thirty-eight industrialized countries to reducing CO_2 emissions to less than 1990 levels by 2012. In reality, however, the actual impact of this agreement has been very limited (Helm 2008).

In addition to the formidable problems of ensuring compliance and implementation, the Kyoto initiative was always vulnerable to the possibility that domestic politics would prove a stronger influence on policy than any commitment to the international public good. The idea of 'common but differentiated responsibilities', which was developed at the 1992 Rio Summit, was an important recognition of the different historical records, responsibility, and circumstances of individual states, but one that proved unable to withstand the subsequent pressure of parochial politics. Some wealthy countries, especially the United States and its close strategic ally Australia, have argued that without binding commitments from the likes of India and China, any efforts on their part are futile and likely to damage their vital industries in the meantime. Whatever momentum Rio managed to develop was further undermined by the unilateral withdrawal of the United States under George W. Bush in 2001. If the most powerful nation on the planet was putting its narrow national interests ahead of its historical leadership role, not to mention its status as the world's largest emitter of CO_2 (at that time), then it was always going to be difficult to persuade any other state to act in the collective international interest. As Roberts and Parks (2007: 48) note,

> When powerful states consistently treat weaker states like second class citizens in areas where they possess structural power, they run the risk of weaker states 'reciprocating' in policy domains where they possess more bargaining leverage. Since climate change is a problem that requires near-universal participation to solve, North-South negotiations have suffered this fate.

These inherent tensions and differing national perspectives also undermined the Copenhagen Climate Change Conference in 2009. Great hopes were held about the prospects of the Copenhagen meeting, too, but the reality was very different. Not only were familiar differences of perspective between the developed and developing economies a major problem, but China was also revealed to be a significant and potentially obstructive actor in the talks. Despite an apparent willingness on the part of the more internationalist Obama administration to push for a meaningful agreement, China proved unwilling to make concessions, effectively derailing any possible coordinated effort on the part of the two principal contributors to the problem. If nothing else, however, China's participation and actions provided an unambiguous reminder of the constraints on American power and of the growing significance of China's, even if it was primarily the power to block. Likewise, it was clear that China was just as vulnerable to domestic pressure and vulnerabilities as the United States was (Christoff 2010).

Nevertheless, the momentum for, and the necessity of, developing multilateral agreements to manage climate change persisted. The 'Paris Agreement' of 2015 was the result of difficult negotiations conducted under the auspices of UNFCCC, between 196 parties, with 175 signing the final agreement. The principal intention of the agreement was to keep global temperature increases to below 2 degrees Celsius. Even that was considered too high for many vulnerable states, but the consensus was that, all things considered, the overall outcome was as good as might have been hoped for. The fact that there was any agreement at all was a significant improvement over Copenhagen and seemed to demonstrate an element of 'learning' about how to conduct such complex negotiations and the necessity of reaching agreements if disaster was to be avoided. None of these considerations had much impact on the new administration of Donald Trump, however, which immediately moved to withdraw the painstakingly negotiated agreement on national interest grounds and the need to 'put American workers first' (Crilly 2017). Claims about the positive impact of diplomacy in inducing 'cognitive change' were left looking rather threadbare by the reassertion of parochial politics (Dimitrov 2016).

Given the continuing primacy of short-term instrumentalism and domestic politics in the definition of 'national interests' and state policy, it is not surprising that many observers have stressed the potentially positive role that nonstate actors can play in influencing environmental outcomes (Biermann and Pattberg 2008). And yet there is a fundamental constraint on the ability of nonstate actors to play a substantial role in the place of national government: states are reluctant to delegate authority in this issue area. Green and Colgan (2013: 494) argue that 'contrary to some claims of a "power shift" from states to different nonstate actors, our findings do not suggest that there is a devolution of power away from the state'. As we shall see, this conclusion is relevant to the Chinese case in particular, where institutionalized political constraints prevent NGOs from playing a prominent part in environmental governance (Gaudreau and Cao 2015).

Despite the continuing importance of states in determining the nature and extent of environmental reforms, however, greater attention has been paid to the potential for environmental nongovernmental organizations (ENGO) to play a decisive role in responding to the growing environmental crisis. It is not difficult to see why. On the one hand, the sheer number of ENGOs working on environmental issues and the undoubted success of organizations such as Greenpeace in raising international consciousness about environmental issues has given them significant public profile (Carter 2007). On the other, many observers have a normative commitment to the idea of greater community participation and the emancipatory potential of environmental issues and consciousness (Cooper et al. 2016). And yet the reality seems to be more prosaic, if paradoxical: 'the very same forces that initially help ENGOs to form and operate, i.e., democratic regime characteristics, eventually constrain their political influence when it comes to pushing democracies toward more cooperative behavior in global environmental governance' (Bernauer 2013: 89).

A key problem for newer, mass movement organizations such as Friends of the Earth and Greenpeace is developing institutionalized mechanisms and processes with which to influence policy without seeming to betray their unconventional founding principles and status as independent critical voices. The fate of various national 'Green' political parties and social movements highlights how difficult it can be for alternative perspectives and values to become an effective part of mainstream politics without appearing to compromise their principles and alienate their supporters (Dryzek et al. 2003). Even in Germany, where a Green political party seemed set to permanently transform domestic politics and attitudes, environmental political influence appears to be in retreat (Tatke 2017). In this regard, Germany's domestic politics, which led to a remarkable *increase* in coal consumption in the wake of the nuclear disaster at Fukushima in 2011, mirror wider problems facing the EU in particular and the prospects for global governance more generally (Hockenos 2017). Simply put, there is an absence of leadership with which to drive national agreement, much less actual action, on climate change.

The change of direction in Germany and the problems afflicting the EU more generally are especially important in this context. For all its recent problems, the EU has been at the forefront of developing and implementing meaningful environmental regulation and reform on its members. The EU's impressive record and policy innovation in this area stands in striking contrast to the familiar failures in other jurisdictions (Quahe 2018). Indeed, the EU epitomizes precisely the sorts of successful strategies and policies that would need to be adopted if regional governance is to be scaled up to the global level. However, Paterson (2009: 152) argues that there are compelling geopolitical reasons for the United States to try and undermine EU leadership in this area, not just because it highlights the failings of America's domestic and international policies, but because it may place the American economy at a long-term disadvantage. Similar sorts of arguments may apply to China, too.

Can China lead climate change adaptation?

For all the possible merits of, and need for, global governance in the area of climate change mitigation in particular, it generally remains conspicuous by its absence. In part, the lack of progress and decisive leadership reflects the unprecedentedly complex nature of the problem. In part, however, the absence of leadership reflects the sorts of structural changes we have considered in earlier chapters in which America's relative decline and the incapacity or unwillingness of others to take action have led to a debilitating leadership deficit. To be fair, it is clear that these sorts of tensions and problems predate the ascendance of Donald Trump and will likely endure after him. Yet Trump's disdain for multilateral cooperation and hostility toward environmental regulation have reinforced long-standing problems. It was precisely this sort of attitude and Trump's withdrawal from the Paris Agreement that led some observers to claim that China had been given the opportunity to exercise global leadership in America's absence (Sanger and Perlez 2017).

There are, however, a number of problems that are likely to inhibit China from taking up the leadership role on climate change that has been abandoned by the Trump administration. First, there is the general problem of whether China can actually provide leadership of a sort that would be widely supported (Beeson 2018b). Second, there is the question of whether China actually wants to provide leadership, given the possible economic and even political costs that might come with such a role (Tiezzi 2014). However, China has one potential 'advantage' that may allow or even compel it to act in ways that other states may not: most states are reluctant to initiate possibly costly domestic reforms because it may disadvantage them relative to other states, which may free ride and gain a competitive advantage (Shue 2011). China's leaders, by contrast, have become increasingly conscious that the environment is becoming a potential source of social unrest (Zhong and Hwang 2015), giving them a powerful incentive to act, even if others do not. China's planners have also realized that they may be able to carve out a leading position in the development of 'green energy' that may offset any short-term pain (Forsythe 2017). Significantly, China is developing this strategy by employing techniques associated with the developmental state, rather than market forces (Chen and Lees 2016). In short, China's response to environmental issues throws this entire issue area into sharp relief and may even offer a new paradigm for responding to this universal challenge.

As with other issue areas, however, China's approach to the problem of environmental management represents a stark and potentially unpalatable alternative to the conventional Western wisdom. China's leaders have developed a form of 'environmental authoritarianism' in which the state plays a central and, where deemed necessary, commanding approach to determining environmental outcomes (Beeson 2010, 2018b). China's model not only represents a very different way of dealing with the – enormous, in

China's case – practical demands of overseeing environmentally sustainable structural change in the economy and the way it operates, but it also raises questions about some fundamental assumptions about the possible drivers of public policy change in this area. The idea that rising living standards could encourage environmental awareness may have some credibility, but it is quite another thing to change that nascent consciousness into political action, much less an effective response. In any case, when rising living standards lead to American-style consumption patterns they may be more of a problem than a solution (Li and Reuveny 2006).

In China's case, there is little doubt that its environmental problems are acute, getting worse, and a source of growing social unrest, especially in the big cities (Economy 2004; Steinhardt and Wu 2016). Not only does environmental degradation potentially undermine social stability and the authority of the CCP, but it also threatens the continuation of the economic growth model that has underpinned the implicit political bargain between the CCP and the wider population that has been the foundation of social stability (Zhong and Hwang 2015). The dilemma facing China's authoritarian regime, especially at a time when Xi Jinping is actually trying to centralize power, is that there is an instinctive reluctance to devolve authority to other agencies and actors (Youwei 2015).

As we saw in Chapter 4, there is a variety of opinions about the 'strength' of the Chinese state and its capacity to keep economic development on track – even without an environmental crisis. What is important to note at this point is that, despite, the authoritarian and 'fragmented' nature of the state in China, it has displayed an ability to coopt new actors into the policy-making process (Mertha 2009), as well as experimenting with, and learning from, their own and others' policy ideas (Heilmann and Perry 2011). Having said that, there are clear limits to the willingness of the state to decentralize authority, and inherent problems with trying to implement state-led structural change given the sheer scale of the undertaking and the fact that much of the sprawling bureaucratic apparatus is riddled with patronage politics, factions, and corruption (Pei 2016; Zeng 2015). It is clear that Xi Jinping recognizes these problems, but it is unclear whether his proposed overhaul and streamlining of the bureaucracy will be able to improve them (Wong 2018). Significantly, however, the environment is one of the areas targeted for reform.

Nevertheless, despite some existing handicaps, the reality is that the authoritarian Chinese state's record in addressing at least some of its environmental problems compares favorably with most Western countries. Perhaps the most striking achievement in this regard is that China is actually reducing the amount of coal it uses (Qi and Lu 2018), despite the fact that it has its own reserves, and the possible cost advantages of exploiting them. As noted, China is also the world's biggest investor in renewable energy. What remains to be seen is whether these sorts of major initiatives in which China's authoritarian state can command a degree of compliance via its own bureaucratic apparatus will translate into meaningful reforms in actual practice at the local level. Here the record seems more mixed and the challenge of ensuring compliance more acute.

Ironically, one problem appears universal: local officials in China are responsive to some of the same sorts of pressures as their counterparts in the West. As Eaton and Kostka (2014: 360) point out,

> local leaders, who bear responsibility for interpreting and carrying out environmental policies, typically have very short time horizons and are not strongly incentivized to take on the difficult business of changing lanes from a growth-at-any-cost model to a resource-efficient and sustainable path.

Adding to the central government's difficulties in ensuring the cooperation of state and provincial governments in implementing policy is the possibility that local authorities not only manipulate the relevant data, but have conflicted priorities: 'to attract investment, local governments tend to make policies that protect enterprises even if they exacerbate pollution' (Qi and Zhang 2014: 208). It is possible that the current reform proposals may go some way to addressing the historical difficulties associated with China's distinctive form of 'fragmented authoritarianism' (Lieberthal 1992) and the sheer scale of the governance and restructuring challenge facing China's leaders. Significantly, for all the theoretical and normative support that the idea of decentralization may enjoy in the West (Ribot 2002), in China it is argued that 'the decentralisation of policymaking and policy implementation in the reform era has created political space for local governments to act as representatives of local interests, rather than as mere agents of the central government' (Lo 2015: 152–3). Hardly surprising, therefore, that Xi is overseeing a major effort to *centralize* state power.

There are, however, additional complications that make this task especially difficult for China and which may place normative and practical obstacles in the way of the adoption of its approach elsewhere. Even before the recent crackdown on dissent and centralization of authoritarian rule (Mitchell and Diamond 2018), the possibility that nonstate actors and civil society might play the sort of role that they have in the West was problematic in China. The possibly understandable reality, especially in the new atmosphere of ideological conformity and heightened domestic social surveillance (Mitchell and Diamond 2018), is that NGOs generally are under increased pressure to literally toe the Party line. As Zhan and Tang (2013: 382) point out,

> unlike a few other domestic civic groups that have attempted to challenge the authoritarian system, Chinese ENGOs have largely adopted a non-confrontational stance toward it. They have in general limited organizational capacity and interest in policy advocacy. Many important environmental issues, such as those related to local environmental victims, they have largely ignored. Most ENGOs also lack extensive grassroots support, and many, especially the larger ones, were in the main founded with financial support provided by overseas foundations, which tend to avoid funding politically sensitive activities.

The long-standing underlying political reality in China, as we saw in Chapter 4, is that the CCP shows no sign of relaxing its grip over the levers of power, and Chinese society as a whole is showing little evidence that it is replicating the West's historical experience and moving inevitably in the direction of greater political liberalization and inclusiveness. On the contrary, at a time when authoritarianism is on the rise across the world, the direction of political travel seems to be in the opposite direction. The crucial issue for the Western democratic powers that have dominated the international system for so long is what the consequences of China's enduring, possibly intensifying authoritarian rule will be for international cooperation generally and in the area of climate change mitigation in particular.

Despite castigating the Trump administration for its environmental policies, it is not clear that China can assume the leadership mantle in this area. China is not only constrained by some of the general problems of leadership noted earlier, but some environmental and resource security issues highlight a potentially irresolvable clash between national interests and possible international obligations. China's policy toward some of its immediate neighbors on questions of water security offers a revealing insight into how it is likely to behave under such circumstances. Efforts to manage the vitally important Mekong River, upon which downstream states such as Thailand, Cambodia, Laos, and Vietnam are highly dependent, have foundered on China's reluctance to bind itself to any multilateral agreement. As Chellaney (2012: 150) observes, 'China does not have a single water treaty with any co-riparian country ... while promoting multilateralism on the world stage, China has given the cold shoulder to multilateral cooperation among river-basin states.'

Although China's leaders have undoubtedly begun to make some meaningful impact on the country's very significant environmental problems, it is far from clear whether such actions will lead to similar consequences at the international level. On the contrary, many observers consider China to be a conservative, status quo-oriented actor in global governance (Yeophantong 2013; Kahler 2013; Wang and French 2014). In fact, some commentators fret that China will prove insufficiently assertive and will in fact help to reproduce the existing order (Kennedy 2012), an order which has thus far made very little impact in addressing the underlying political, economic, and institutional dynamics that constitute the current system. For all its possible achievements at the domestic level, authoritarian rule, and the necessity of maintaining domestic legitimacy and/or control at all costs, may ultimately prove an obstacle to international collective action.

Concluding remarks

This chapter has considered the Chinese experience in some detail because it is now the largest single contributor to damaging greenhouse gas emissions and the principal alternative to democratic and/or market-based responses to the challenge of climate change. The paradox here is that while China's leaders may be making some progress to address the domestic consequences of rapid industrialization and their formerly cavalier attitude to the natural environment, without action on the international front, such efforts may prove futile. True, improving the air quality in China's big cities may go some way to placating an increasingly restive urban population, but it may mean little without addressing the overall circumstances that underlie *global* warming. The simple reality is that no country can escape the consequences of runaway climate change, even if some are better placed than others to manage its short-term impacts. In the longer-term, however, China is just as exposed to the potentially catastrophic consequences of declining agricultural productivity, water shortages, and rising sea levels. Guangzhou, Shenzhen, and Shanghai may be emblematic of China's rapid economic and industrialization but they are all acutely vulnerable to rising sea levels, flooding, and environmental crisis (Kimmelmann 2017).

While the imperative for action may look overwhelming, the difficulty of knowing quite how to address such an unprecedented and monumental global problem makes effective collective policy development difficult – even without the sort of climate denial and short-termism that distinguishes the Trump regime. Set against such epic problems, discussions of global governance and the prospects for rational debate, deliberative democracy, or any of the other well-intentioned but improbable 'solutions' look almost comically at odds with the inexorable and destructive logic of unmitigated climate change. The danger is that the problems will become so acute in a relatively short period of time that authoritarian and brutal responses may become the norm as states seek to maintain control. Growing numbers of environmental refugees may be the principal victims of an increasingly unforgiving international environment. Europe and North America are already moving to limit flows of migrants, something that will only push the problem back onto those countries least able to do anything about it – and possibly least responsible for the problem of climate change in the first place, of course.

There is a real possibility, therefore, that the environment will rapidly emerge as the definitive security problem of the twenty-first century, acting as a 'threat multiplier' that exacerbates already formidable developmental challenges in large parts of the world. In such circumstances, it may seem fanciful and Utopian to consider whether world leaders may be able to come together to develop new ways of maintaining collaborative and peaceful relations. If anything meaningful is to be done, however, that would seem to be vital, no matter how unlikely it may seem to judge by the historical record. The next chapter considers this even more formidable challenge.

9

Governing Global Security

Security cooperation of any sort is, if much of the theoretical literature is to be believed, inherently unlikely. According to realists in particular, states are always concerned about their own security above all else, suspicious of their peers, and determined to do all they can to increase their power relative to that of potential rivals. The international system is, the argument goes, one characterized by zero-sum games and a Darwinian struggle for survival (Morgenthau 1973). Unsurprisingly, realists are skeptical about the prospects for cooperation and dismissive of the role of institutions, other than as instrumental mechanisms with which states can pursue what are ultimately national interests (Mearsheimer 1994/95). The best that can be hoped for is a durable balance of power in which stability is maintained by a rough equivalence in strategic resources (Walt 1985). Looking around the world today, it is hard to argue that realists have some persuasive evidence at their disposal in support of this rather gloom-inducing view of international relations.

And yet, as Alexander Wendt (1992) famously claimed, 'anarchy is what states make of it'. In other words, while there may be some basic 'structural' features of the international system, this does not necessarily dictate the way that individual states will respond to it. While there may, indeed, be no reliable transnational authority standing above individual states capable of resolving disputes and enforcing order – even justice, perhaps – this does not mean that the world is entirely ungoverned or that cooperation is impossible. On the contrary, previous chapters have detailed the extent to which the world *is* governed, even in the most complex issue areas, such as climate change. True, these efforts may not be terribly effective at times, and great powers may have more say than small ones in determining the precise nature of governance processes, but the larger point stands: if the world really was as irredeemably conflict-prone, self-serving, and brutal as realists claim, even modest levels of cooperation and the very real positive-sum gains they have generated would not have occurred.

Indeed, perhaps the most remarkable, empirically robust feature of the contemporary international system is that interstate wars are rare and have been for decades (Goldstein 2011). To be sure, there is plenty of chaos and mayhem around the world, but it is invariably a consequence of state failure, civil war, or some other 'domestic' problem. War between states has gone into precipitate decline and, at this stage, at least, shows no real signs of recommencing – despite the bluster and reckless actions of hegemonic rivals, rising powers, and rogue regimes. All of this could change in an instant, of course, but the fact that the world has witnessed *any* diminution in the supposedly universal proclivity for violence and self-aggrandizement on the part of states is remarkable and needs explaining. The perceptions leaders have about themselves and their counterparts in other states are clearly a crucial part of any explanation of the declining role of violence in resolving interstate relations (Legro 2005). Either way, diminished conflict is a welcome antidote to the prevailing realist wisdom that continues to exert such a baleful influence on policymakers and the populations they claim to represent (Snyder 2009).

This chapter begins by considering why interstate violence might have declined, and what lessons we might draw from this happy and largely unexpected turn of events. Once more the EU has provided a powerful and enduring model of what can be achieved in propitious circumstances. Unfortunately, it is far from clear whether this fortunate state of affairs can be maintained in Europe, let alone exported to parts of the world where violence and state failure appear endemic and resistant to remedy (Milliken and Krause 2002). Nevertheless, there are grounds for – very – cautious optimism. East Asia has proved surprisingly stable and conflict-free, and some observers believe that the creation of regional 'security communities' has been part of the explanation (Acharya 1995). The key question is whether forms of regional and even global security governance are actually feasible and whether the European and Asian experiences offer a way of resolving some of the world's more enduring security challenges. A failure to develop security governance mechanisms may mean that all the other issue areas considered in this book may become even more unmanageable in the absence of a degree of order, predictability, and security.

Is peace possible?

Believing that human beings have the capacity to live peacefully means accepting some major, currently unfashionable, rather teleological, and possibly Eurocentric claims about the nature of social reality and the course of history. Ever since the Enlightenment, there has been a belief not only that 'progress' is possible, but that Europe has been in the vanguard of developing new, more rational, scientifically based ways of understanding the world (Kant 2003 [1795]). We think about ourselves and our capacity to act in and on the world differently as a consequence. Even in areas such as social policy, there was a sense that 'good' ideas would win out over bad, and that expertise and technocratic rationality would produce a better world (Fischer 1990). Not only were such beliefs part of the postwar social compromise established across much of the West in the aftermath of the Second World War (Castles 1998), but historically they help to explain the technological and economic advantages enjoyed by the dominant Western economies, too (Mokyr 2017).

In the aftermath of humanity's bloodiest and most destructive century and the current absence of effective leadership within and across state borders, the idea that we have an ability to learn from experience and to avoid painful, unproductive experiences, and costly mistakes looks rather implausible. And yet our collective ability for reflection and improvement is a distinctively human quality and one that is, according to Stephen Pinker, the reason violence is in decline, and not just the interstate variety. As Pinker (2012: 642) puts it: 'For all their foolishness, modern societies have been getting smarter, and all things being equal, a smarter world is a less violent world.' It is not necessary to agree with Pinker's optimistic reading of our collective destiny to recognize that there has been a marked diminution in state-sponsored organized violence of the 'traditional' sort and that this is just as an important empirical fact as is the relentless (and pointless) carnage that continues in places such as Syria. The question is why any such process has happened at all, even if it remains highly uneven and with no guarantee that it will endure.

Big bang theory

One explanation that is especially relevant to a discussion of security issues in particular revolves around the nature of modern weapons systems. Since the Second World War and the first – and thus far the only – use of nuclear weapons, it has become apparent to even the most hawkish and cold-blooded of strategists that the use of such devices threatens to be catastrophically destructive for the combatants, to say nothing of the rest of humanity who may be innocent bystanders (Mueller 1989; Väyrynen 2006). The scale, unpredictability, and difficulty of knowing quite what 'winning' such a war might look like has, so far, acted as a powerful disincentive for military strategists and megalomaniacs alike. In this sense, at least, there is some basis for the argument that policymakers are at heart 'rational' and capable of making informed judgments about various strategic options. Having said that, arguments about the possible benefits about the widespread possession of nuclear weapons look highly implausible (Gerzhoy and Miller 2016), especially when they may fall into the 'wrong' hands and be used by highly motivated terrorists who seem impervious to the norms of 'appropriate' nuclear strategizing (Allison 2004).

Given that nuclear weapons present an immediate existential threat like no other, it is possible to argue that they also represent the most consequential challenge to any idea of global governance. Paradoxically enough, however, some prominent international relations theorists argue that the scale of the threat posed by nuclear weapons actually makes cooperation an essential, inescapable necessity. Deudney (2007: 35), for example, claims that 'situations of anarchy combined with intense violence interdependence are fundamentally perilous for security ... in this situation government, some authoritatively binding arrangement of restraint, is necessary for security.' Likewise, Wendt (2003) argues that the creation of a world state is the inevitable consequence of the need to control unprecedented potential levels of organized violence. The implications of these arguments will be taken up in more detail in the concluding chapter. The point to emphasize here is that the dialectical interaction between political and military power discussed in Chapter 1 remains a defining feature of the contemporary era, too, and one which has assumed an even more compelling logic and urgency.

Any form of global governance worthy of the name will have to be capable of dealing with matters of life and death. Given that there are now more guns than people in the United States, that there are nearly 900 million firearms in the world, that spending on weapons around the world topped $1.5 trillion, and that the number of nuclear powers has grown and looks likely to increase further, the record of achievement looks modest, at best (Tovey 2016). There has, however, been some progress, which suggests that reform and management even in this most combustible and sensitive issue area remains a possibility. It is important to remember that the establishment of the United Nations (UN) was driven first and foremost by the recognition that horrors like the Second World War had to be avoided, and not just on moral grounds. One unambiguous lesson that emerged from this conflict was that the costs of modern warfare in blood and treasure were simply becoming too great to be borne. Perhaps 80 million died during the Second World War, of whom the vast majority were civilians.

Institutional responses

It was against this bloodstained backdrop that the UN was established in 1945 with the explicit aim of preventing another such conflict. Given the history of earlier efforts to achieve something similar via the League of Nation between the two world wars, skepticism may have been justified. After all, E.H. Carr (1998 [1939]), one of the leading lights in the realist pantheon, produced a devastating and still influential critique of the failings of the League and the Utopian thinking that he claimed informed it. The basic failing of the League and other such well-intentioned efforts to moderate the behavior of sovereign states was that it did not take account of differences in national power and states' willingness to use it: ultimately might determines what is right, according to Carr.

The League's failings are well known and extensively documented (Walters 1965; Mazower 2012), but they are worth recalling, if only as a reminder of just how difficult it is to influence the actions of autonomous states, especially where vital questions of national security are considered to be at stake. As with the UN, though, when the League was established in 1920, in the aftermath of the 'war to end all wars', it looked like an organization that was in the right place at the right time. While it is easy to be dismissive of the League's failures in hindsight, it is noteworthy that for the first time the notion of a *collective* approach to security was taken seriously; likewise, the idea that international disputes should be resolved through negotiation and arbitration became one of its founding principles. Crucially, however, the League was undermined by the failure of the United States to join and by its own lack of any enforcement capacity. The failure to rein in rising authoritarian powers in Germany and Japan has ominous parallels with our own time, which is why its possible lessons are worth trying to distill.

Despite the possible salience of the League's experience, the UN has not been able to overcome similar problems. On the plus side, it has not caused the UN to collapse, the sometimes-lukewarm support of the United States, notwithstanding. A number of key compromises and handicaps have been built into the UN from the outset, though, and these have limited its ability to influence or constrain the actions of its members at times, especially the more powerful ones. While the idea of sovereign equality might be good in theory, it is scarcely realized in practice (Lake 2003). A noteworthy and enduring illustration of the gap between rhetoric and reality was enshrined in the UN Security Council (UNSC), in which a small, unrepresentative group of powerful states continue to wield an anachronistic veto power over key issues of international security (Malone 2004). Similarly, the necessity of recognizing individual state sovereignty has from the outset made it difficult for the UN to 'intervene' in the internal affairs of member states, even when they threaten harm to their own people or to other states (Diehl et al. 1996).

The highpoint of UN activism in this context was the development of the 'responsibility to protect' (R2P) doctrine. In the aftermath of a number of high-profile violations of human rights and security on Rwanda and Srebrenica, the 'international community', and more specifically the UN, tried to establish framework for ensuring that such mass atrocity crimes could not happen again. Crucially, the notion of sovereignty was recast so as to make states responsible for the security of their citizens. In the event of states not fulfilling their responsibilities and actually violating their own citizens' basic rights, the international community has the authority – perhaps even the moral obligation – to intervene, even if this meant violating the normally sacrosanct idea of national sovereignty. Significantly, the basic principles underlying R2P were endorsed by more than 150 world leaders at a specially convened Summit to consider future forms of humanitarian intervention (Luck 2008).

Well-intentioned, necessary, and potentially transformative as the R2P idea may have been, however, its realization and current status have been and are problematic. Not only does the highly politicized and frequently divided UNSC ultimately authorize possible interventions, but the few occasions where they have occurred in conflicts in places such as Darfur and especially Libya, where direct force was used, have not gone well. Translating noble words into effective deeds is, as one of the most prominent contributors to this debate points out, a difficult process and one that makes R2P a 'radically unfinished program' (Bellamy 2009: 118). The fact that some members of the UNSC are highly protective of their own domestic sovereignty, cautious about establishing principles that might be applied to them and – in Russia's case in particular – actively involved in propping up the likes of Bashar al-Assad, a flagrant violator of the Syrian people's human rights, does not bode well for the R2P principle's prospects.

Having said that, the UN has undoubtedly done useful and important work that might not have happened at all if it had not existed. The UN's Treaty on the Non-Proliferation of Nuclear Weapons, for example, does seem to have limited their spread, although there has been little progress in moving toward their elimination, despite high-profile support from the Obama administration and others (Shultz et al. 2007). Predictably enough, perhaps, the Trump regime is dedicated to 'modernizing' its America's nuclear arsenal, in part, no doubt, as a response to Russia's ambitions to do the same (Panda 2018). It is also worth noting that the Trump administration's efforts to convince North Korea to give up its nuclear weapons have been just as unsuccessful as all of his predecessors (Mead 2018).

Nevertheless, while the UN's peacekeeping operations have come in for more than their fair share of criticism, they have often done what the label suggests and actually kept the peace in the most challenging of circumstances (Howard 2008). A number of points are worth emphasizing about their operations in the context of a discussion about possible security cooperation. First, UN peacekeeping activities have a *collective* basis and are funded by member states. Second, the costs of such activities are not great and only amount to 0.5 percent of overall military expenditures, or 1.4 percent of the United States' defense budget (Clarke 2016). Third, for all their inherent difficulty and even danger, they have been surprisingly successful at times. Some of the more important achievements in this context are the initial policing of the demilitarized zone between North and South Korea, allowing peace to be established and sustained in countries such as El Salvador and Mozambique, as well as attempting to maintain stability between Israel and its neighbors (Bellamy et al. 2010). To be sure, there have been spectacular failures, too, most notably in Rwanda and Srebrenica, but the overall point remains: UN peacekeeping efforts demonstrate that security cooperation not only can occur, but can be effective if adequately resourced and supported by the major powers.

In discussions of this sort it is too easy and common to focus on the failures and neglect the successes. This possibility is even more apparent in the case of those regions in which peace is actually the norm and peacekeeping interventions are unnecessary. For all of the apparent chaos in the world at present, it is worth remembering that large parts of the world remain almost entirely unaffected by conflict, save for occasional relatively low impact – in material terms, at least – terrorist attacks of one sort or another. This is not to understate their overall psychological impact, of course. On the contrary, there is little doubt that, despite the very low numbers of casualties such attacks generate when compared with conventional wars, they have a disproportionate impact on targeted populations, as is their intention, of course (Silke 2003). A sense that the security situation is out of control, that governments lack effective tools or even the will with which to respond to such outrages, is pervasive among the hitherto secure liberal democracies that have become unused to violence of this sort.

Peace in our time?

In this regard, Western Europe in particular is a victim of its own remarkable success. For more than half a century a region that has for hundreds, if not thousands, of years been synonymous with violence inspired by sectarian, religious, and ideological causes of one sort or another has largely been at peace. True, there have been problems in Ireland, Spain, and elsewhere, but it is important to remember that this is the continent that pioneered industrialized genocide and which was the epicenter of the two largest conflicts the world has ever known. By these standards, the efforts of ISIS, al-Qaeda, and their imitators and offshoots look rather ineffectual and amateurish.

The key question for comparative and prescriptive purposes is: how did the Europeans manage to transform their continent from being perhaps the most violent and unstable place on the planet to being one of its most peaceful – and prosperous? The fact that the EU simultaneously oversaw a hugely successful process of economic reconstruction and development in the postwar period is plainly a key part of the story. We have already seen how a distinctive dialectical relationship between war and politics was responsible for the rise of the European state. The relationship between conflict – or its absence – remains pivotal today. The state became important in Europe because it 'solved' basic problems of coordination, organization, and stability, providing the basis for rule-governed behavior and the social and political stability within which economic activity could take off (North et al. 2009). The achievement of the EU was that, for the first time in human history, it managed to scale up this process to a continental size, incorporating formally independent sovereign states into the project in the process.

There is a rich and persuasive literature about the possibly pacifying influence of economic development (Gartzke 2007; Mueller 2010). There is an equally extensive literature on 'democratic peace theory', which claims that democracies are much less likely to go to war with each other (Russett 1995), even if some of them are less inhibited when it comes to attacking nondemocracies. Students of comparative politics have long claimed that there is a tipping point, where per capita incomes reach a certain level and democratic transformation becomes more likely and sustainable (Przeworski et al. 2000). Even if we recognize that there are some noteworthy exceptions to this thesis, such as Singapore and perhaps China itself, it is clear that those parts of the world that are most stable and peaceful are generally those where economic development has been, or is becoming, successful and sustained. Simply put, citizens have more reason to feel satisfied with their lives and prospects; they have a stake in the future. Significantly, there is also an external, international dimension to this story.

Liberals, particularly those that take economic issues seriously, have long argued that there is a positive link between international economic integration and the declining prospect of war. 'Liberal interdependence theory' posits that as formerly, discrete national economies develop higher levels of interaction, not only do the borders of national economies become blurred, but the political elites in these countries come to recognize that they have too much to lose by initiating conflicts that are unlikely to produce winners, and which may wreck the economies upon which the legitimacy of their regimes depends (Keohane and Nye 1977). This applies just as much to authoritarian regimes as it does to democratic ones. Indeed, given that autocrats may have no other source of legitimacy, they may have an even bigger stake in ensuring that the preconditions for economic development remain in place (Gilley 2014).

Liberal interdependence

Having said that, and at the risk of mixed metaphors, economic interdependence is not a magic bullet. Relations between China and Japan, for example, are notoriously acrimonious despite highly integrated economies that follow the supposed logic of comparative advantage theory (Yahuda 2006). At times, nationalist forces have managed to jeopardize the entire basis of the relationship and there are signs that Japanese investment is being redirected as potentially footloose MNCs reconsider the security of long-term investment in China (Shirouzu and Takada 2014). It is also clear that the Chinese government is prepared to use its growing geoeconomic leverage to pursue nationalist goals, as we saw in Chapter 4. China's explicit willingness to link security and economic issues was clear in its dispute with South Korea over the latter's decision to install an American missile defense system (Volodzko 2017), and in China's abortive effort to use rare earths as a bargaining chip in its relationship with Japan (Bradsher 2010).

And yet, for all its troubled history, Japan illustrates just how much can change given propitious historical circumstances. Not only did Japan, like Europe, benefit from American aid and assistance in the aftermath of the Second World War, but it developed a similar focus on economic rather than strategic development. In Japan's case, perhaps, this is even more understandable given its disastrous participation during the war, its consequent economic and social devastation, and the fact that it was attacked with nuclear weapons. Whatever the causes may have been, however, the result was startling. On the one hand, Japan literally rose from the ashes to become the second largest economy in the world in little more than twenty years. On the other, its people and political leaders largely rejected the militaristic ethos that had led them into such epic folly, resulting in a deep-seated normative aversion to war (Katzenstein 1996).

As a result, Rosecrance (1986) has argued that Japan has effectively pioneered a new form of 'trading state', which prioritizes economic development and which spends much less than 'normal' countries on its own defense. Again, there are some very distinctive, possibly unique, historical circumstances that help to explain Japan's seemingly aberrant approach to its own national security, not the least of which has been its strategic subordination to, and reliance on, the United States as a military protector (Pyle 2007). Nevertheless, the fact that *any* country can seemingly flout the supposedly timeless, universal conventional wisdom and 'get away with it' is noteworthy. It has also been a feature of the EU's highly successful approach to development with all its associated confidence-building benefits. Yet both the EU and Japan are routinely criticized by the United States for their failure to 'burden share' and for free-riding on America's still massive defense spending, which remains as large as the next seven countries combined, including China and Russia (McCarthy 2018).

The realists who dominate strategic debate and set the parameters for subsequent policy generally see such levels of spending as essential. The justifications can stretch credulity, however. The argument that high levels of defense expenditure is the cost for protecting freedom and maintaining vigilance and ultimately peace is rather undermined by the fact that the United States has been at war for most of its history. While some argue that there are important intellectual and industrial spin-offs from lavish spending on arms (O'Hanlon 2015), such arguments look implausible given America's ever-growing indebtedness and inability to pay for existing commitments, let alone those proposed by the Trump administration (Shear and Steinhauer 2017). The great paradox of defense spending is that we hope it is wasted, and that we never actually need to use it, as it could unleash all of the horrors and damage discussed above. In the meantime, however, not only do we collectively waste incomprehensibly large sums of money on ever more lethal weapons systems, but such scarce resources are not available for more useful tasks, such as rebuilding the wastelands created during former and current conflicts.

It is not necessary to be a starry-eyed peace activist to recognize that arms expenditures are essentially wasteful and arguably do little for the sort of 'human security' that is the key concern of the vast majority of the world's population, and a feature of new thinking about the nature of security (Newman 2010). The question, as ever, is what sorts of conditions would actually be necessary to create an international context in which it actually made sense to reduce rather than continually increase spending on military assets. This is not an idle or fanciful question. On the contrary, in the aftermath of the end of the Cold War – which was entirely unpredicted by the policymaking and scholarly communities – there was much talk about the expected 'peace dividend' that many had expected would result (Markusen 1992). As we now know, the actions of George W. Bush did more than anything else to undermine this prospect, but it remains the case that much of the world continues to be remarkably secure by historical standards.

Security communities

Nevertheless, there is a substantial literature that points to the continuing existence of security communities in different parts of the world, and which suggests that their existence helps to explain the durability of peace. According to Adler and Barnett (1998: 30), a security community can be said to exist when there is a 'transnational region composed of sovereign states whose people maintain dependable expectations of peaceful change'. Despite the rather demanding – and from a realist perspective, inherently unlikely – conditions underpinning this definition, there are important examples of this phenomenon, and not just in Europe. On the contrary, Acharya (2001) argues that the same sort of sense of community and collective identity that Karl Deutsch (1969) argued was such a distinctive and important part of the European experience can also be found in Southeast Asia. For all the criticisms that are often made about the EU's capacities as an effective security actor (Froitzheim et al. 2011), there is little question that – until recently, at least – it fulfilled expectations about the nature and benefits of a security community. The same cannot be said about Southeast Asia.

Although much is made about the development of a distinctive normative agenda and diplomatic style under the auspices of the Association of Southeast Asian Nations (ASEAN), the so-called 'ASEAN way' of consensus, voluntarism, and informality has always had its limitations. Even at the height of its powers, ASEAN's capacity to act decisively and influentially has always been limited by its own internal differences and a preoccupation with protecting domestic sovereignty (Jones and Smith 2007). Difficult, potentially divisive issues have tended to be studiously avoided, lest they cause disagreement and undermine notional solidarity. Nevertheless, interstate war did essentially disappear in Southeast Asia – as it did nearly everywhere else on the planet, of course. The challenge for ASEAN supporters, such as Kivimäki (2014), has always been to demonstrate why the grouping should take the credit for a worldwide phenomenon. The reality is that ASEAN and its potentially important offshoots, such as the ASEAN Regional Forum (ARF), lack the power to act decisively to keep the peace or enforce agreements (Emmers and Tan 2011).

ASEAN's potential vulnerabilities and shortcomings always lurked beneath the surface of its soaring rhetoric and endless meetings. Now, however, thanks to China's increasingly 'assertive', not to say aggressive and expansionist policies in the South China Sea, ASEAN's ineffectiveness and vulnerability to great power politics have been brutally exposed. The simple reality is that China has exercised a highly effective divide and rule strategy, in which it has effectively bought off a key client state in the form of Cambodia and guaranteed itself a proxy veto over ASEAN policy. ASEAN's collective form of diplomacy and decision-making is especially vulnerable to this sort of divisive strategy and it has subsequently proved unable to come to a collective position on what is arguably the single most important security challenge it has faced since its inception (Beeson 2015).

The limits to European influence

Unfortunately for those interested in the prospects for collective governance in this issue area, it is not only the comparatively weakly developed institutional architecture of Southeast Asia that appears unable to cope with the rapidly evolving international order. On the contrary, the EU is also experiencing a series of internal and external challenges to its authority and ability to maintain the sort of stability that had seemed to define it. Internal divisions have become more apparent and intense as a consequence of the GFC and the policy prescriptions handed down to some of the EU's smaller, poorly performing (and governed) economies, such as Greece. At the same time, however, Russia – another assertive authoritarian power – has taken advantage of the EU's problems and apparent weakness to reassert itself in its 'near abroad' (MacFarlane and Menon 2014). The EU's – and, more problematically still, NATO's – entire strategy of Eastward expansion has been thrown into doubt by a Russian leadership keen to restore what is seen as its rightful place in the international scheme of things.

Adding to the EU's problems is the fact that Turkey, Europe's supposed bridgehead to Asia and exemplar of the EU's positive normative influence, has also taken a decisively authoritarian and destabilizing turn (Fisher 2018). The rather sobering point to emphasize is that much has been made, especially by the Europeans themselves, about the pioneering importance of 'normative power Europe' and its potential to promote a process of policy and even normative transfer to other 'less developed' and/or modern parts of the world (Manners 2002; Beeson and Stone 2013b). In some ways, of course, this is highly reminiscent of the sorts of policies the United States developed at the height of the Cold War. In America's case, however, they were backed with considerable geopolitical and geoeconomic leverage, and American policymakers were frequently prepared to turn a blind eye to political leaders and practices of which they did not normatively approve (Beeson 2014a). Neither was the United States constrained by an agreement to help sort out a migration crisis; Europe, by contrast, is heavily reliant on the increasingly authoritarian government of Recep Erdogan (Samuels 2017).

The EU's diminished authority and influence is a problem for a number of reasons as far as global governance is concerned. First, it raises serious doubts about the circumstances in which 'good' ideas will be taken up. If global governance is to be realized not only will stable security relations have to be part of the overall package, it is not unreasonable to assume, but the ideational basis and operational principles of any prospective form of 'security governance' would also need to be voluntarily taken up by members of any international community worthy of the name. While there may be some grounds for forcefully intervening to build peace and remove the odd despot on the road to collective security governance, the largely peaceful transfer and uptake of the norm of nonaggression also seem essential. This is why the apparent decline in the influence of the EU as a role model and actor is potentially so disastrous: if the most successful and secure regional security community yet devised cannot exert a benign and positive influence, who can?

Security governance

There are currently some alternative visions on offer, but they may not lead inexorably to effective global governance. Unsurprisingly given the EU's track record of encouraging strategic stability and promoting cooperation between former foes, it has been the focus of the most analytical attention. There is a growing literature that seeks to account for this success and conceptualize it using the language of governance. An influential formulation by Webber and colleagues (2004: 8) suggests that *security* governance

> comprises five features: heterarchy; the interaction of a large number of actors, both public and private; institutionalization that is both formal and informal; relations between actors that are ideational in character,

structured by norms and understandings as much as by formal regulations; and, finally, collective purpose.

This conception describes many of the features that distinguish the EU generally, and which have enabled its distinctive and frequently highly successful approach to encouraging cooperative behavior across national borders and at different scales. Yet, while it might be easy to suggest in broad theoretical terms what is required to allow cooperative security governance to occur, it is much harder to realize in practice, especially where national sovereignty is either uncertain or jealously guarded, as it is in Southeast Asia, for example (Beeson 2014c). Even more fundamentally, where the very foundations of domestic security are uncertain and the role of the military is primarily about responding to possible *internal* rather than external threats, then the prospects for effective security governance at even the regional level are not good (Beeson and Bellamy 2008).

One of the founding fathers – interestingly, they were (and are) predominantly men – of realist thinking, Hans Morgenthau, recognized that domestic politics profoundly influenced the nature of national policy and the thinking that informed it. In the context of a discussion about the prospects for security governance, domestic factors remain a potentially implacable obstacle to more collective approaches to security issues in particular. As James Sperling (2010: 14–15) points out, as a result

> each state will face different, yet overlapping, vulnerabilities and insecurities which, in turn, may produce alternative and possibly competing national security agenda. Similarly, the ability of national elites to meet those vulnerabilities and insecurities will be shaped and limited by the imperatives, prescriptions and proscriptions of the national security culture. The precise variations in state structure and national security culture between two or more states will create a context that is (un)favourable to bilateral or multilateral security cooperation.

It ought not to need emphasizing that states have remarkably different security or strategic cultures (Bloomfield 2012). The fact that China and the United States both consider themselves to be 'exceptional' great powers with interests and even responsibilities that extend well beyond their national borders gives them a perspective that is entirely different from a so-called middle power such as Canada or Indonesia, a 'rogue' state such as North Korea, or a failing state such as Somalia. Unless we understand the sorts of historically contingent factors and material capabilities that help to define national strategic cultures and the policies they engender, we shall not be able to identify, much less do anything about, the reasons states do not wish or are not able to cooperate on security questions. For the purposes of this discussion, the key point is that the existence of different security cultures highlights the possible importance of discourse and identity in determining expectations about even the possibility of cooperation (Lock 2010: 700).

Reconciling competing objectives

Given that many observers think the United States and China are currently on an inevitable collision course that may end in outright conflict (Allison 2017), it is important to say something about their respective positions. Any significant move toward meaningful global governance will obviously necessitate the cooperation and participation of the world's two most significant actors. Even if we do not accept that there is anything inevitable about the course of international relations in particular or human history more generally, the actions of great powers are also a consequence of their material capabilities and the strategic cultures that help to determine how such resources ought to be deployed.

We know a lot about how American policymakers and grand strategists think about the world because we have had half a century or more to see how it operates when the United States is the most powerful and unconstrained nation on earth (Bacevich 2002; Green 2017). True, the bipolar structure of the Cold War and the formerly formidable strategic presence of the Soviet Union kept the United States in check to some extent, but American power has been informed by distinctive values and systematically deployed in pursuit of essentially national interests for many years (Smith 1994; Latham 1997). What makes American foreign policy so consequential, of course, is that it remains by far the most powerful strategic actor in the world, albeit not an omnipotent one (Beckley 2015; Posen 2003). Nevertheless, the basic contours of American grand strategy are likely to remain in place, according to Layne (2017: 267), because the strategic culture and the 'foreign policy establishment' from which it emerged remain wedded to a core set of beliefs.

There is an important, but often neglected, distinction in conceptions of hegemony: it can be either persuasive or coercive. If a form of collective security governance is to be achieved and sustained, the central role played by norms and ideas means that if hegemonic leadership of some sort remains part of the picture – at least in the transitional stage – then hegemony will need to be the persuasive variety. If nothing else, long-term changes in the distribution of material power and capabilities mean that 'effective' forms of coercion are simply infeasible, for the sorts of reasons discussed earlier in the chapter. It is possible that the increasingly hawkish Trump administration may not recognize this or the possible value of America's 'soft power' and institutionalized influence; which is why Trump may be the single biggest threat to the liberal rules-based order (Haas 2018), which so many hope will endure and influence China's behavior in turn. Unfortunately for advocates of such views, the evidence about the impact of American values on China is far from conclusive.

Will China change everything?

As we have seen in earlier chapters, the evidence about the degree of socialization that has occurred among China's elites and the general population is ambiguous and dependent on context. However, it is possible to make a few plausible generalizations about China's policy in the security domain. First, as with some of China's smaller neighbors, there are real limits to China's willingness and ability to cooperate – or there are along liberal lines, at least. National sovereignty is an especially sensitive issue for the leaders of authoritarian regimes. This does not mean that there is no basis for regional or even global cooperation at some stage. What it may mean, however, is that the rules and operating principles that govern such processes will need to be ones that even authoritarians can live with. In this regard, the sort of undemanding and accommodating security community that ASEAN has developed may be entirely acceptable, if ineffective (Beeson 2015). Indeed, the reality is that China, like many other Asian states, takes a much more 'comprehensive' view of security than is customary in the West (Alagappa 1998). Rather than seeing security as simply referring to traditional concerns about weapons systems, strategic doctrines, and relative military capabilities, China's leaders see economic and technological development as intrinsically linked to overall security. Such differing conceptual and policy frameworks have the potential to make an already difficult issue even more complex, as potentially incompatible perspectives are brought to bear on what are vital national interests.

The ARF is an example of an Asian-style security organization that, despite being unambiguously in the right place at the right time, was from its inception 'built to fail' (Emmers and Tan 2011). As with other Asian institutions discussed in Chapter 6, the ARF has no capacity to compel its members to adhere to any agreement, even in the unlikely event that it was able to come up with one. More importantly, perhaps, and rather discouragingly for advocates of collective approaches to resolving difficult security problems, key issues such as the status of Taiwan, North Korea, and China's territorial claims in the South China Sea are simply not discussed for fear of upsetting some of the affected parties. While it is true that there is some innovative confidence-building activity occurring within supportive 'Track 2' mechanisms, such as the Council for Security Cooperation in the Asia Pacific (CSCAP), the net result of these official and semi-official efforts is rather underwhelming (Ball 2000).

The second point to emphasize, therefore, is that China is the most important example of an Asian state that remains impervious to Western-style legalistic norms and practices, and carefully controls the extent and nature of its engagement with international organizations (Chin and Thakur 2010). Whatever the merits of China's territorial claims may be, they are widely seen as a threat to the rules-based order, especially in the wake of China's rejection of an independent tribunal's adverse ruling (Phillips et al. 2016). Much the same sort of criticism might be made about the United States and its unwillingness to even sign the United Nations Convention on the Law of the Sea (UNCLOS) (Patrick 2012), of course, but this only highlights how the actions of great powers act as obstacles to, rather than facilitators of, international security cooperation. Even more deflating for admirers of ASEAN's potential diplomatic influence, the organization has been effectively neutralized by China's skillfully executed policy of divide and rule, in which it has effectively bought Cambodia's support against its fellow ASEAN states. For a consensus-based organization such as ASEAN, this is a potentially fatal flaw (Beeson 2016).

An even more consequential third observation is about the possible implications of Chinese military spending and modernization, which has been a major focus of attention for many outside observers, especially from the United States (Liff and Ikenberry 2015; Shambaugh 2002). While China's defense spending may still be a relatively small proportion of the United States', and while its weapons systems may not be judged to be as 'good', nor its military as battle-hardened and tested, there has been a growing chorus of alarm pointing to China's growing military capacity and its possible ambitions to achieve regional hegemony and displace the United States (Mattis 2018). Even if China refrains from using force – and risking a direct confrontation with the United States in the process – it is difficult to see how it can play a constructive role in regional security, let alone the global version. There are potentially irreconcilable territorial claims as well as concerns about the rule of law and freedom of navigation that would seem to make cooperation difficult if not impossible. Likewise, the fact that China's leadership reserves the right to use force to resolve what it sees as a domestic problem in Taiwan provides a reminder of the totemic and non-negotiable nature of some regional security issues (Beeson and Li 2014; Kaplan 2012).

Finally, it is not at all clear that the thinking of China's elites is being significantly transformed in the direction of new modes of cooperation, rather than the continuing pursuit of essentially national interests. As we have seen in earlier chapters, there are limits to the degree of 'socialization' that is occurring as China's policymakers become more involved in international organizations and agreements. This is especially the case in the area of security cooperation where China's historical concern about the constraining impact of 'American hegemonism', and an instrumental approach to achieving what are overwhelming nationally focused foreign policy goals, means that some issues simply remain nonnegotiable. Indeed, Friedberg (2011: 54) argues that 'the notion that China's participation in international institutions is helping to "socialise" its elites and to bring them around to what are essentially Western liberal internationalist ways of thinking about world politics smacks of self-congratulation, if not self-delusion'.

While there is plainly something in such claims, it neglects a subtler point: realist thinking has a long history in China (Johnston 1995); ironically it is one that is being reinforced rather than reduced by the exposure of Chinese students to American international relations theory and teaching (Qin 2009). The fact that John Mearsheimer is so highly regarded in China is no coincidence, nor is the prominence of China's own realist thinkers such as Wang Jisi and Yan Xuetong (Beeson and Zeng 2017). Significantly, realist ideas and thinking dominate the discussions of strategic issues among scholars in China and the sorts of recommendations they subsequently make to the national government (Zeng 2016). At best, and despite the rhetoric about win–win diplomacy, this is promoting interest in a new form of great power relations between the world's only unambiguously great powers, China and the United States (Xi 2014b); the prospects for lesser entities and more inclusive forms of collective governance in such circumstances are not encouraging. At worst, it may not be able to head off a conflict some see as inevitable.

The coming war with China?

If there is one thing that unambiguously capable of putting an end to any prospect of global governance it is a war between the world's two most powerful states. Indeed, worrying about global governance would be the least of our

troubles in such a potentially apocalyptic scenario, which is why many people continue to think it is inherently unlikely. And yet some observers have
been predicting the 'coming conflict with China' for decades (Bernstein and
Munro 1997). Such fears seem to have dissipated as China became more
deeply integrated into the international order and showed every sign of
becoming a 'responsible stakeholder'. Recently, however, there has been a
resurgence of predictions about the possibility – even the inevitability – of
a war between China and the United States. In this context, the territorial
disputes in the South China Sea are a possible symptom rather than the fundamental cause of potential problems. It is important to outline briefly the
basis of such claims because if they are credible then much of the preceding
discussion is unlikely to be of even academic interest in the long run.

Graham Allison is the most prominent exponent of the idea that a military confrontation between China and the United States may be difficult
to avoid. He bases this assertion on the historical record of relationships
between rising and declining powers. The so-called Thucydides' trap is a
consequence of the difficulty of reconciling the ambitions and dissatisfaction felt by a rising power and the desire of the existing hegemon to maintain
the status quo. The reluctance of the dominant power to accommodate the
wishes of its increasingly powerful and unhappy rival increases tensions
between the two, which the historical record suggests generally leads to
war. As Allison (2017: 184) rather starkly puts it, 'on current trajectories, a
disastrous war between the United States and China in the decades ahead is
not just possible, but much more likely than most of us are willing to allow'.

As noted, these kinds of claims have been around for a long
time. Significantly, however, they have been made not just by journalists,
but by some of the leading IR scholars of the day. Long before Allison
predicted conflict, Robert Gilpin (1981) had argued that the tensions
generated by possible 'hegemonic transitions' might only be resolved
through war and the coercive establishment of a new order (also see
Organski 1968). Even liberals have recognized that major wars create
the conditions in which rising powers can actively create a new order in
ways that might not have been feasible otherwise (Ikenberry 2001). This
was, after all, the American experience in the aftermath of the Second
World War. The question is whether liberals are also right to be optimistic about the supposedly pacifying effect of liberal interdependence. In
other words, are policymakers sufficiently rational and capable of making
informed judgments about the best ways of pursuing national interests?
Even more importantly, perhaps, can policymakers cope with unforeseen
events, miscalculations, or the sorts of accidents that could occur as tensions ramp up and military confrontations escalate?

The short answer, of course, is that we don't know. For all the sophistication of some of the theoretical models that have been developed, and the exhaustive mapping of historical precedents, it is impossible to say anything definitive about what will happen next week, never mind the next decade or century. There are, however, some encouraging signs and precedents. The experience of even the limited use of nuclear weapons has seemingly had a sobering and instructive influence on subsequent generations of policymakers. It is difficult to imagine the circumstances in which full scale nuclear war might actually be considered rational or be in any sense winnable.

There have also been some plausible suggestions made about the possibility of developing something like a nineteenth-century concert of great powers in Asia (White 2012). If successful, such a model could be replicated elsewhere. A concert of powers might even give a greater sense of purpose and credibility to extant security organizations, which might be made more effective and capable of encouraging, even demanding, that states behave in ways that are likely to decrease the chances of unwanted and unwinnable conflicts. Caveats are, I'm afraid, unavoidable however. Having said that, such ideas are a moderately optimism-inducing reminder that the future is open-ended and that nothing is inevitable. As we shall see in the concluding chapter, even world government could be a possibility, although I wouldn't bet the house on it.

Concluding remarks

This chapter has highlighted some of the many potential obstacles that stand in the way of effective cooperation in the security arena. In some ways this is entirely unsurprising, and not just because of the absence of effective international leadership at this moment in history. On the contrary, realists are right to point out that security concerns remain nonnegotiable issues for many nation-states and they are reluctant to do anything that they consider may undermine this or threaten their ability to act autonomously if necessary. While realist logic may be understandable, it is ultimately self-defeating and arguably at odds with some of the more important developments of the last half-century or so.

On the one hand, we know from painful historical experience that no matter how much individual nations spend on weapons systems, it can never unequivocally guarantee national security – or satisfy the insatiable demands of military planners and strategists. There is no weapons system or technological innovation that a defense official would willingly forgo, no matter how expensive or unlikely its use. This is a serious problem for the world's wealthiest countries; it is entirely unjustifiable for poor states with more pressing issues of human security to resolve. This is not simply a patronizing observation from a fortunate denizen of the privileged north either: unless basic questions of human security are addressed, they are all too likely to spill over into serious domestic conflicts of a sort that seem sadly endemic in much of the would-be developing world. Equally pertinently, we know from history that arms races generally end badly and do nothing to ensure sustainable peace.

On the other hand, and rather more encouragingly, we also know that it is possible to generate sustainable patterns of peaceful, stable international relations, if only at a regional level. The reality is that interstate war is rare; close, institutionalized regional relations appear to have something to do with this. The EU stands as an enduring reminder that peace and prosperity can go together, and that this can entirely transform the way that former foes think about each, to the point where war between some countries seems utterly unthinkable. It is not just a European phenomenon either: the Asian experience suggests this can occur elsewhere, too. The fact that the world's longest land border between Canada and the United States remains entirely undefended is not simply a calculation on Canada's part that they cannot defend themselves against the more powerful United States – however rational and sensible that may actually be – but a recognition that there are no conceivable circumstances in which the United States would actually *want* to invade Canada. Even Donald Trump's eccentric foreign policies haven't managed to overturn that assumption (Baker 2018).

The remarkable postwar history of Japan suggests that there are other paths to 'national greatness' and that militarism can be repudiated. Even more importantly, perhaps, the Japanese experience suggests that the 'logic' of war and conquest may have changed in profoundly important ways: Japan's empire-building efforts before the Second World War may have ended in disaster, but it was able to achieve precisely the same goal of economic and resource security in the aftermath of the war peacefully through direct foreign investment (Beeson 2014b). The fact that we have even a limited number of successful alternatives to the apparently universal dynamics that realists claim affect all states is significant and optimism-inducing. True, there are many obstacles to other states replicating these achievements, or of scaling up such approaches to security to a regional or global level, but the empirical record suggests that the potential is at least there. The concluding chapter considers whether it can be realized.

10

The Future of Global Governance

It's tough to make predictions, especially about the future.

Yogi Berra

A map of the world that does not include Utopia is not worth even glancing at.

Oscar Wilde

Men make their own history, but they do not make it as they please; they do not make it under self-selected circumstances, but under circumstances existing already, given and transmitted from the past. The tradition of all dead generations weighs like a nightmare on the brains of the living.

Karl Marx

By this stage, the reader may be forgiven for thinking that this chapter looks rather pointless. After all, the previous chapters have gone into quite some detail about the problems confronting effective global governance – even for the declining numbers of people who still think it's possible in theory and a good idea in principle. Paradoxically enough, however, some of the

192

smartest people on the planet – or among international relations scholars, at least – think that not only is global governance possible and necessary, but world *government* is actually desirable and necessary, too. This concluding chapter considers some of these arguments in detail; it also considers what the world might look like without some form of 'good enough' global governance. The inescapable reality would seem to be that 'we' – in this case simply members of the human race – aren't likely to survive without some type of effective global governance, or not in some form we might consider 'civilized' at least.

At the outset, it is important to recognize that simply mentioning the word 'civilization' invites criticism, and consequently merits a few initial disclaimers. It is not necessary to subscribe to some sort of Huntingtonian (Huntington 1996) idea about a possible 'clash of civilizations', or even to believe that some civilizations are 'better' than others to recognize that contingent cultural values continue to shape the way that people think about themselves and their relationship to the world. At whatever 'scale' individual identity is formed or expressed, at some level, at least, it will reflect specific historical circumstances and the still overwhelmingly national contexts in which people exist. As I shall explain, this is a particular challenge for advocates and theorists of cosmopolitanism and/or transnational social movements: the reality would seem to be that whatever progress cosmopolitan ideas may have made seems to be rapidly unraveling in the face of a worldwide resurgence of populism and nationalism.

These sorts of issues and questions have frequently been caught up in contemporary debates about the importance of preserving 'Western values'. Plainly, some participants in the so-called history wars have ideological axes to grind and are not reliable witnesses when it comes to deciding whether progress is actually possible and what it might look like if it is (Smyth 2016). And yet anyone who is seriously interested in the idea of global governance has to think about the norms and principles that are associated with international cooperation, even if they don't like the ones that currently influence its practice. Anyone advocating a move toward world government might be expected to have an even greater responsibility to explain and justify its underlying rationale; some of them do, which is what makes their work so interesting and worthy of consideration. Before doing so, however, it is important to (re)consider some of the material and ideational forces that have got us collectively to this point.

The perils and necessity of extrapolation

Yogi Berra knew whereof he spoke. It is difficult to say anything sensible about the future at the best times; many think the current historical moment is anything but. Despite the apparent uncertainty, it has been persuasively argued that not only is progress unambiguously possible, but the quality of life, particularly for many Westerners who have inherited the achievements of the Enlightenment, at least, is unsurpassed in many ways (Pinker 2018). Realists might retort that all of the prosperity and progress hangs by a thread and could disappear at any moment in the proverbial puff of smoke, albeit the rather large and mushroom-shaped variety. With Donald Trump in the White House and threatening to rain 'fire and fury' on the likes of North Korea, and questions being raised about his mental stability, such fears look more credible than ever before (Drew 2017). This was true even before Trump appointed John Bolton – someone who has advocated a preemptive strike on North Korea – as a key security advisor (Friedman 2018). And yet, by the time this book is published, Trump's admirers hope he may have resolved the Korean crisis and received the Nobel Peace Prize.

If things are confusing strategically, they are no less clear as far as the global economy is concerned. Indeed, 'black swan events', or unexpected, improbable developments that no one saw coming, are seemingly part of the fabric of contemporary existence, but they are especially prominent in the notoriously skittish money markets (Skidelsky 2009; Taleb 2007). Marxists might argue that they were entirely unsurprised by the recurrence of crises in the global economy, given that they see such events as an inevitable expression of the irreconcilable contradictions embedded in capitalist social relations (Harvey 2010). But many have been taken unaware by recent events, including within the ranks of mainstream academic economists (Krugman 2012). Such myopia matters because it suggests a worrying inability to think critically and nonideologically about key developments in the global economy. As we saw in earlier chapters, many Western observers have had difficulty coming to terms with the possibility that East Asia successfully developed not by following the West's economic prescriptions and advice, but by ignoring them.

Differences of opinion about some of the most important historical developments of recent years matter because many analysts and observers may be misreading the possible course of economic development, too. Given the history of the last decade or so, this is not entirely surprising, perhaps: instability and unpredictability seem to be the order of the day. Trying to make sense of what might happen to economic activity in China and America is still important, however, if only because such judgments have the capacity to influence the behavior of equity and bond markets in dramatic ways. There are other, arguably more important, reasons for the thinking about the future direction of, and relationship between, the world's two largest economies, though. As we have seen, transformations in the relative material and 'structural' importance of the broadly conceived American and Chinese economies have the potential to spill over into their interrelationship, and not just in the form of trade wars. On the contrary, the rise of China's economy will inevitably lead to the PRC becoming more influential, possibly even triggering a process of 'hegemonic transition'.

Or it may not. Many – especially in the West – have long predicted that China faces possible unresolvable economic problems and may even face collapse (Chang 2002; McMahon 2018). If China's heavily indebted corporate and banking sectors don't undermine the PRC, its inflexible political structures will inhibit social dynamism, ultimately causing a multidimensional economic, political, and potentially strategic crisis (Pei 2006), the argument goes. It's possible. Indeed, if there is an economic crisis in 'communist' China it's hard to see how this wouldn't turn into a crisis of legitimacy for the CCP as well. Under such circumstances the chances of China's leadership focusing on an external enemy to divert attention from their own shortcomings and domestic problems would have to be high. Having said that, China's leaders have thus far defied the skeptics and the prognostications of Western political theorists and economists and kept the China dream well and truly alive.

But if it is impossible to say anything definitive about the current state of the global economy or about the international order in which it is embedded, there is one area in which it is possible to make predictions with slightly greater confidence. The natural environment is in serious trouble and it is likely to get worse. While there may be a good deal of uncertainty about the exact numbers and the precise effects of global warming, only the willfully ignorant or deceptive would deny that it will have a major impact on the environment and by extension on human society. This looming crisis doesn't mean that anything will be done to mitigate its impact, of course. But it does help to make the theoretical case for the unavoidable necessity of collective action and for developing the mechanisms with which such actions might actually be taken. This is where we arrive at the discussion of world government – however unlikely a prospect it may seem.

The cosmopolitan alternative

Oscar Wilde – author of this chapter's second epigraph – may not have known too much about global politics, but he did have a way with words. It is noteworthy and revealing that large numbers of Chinese people seem to take the idea of the 'Chinese dream' entirely seriously. Restoring the nation's place and status is seen as a worthwhile project and part of a general improvement in the well-being of ordinary citizens. These remarks are not intended to justify either China's increasingly authoritarian political system, its 'assertive' foreign policies, or the damage it has inflicted on the environment domestically or elsewhere. My point is that it is still possible to speak of the Chinese dream in a way that is simply no longer true about the American variety. It has long been established that living standards for many in the United States are actually falling, and the optimism-inducing, legitimacy-enhancing idea that 'ordinary' Americans will surpass the achievements of their forebears no longer holds (Tankersley 2016).

Even more troublingly, in my view, is the apparent long-term disenchantment with the EU across much of Europe, especially when combined with the rise of populism and reactionary politics. For all its undoubted problems, the EU remains the best and most developed example of transnational cooperation the world has yet seen. The collapse of the EU, or its decline into an ineffectual shadow of its former self, would be a major blow, not only to the economic, political, and strategic significance of Europe, but also to our belief in the possibility of addressing big problems collectively. This is an especially acute and poignant problem for Europe because we know only too well what Europe can look like without a collective sense of purpose and even identity.

Given the apparent rejection of the European ideal by so many of that continent's citizens, this might seem an especially inauspicious time to discuss the merits, let alone the actual possibility, of developing a cosmopolitan identity and orientation to the world. As even one of cosmopolitanism's most prominent champions has been forced to concede, 'when cosmopolitanism meets state interests under economic pressure, the former is often cast aside ... many European states are cosmopolitan when it comes to championing ideals, but remain sectarian when it comes to their implementation' (Held 2016: 244). Quite so. Consequently, some of the more sophisticated advocates of a cosmopolitan disposition recognize that however desirable the political and moral unification of the entire human race might be in theory, in practice 'human subjects cannot perceive the world other than through the distorting lens of language and culture' (Linklater 1998: 48). This is a problem even in the contemporary United States, which is a direct product of the Enlightenment project and the 'Western' values it embodied. It is a potentially an insurmountable obstacle to developing a common cause with countries where different cultural values continue to prevail, as they do in China, of course.

The idea that we might inhabit a post-ideological world in the aftermath of the Cold War looks like wishful thinking. China has embarked on a state-led project of national renewal that is predicated on a systematic campaign of indoctrination and discursive control that is uncomfortably reminiscent of the Cultural Revolution, a period with which the Chinese state and people have yet to come to terms. The United States is arguably little better. The Trump administration's preoccupation with 'fake news' and the propagation of 'alternative facts' would seem to have rendered the possibility of a Habermasian-style 'ideal speech community' – the necessary foundation for any 'rational' consideration of policy options and modes of governance – all but impossible. Or perhaps one should say, impossible within the dominant political discourses of China or the United States. Fortunately, it is still possible to conduct an academic debate about such issues, even if the potential audience is likely to be small, unrepresentative, and elitist. At this stage of human development, however, these may be the only people who take cosmopolitan ideas, much less the notion of world government, remotely seriously.

Is world government the (only) answer?

Nevertheless, for the likes of Andrew Linklater (1998: 49) the great merit of a 'thin' account of cosmopolitanism is that it 'provides a critique of domestic and international political arrangements'. Much the same could be said about the idea of world government: it is inherently unlikely, but at the very least it provides us with a possible perspective for thinking about the problems with existing forms of global governance. Again, and without wanting to unduly labor the point, the 'us' in question is notionally the human race but in reality a relative handful of people interested in such issues with all the inherent problems of self-selection and bias that inevitably entails. People interested in 'saving the world' are likely to have very different views from those who are pursuing their own or even the purported national interest. Indeed, people at different points of the life cycle might be expected to take a different position on rising sea levels over a 50–100-year period, for example, than someone like Donald Trump, who has already used up his biblical allocation of three score and ten years. One might even suppose that anyone with children might be predisposed to taking a longer view of planetary sustainability, but that is plainly not the case either.

There are, however, issues and contexts in which self-interest, especially the enlightened variety, might actually encourage the development of something like a world state, it is claimed (Ulas 2016). Climate change is the definitive test of our capacity to act collectively and to develop mechanisms with which to organize our efforts, but it is not the only one, of course. Some of the other enduring problems that we all face, albeit with different degrees of urgency, such as economic inequality, managing migration, and international security generally, to name only the most pressing, would seem to necessitate very high levels of coordination and cooperation. For those readers who think that this sort of cooperation is inherently implausible (or undesirable), it is important to recognize the foundations of such an international order are actually already in place, and not just in the EU. As prominent political theorist Robert Goodin (2013: 151 & 53) observes, 'in certain essential respects, world government is already with us ... Indeed, we have about as much of a world government as the United States had a federal government on the eve of the nineteenth century'.

All of the institutions, relationships, networks, and actors that we have considered in earlier chapters are – for all their manifold shortcomings – remarkable for the fact that they exist at all. There is plainly something very different about the way the world is organized now than there was when the nation-state emerged in Europe, let alone when Thucydides was reporting on the Peloponnesian War around 400 BC. This has not stopped large numbers of international relations specialists from claiming that precisely the same dynamics determine interstate relations now as they did two thousand years ago. And yet one of the benefits of historically informed comparative analysis is that it forces us to recognize that other histories have existed and other futures are possible. Whatever comes of China's contemporary ascent, its history is an instructive reminder about the potentially centripetal impact of interstate war. Put differently, rival states and the political elites that control them can come to recognize the potential value in cooperation and the creation of a peace-keeping, order-imposing Leviathan on a transnational scale.

Some readers will no doubt object that China's Warring States period was also a couple of thousand years ago and it makes no more sense to draw conclusions from that time than it does to make inferences based on the experiences of the ancient Greeks. Perhaps so. But there is also a compelling new logic in contemporary strategic relations that some observers argue is – or should be – forcing states to consider the merits of collaboration and even world government. Daniel Deudney (2007), for example, suggests the control of nuclear weapons is an essential prerequisite for achieving meaningful and sustainable international security. Consequently, arms control ought to be the paramount concern of states, and this can only be achieved by moving toward world government. Deudney's vison is one based on what he calls 'negarchy', which is neither anarchic nor hierarchical, but one in which differentials of state power are consciously negated in order to preserve the status quo. Unfortunately, perhaps, even Deudney thinks this is an improbable development, and that 'the most likely outcome of the current and emergent constraints and opportunities is not a nuclear union of restraint, but rather the incremental extinction of political liberty' (Deudney 2007: 264).

I have made similar sorts of dispiriting arguments about the possible consequences of failing to address climate change (Beeson 2010). Indeed, making these sorts of arguments is depressingly easy and all too plausible. The all too obvious obstacles to realizing a world government or world state is possibly one reason why some of the most influential – among international relations scholars, at least – advocates of the idea argue that a longer time frame is appropriate when thinking about its prospects. Alexander Wendt (2003) is, indeed, one of the most prominent IR specialists alive today, and he suggests that a 100–200-year period may be required for a world state to appear. He may be right, but it does beg the question of what the world might look like by then without world government in the meantime, and why anyone alive today should actually care. This is not a flippant point: without some sense of world government, or even more modest forms of global governance is actually realizable, it is difficult to see how much progress will be made.

To be fair, it is important to acknowledge that there are a number of proposals about how such a world government or state might be realized, or at least brought into sharper focus (Cabrera 2006, 2010). One of the preconditions for such moves is a change on consciousness, and not just on the part of current crop of nationally based elites who have potentially much to lose from any transformation of the existing structures of governance. Idealists might argue that we all have much to gain by saving the planet, of course, but it is difficult to see such arguments cutting much ice with the likes of Donald Trump. Without enlightened leadership, it is difficult to see how or why the populations of any country could come to develop a notion of themselves as 'citizens of the world' and allow democratic processes to be scaled-up to a global level, which many prominent observers claim is a precondition for effective global governance (Falk 1993; Held 2004). At a time when confidence in democratically elected politicians is at historically low levels, and many young people have lost faith in democracy as a system, the preconditions for acting on issues such as climate change – especially in the time available – are not good, to put it mildly. Indeed, as Henry Shue (2011: 17) points out, when it comes environmental mitigation in particular, 'our politicians have failed to be worthy of our scientists or of the trust we citizens have placed in them'.

Rethinking global governance

Karl Marx, the author of the famous passage from *The Eighteenth Brumaire of Louis Bonaparte*, which provides this chapter's third epigraph, did know something about the politics and economics of his time, even if there is still much debate about the conclusions he came to as a consequence. But whatever the reader may think about Marx's teleological view of history and the supposedly inevitable demise of capitalism, he had a point about the material circumstances we inherit – and bequeath to those who come after us, of course. It is already painfully apparent that climate change is having a disastrous impact on large parts of the world, fueling conflict and driving the sorts of mass migration that are beginning to undermine social stability in the privileged enclaves of the West. Some of the dystopian visions of zones of peace and conflict may prove to be incorrect only in as much as the 'zones' may prove more porous and difficult to preserve than seemed likely. Or they will unless authoritarian governments unleash the formidable powers of nation-states on those unfortunate enough not to belong to one, or one worthy of the name, at least.

If Marxist-inspired environmentalists are correct in the arguments they make about the incompatibility of a capitalist mode of production and rampant consumerism with a sustainable environment (Foster et al. 2010; Kovel 2007), then the prospects for effective action are bleak indeed. Even believers in the possibility of an effective global civil society recognize the difficulty of aligning this with a vision of endless consumption on a planetary scale (Keane 2003: 79). In addition, the relatively slow unfolding of the environmental crisis means that there is unlikely to be a GFC-style moment when the world's most powerful actors come together to stave off catastrophe. More fundamentally, it is also unlikely that there will be a similar alignment of economic interests and political will, especially when environmental degradation is disproportionately affecting the least powerful, poorest members of the global population first. One thing 'radical' scholarship does usefully highlight in this context is the continuing uneven nature of development and, not to mention, the concomitant lack of influence and power this creates when it comes to having an influence in the way the world is organized.

One of the most difficult questions to answer about such enduring forms of inequality, of course, is just what can be done to overcome them. It is not necessary to subscribe to conspiracy theories about the IFIs and their powerful state sponsors deliberately working against the interests of the poor – although alarming numbers of people do, of course – to recognize that some problems are deep-seated, 'structural', and not helped by possibly well-intentioned but misguided policy prescriptions from 'the West' (Easterly 2006). Having said that, millions of people have been lifted out of poverty, not least because of the rise of China and the state-led East Asian economic miracle. Differences of opinion about the 'right' model of development are likely to be a continuing source of disagreement as a consequence, and one that is overlaid with similar debates about the most effective forms of political organization at the national level. For some observers, the great hope in this regard is some sort of synthesis of the best aspect of 'East' and 'West', in which 'knowledgeable democracy' is reconciled with 'accountable meritocracy' (Berggruen and Gardels 2013: 13). Given that this model involves a lot of 'involving and devolving', it is difficult to see it being enthusiastically embraced by the growing number of authoritarian state-capitalist regimes around the world (Bremmer 2010).

Perhaps the key issue to consider when 'rethinking' global governance is about the future role of the state: will it 'wither away' (as Marx thought), will it become the last defense of privileged elites in a sea of troubles, or will it play an indispensable role as the architect of new forms of transnational cooperation? For some scholars, the best we can hope for is a form of 'good enough' governance, in which governments are 'operating in many venues simultaneously, participating in a bewildering array of issue-specific networks and partnerships whose membership varies based on situational interests, shared values, and relevant capabilities' (Patrick 2014: 62). There is plainly something in this idea as description of contemporary reality. But the distinguishing feature of contemporary governance arrangements is that such arrangements are failing and not 'good enough' at all.

For all its possible problems and checkered historical role, the state – or powerful states, at least – remains the most important political force in world affairs. Despite the attention that is currently given to new social movements, nonstate actors, and actions at different scales, the reality is that, for better or worse, it is still states that are quite literally calling the shots. This was true before the rise of the new authoritarians and world's growing list of problems; it is doubly so now. The EU is discovering just how difficult it is to maintain a credible, genuinely transnational political identity and capacity in the face of seemingly irreconcilable differences of opinion about divisive problems. As Plesch and Weiss (2015: 202) rightly point out, 'nonstate actors can make and have made essential contributions to global problem solving. Not to put too fine a point on it, however, they can do little to safely manage geopolitical competition or control the spread of advanced weapons – let alone eliminate poverty, thwart pandemics, fix climate change, ensure macroeconomic stability, agree on inter-national standards, or halt mass atrocities.'

Intergovernmental organizations *can* work, and nonstate actors *can* be empowered to make a contribution to solving collective action problems, but only if they are given the authority to do so by the world's most powerful states. It is, after all, states that sign off on and respect inter*national* agreements, or authorize and legitimate the activities of other actors in specific issue areas. As the Trump administration's recent actions remind us, they can also walk away from agreements as well. In such circumstances, we have to consider the possibility that we won't find ways to address climate change in particular and we need to think seriously about what that might mean for governance of any sort. Rethinking global governance may mean recognizing that there may not be answers to complex questions that don't involve states, and that there may not be any good answers at all.

A sobering illustration of the latter possibility is that defense agencies around the world are currently workshopping the consequences of a radically deteriorating environment. As Parenti (2011: 11) points out, 'the Pentagon and its European allies are actively planning a militarized adaptation [to climate change], which emphasizes the long-term, open-ended containment of failed or failing states'. Earnest debates about the way the natural environment has become 'securitized' look rather less important than actually thinking about what the refocusing of national security policies may mean in actual practice. Debates about 'good governance' are not likely to be of even academic interest under such circumstances.

There are, however, some glimmers of hope. Enlightened and even ethically informed self-interest could, Peter Singer (2002: 13) argues, provide a compelling reason to address economic inequality and much else. Skeptics may wonder about the prospects of seeing the words 'ethically informed' and Donald Trump in the same sentence, but leaders do change, and we must hope that America's democratic institutions will ultimately prevail.

The great hope is that future readers in a post-Trump era may wonder what all the fuss was about. But it is important to remember that while the world may have forgotten or become resigned to the horrors and blunders that the unilateralism of George W. Bush unleashed on the world, their legacy lives on – not least in the practical and ideational difficulties that confront subsequent generations of policymakers interested in international cooperation. The rise of Trump and the new authoritarians is a potent expression of the contempt that they and their supporters have for internationalism.

Advocates of international cooperation must, therefore, hope that many of the international institutions that were created under the auspices of American hegemony will survive and prove effective. For all the criticisms that are all too easily made about organizations such as the WTO and the UN, they do embody some important principles about the possibility, at least, of collaboration, problem-solving and collective action. The same can be said even more forcefully about the EU; the symbolism of the EU's demise or decline into institutionalized irrelevance would be long-lasting and uniformly negative. Its fate may give us the best indicator of the prospects for effective transnational governance more generally: if the EU with its established and historically effective patterns of institutionalized cooperation can't survive within the relatively conducive context of Western Europe, the prospects for global governance look remote indeed. For those interested in rethinking global governance, we may have to think about what the world looks like in its absence.

Bibliography

Abernathy, D.B. (2000) *Global Dominance: European Overseas Empires, 1415–1980* (New Haven, CT: Yale University Press).

Abu-Lughod, J. (1989) *Before European Hegemony* (New York: Oxford University Press).

Acemoglu, D., Johnson, S., and Robinson, J.A. (2001) 'The colonial origins of comparative development: An empirical investigation', *The American Economic Review* 91(5): 1369–1401.

Acemoglu, D. and Robinson, J.A. (2006) *Economic Origins of Dictatorship and Democracy* (Cambridge: Cambridge University Press).

Acemoglu, D. and Robinson, J.A. (2010) 'Why is Africa poor?', *Economic History of Developing Regions* 25(1): 21–50.

Acemoglu, D. and Robinson, J.A. (2012) *Why Nations Fail: The Origins of Power, Prosperity, and Poverty* (New York: Crown).

Acharya, A. (1995) 'A regional security community in Southeast Asia?', *Journal of Strategic Studies* 18(3): 175–200.

Acharya, A. (1997) 'Ideas, identity, and institution-building: From the "ASEAN way" to the "Asia-Pacific way"', *The Pacific Review* 10(3): 319–346.

Acharya, A. (2001) *Constructing a Security Community in Southeast Asia: ASEAN and the Problem of Regional Order* (London: Routledge).

Acharya, A. (2012) 'Comparative regionalism: A field whose time has come?', *The International Spectator* 47(1): 3–15.

Acharya, A. (2014) *The End of the American World Order* (Cambridge: Polity Press).

Acharya, A. and Johnston, A.I. (2007) 'Conclusion', in A. Acharya and A.I. Johnston (eds), *Crafting Cooperation: Regional International Institutions in Comparative Perspective* (Cambridge: Cambridge University Press): 244–278.

Adler, E. and Barnett, M. (1998) 'A framework for the study of security communities', in E. Adler and M. Barnett (eds), *Security Communities* (Cambridge: Cambridge University Press): 29–65.

Alagappa, M. (1998) 'Asian practice of security: Key features and explanations', in M. Alagappa (ed.), *Asian Security Practice: Material and Ideational Influences* (Stanford: Stanford University Press): 611–676.

Albert, M. (1993) *Capitalism Vs. Capitalism* (New York: Four Wall Eight Windows).

Allison, G. (2004) *Nuclear Terrorism: The Ultimate Preventable Catastrophe* (London: Macmillan).

Allison, G. (2017) *Destined for War: Can America and China Escape Thucydides's Trap?* (Boston: Houghton Mifflin Harcourt).

Amin, S. (1978) 'Unequal development: An essay on the social formations of peripheral capitalism', *Science and Society* 42(2): 219–222.

Amsden, A.H. (2001) *The Rise of "The Rest": Challenges to the West from Late-Industrializing Economies* (Oxford: Oxford University Press).

Amyx, J. (2004) 'Japan and the evolution of regional financial arrangements in East Asia', in E.S. Krauss and T.J. Pempel (eds), *Beyond Bilateralism: US-Japan Relations in the New Asia-Pacific* (Stanford: Stanford University Press): 198–218.

Anderson, P. (1996) *Passages from Antiquity to Feudalism* (London: Verso).

Andrews, D. (1994) 'Capital mobility and state autonomy: Toward a structural theory of international monetary relations', *International Studies Quarterly* 38: 193–218.

Angell, N. (2012 [1910]) *The Great Illusion* (New York: Bottom of the Hill).

Anievas, A. and Nisancioglu, K. (2015) *How the West Came to Rule: The Geopolitical Origins of Capitalism* (London: Pluto Press).

Arias-Maldonado, M. (2007) 'An imaginary solution? The green defence of deliberative democracy', *Environmental Values* 16(2): 233–252.

Arrighi, G. (1994) *The Long Twentieth Century: Money, Power, and the Origins of Our Times* (London: Verso).

Ashley, R.K. (1984) 'The poverty of neorealism', *International Organization* 38(2): 225–286.

Aston, T.H. and Philpin, C.H. (1987) *The Brenner Debate: Agrarian Class Structure and Economic Development in Pre-Industrial Europe*, vol. 1 (Cambridge: Cambridge University Press).

Athukorala, P.C. (2009) 'The rise of China and East Asian export performance: Is the crowding-out fear warranted?', *World Economy* 32(2): 234–266.

Avant, D.D., Finnemore, M., and Sell, S.K. (2010) 'Who governs the globe?', in D.D. Avant, M. Finnemore, and S.K. Sell (eds), *Who Governs the Globe?* (Cambridge: Cambridge University Press): 1–31.

Babb, S. (2007) 'Embeddedness, inflation, and international regimes: The IMF in the early postwar period', *American Journal of Sociology* 113(1): 128–164.

Babb, S. (2012) 'The Washington Consensus as transnational policy paradigm: Its origins, trajectory and likely successor', *Review of International Political Economy* 20(2): 268–297.

Bacevich, A.J. (2002) *American Empire: The Realities and Consequences of US Diplomacy* (Cambridge, MA: Harvard University Press).

Bacevich, A.J. (2005) *The New American Militarism: How Americans Are Seduced by War* (Oxford: Oxford University Press).

Baker, A. (2010) 'Restraining regulatory capture? Anglo-America, crisis politics and trajectories of change in global financial governance', *International Affairs* 86(3): 647–63.

Baker, A. (2014) 'Varieties of financial crisis, varieties of ideational change: How and why financial regulation and macroeconomic policy differ', *New Political Economy* 1–32.

Baker, P. (2018) 'Trump shakes up world stage in break with U.S. allies', *New York Times*, June 8.

Baldwin, R. (2016) *The Great Convergence* (Cambridge, MA: Harvard University Press).

Ball, D. (2000) *The Council for Security Cooperation in the Asia Pacific (CSCAP): Its record and its prospects*: Strategic and Defence Studies Centre, Research School of Pacific and Asian Studies, Australian National University).

Ball, M. (2018) 'Peter Navarro used to be a Democrat. Now he's the mastermind behind Trump's trade war', *Time*, August 23.

Barber, T. (2017) 'Europe's new political divisions', *Financial Times*, May 14.

Barbier, E.B. (2010) *A Global Green New Deal: Rethinking the Economic Recovery* (Cambridge: Cambridge University Press).

Barnett, M. and Duvall, R. (2005) 'Power in global governance', in M. Barnett and R. Duvall (eds), *Power in Global Governance* (Cambridge: Cambridge University Press): 1–32.

Barnett, M. and Sikkink, K. (2009) 'From international relations to global society', in R. Goodin (ed.), *The Oxford Handbook of Political Science* (Oxford: Oxford University Press): 748–768.

Bayly, C.A. (2004) *The Birth of the Modern World, 1780–1914* (Oxford: Blackwell).

Beckley, M. (2015) 'The myth of entangling alliances: Reassessing the security risks of US defense pacts', *International Security* 39(4): 7–48.

Beddoes, Z.M. (2013) 'Europe's reluctant hegemon', *The Economist*, June 15.

Beeson, M. (2001) 'Globalization, governance, and the political-economy of public policy reform in East Asia', *Governance – An International Journal of Policy and Administration* 14(4): 481–502.

Beeson, M. (2005) 'Rethinking regionalism: Europe and East Asia in comparative historical perspective', *Journal of European Public Policy* 12(6): 969–985.

Beeson, M. (2006) 'American hegemony and regionalism: The rise of East Asia and the end of the Asia-Pacific', *Geopolitics* 11(4): 541–560.

Beeson, M. (2008) 'The United States and East Asia: The decline of long-distance leadership?', in C.M. Dent (ed.), *China, Japan and Regional Leadership in East Asia* (Cheltenham: Edward Elgar): 229–246.

Beeson, M. (2009a) 'Geopolitics and the making of regions: The fall and rise of East Asia', *Political Studies* 57: 498–516.

Beeson, M. (2009b) 'Developmental states in East Asia: A comparison of the Japanese and Chinese experiences', *Asian Perspective* 33(2): 5–39.

Beeson, M. (2010) 'The coming of environmental authoritarianism', *Environmental Politics* 19(2): 276–294.

Beeson, M. (2011a) 'Can Australia save the world? The limits and possibilities of middle power diplomacy', *Australian Journal of International Affairs* 65(5): 563–577.

Beeson, M. (2011b) 'Crisis dynamics and regionalism: East Asia in comparative perspective', *The Pacific Review* 24(3): 357–374.

Beeson, M. (2013a) 'Can China lead?', *Third World Quarterly* 34(2): 235–252.

Beeson, M. (2013b) 'Living with giants: ASEAN and the evolution of Asian regionalism', *TRaNS: Trans-Regional and -National Studies of Southeast Asia* 1(2): 303–322.

Beeson, M. (2014a) *Regionalism and Globalization in East Asia: Politics, Security and Economic Development*, 2nd edn (London: Red Globe Press).

Beeson, M. (2014b) 'Security in Asia What's different, what's not?', *Journal of Asian Security and International Affairs* 1(1): 1–23.

Beeson, M. (2014c) 'Security governance in Southeast Asia: The paradoxes of cooperation', in J. Sperling (ed.), *Handbook on Governance and Security* (Cheltenham: Edward Elgar): 273–288.

Beeson, M. (2015) 'Can ASEAN cope with China?', *Journal of Current Southeast Asian Affairs* 35(1): 5–28.

Beeson, M. (2016) 'Multilateralism in East Asia: Less than the sum of its parts?', *Global Summitry* 2(1): 54–70.

Beeson, M. (2017a) 'Alternative realities: Explaining security in the Asia-Pacific', *Review of International Studies* 43(3): 516–533.

Beeson, M. (2017b) 'Globalization and governance', in M. Beeson and N. Bisley (eds), *Issues in 21st Century World Politics*, 3rd edn (London: Macmillan Education): 83–96.

Beeson, M. (2017c) 'Why has leadership in the Asia-Pacific proved so elusive?', *Chinese Political Science Review* 2(4): 567–581.

Beeson, M. (2018) 'Geoeconomics with Chinese characteristics: The BRI and China's evolving grand strategy', *Economic and Political Studies*, 6(3): 240–56.

Beeson, M. (2018a) 'Geoeconomics isn't back – it never went away', *The Interpreter*, September 2.

Beeson, M. (2018b) 'Coming to terms with the authoritarian alternative: The implications and motivations of China's environmental policies', *Asia & the Pacific Policy Studies,* 5(1): 34–46.

Beeson, M. (2018c) 'Geoeconomics with Chinese characteristics: The BRI and China's evolving grand strategy', *Economic and Political Studies* 6(3): 240–256.

Beeson, M. and Bell, S. (2009) 'The G-20 and international economic governance: Hegemony, collectivism, or both?', *Global Governance* 15(1): 67–86.

Beeson, M. and Bell, S. (2017) 'The impact of economic structures on institutions and states', in T. Dunne and C. Reus-Smit (eds), *The Globalization of International Society* (Oxford: Oxford University Press): 284–303.

Beeson, M. and Bellamy, A.J. (2008) *Securing Southeast Asia: The Politics of Security Sector Reform* (London: Routledge).

Beeson, M. and Broome, A. (2010) 'Hegemonic instability and East Asia: Contradictions, crises and US power', *Globalizations* 7(4): 479–495.

Beeson, M. and Higgott, R. (2005) 'Hegemony, institutionalism and US foreign policy: Theory and practice in comparative historical perspective', *Third World Quarterly* 26(7): 1173–1188.

Beeson, M. and Higgott, R. (2014) 'The changing architecture of politics in the Asia-Pacific: Australia's middle power moment?', *International Relations of the Asia-Pacific* 14(2): 215–237.

Beeson, M. and Islam, I. (2005) 'Neoliberalism and East Asia: Resisting the Washington consensus', *Journal of Development Studies* 41(2): 197–219.

Beeson, M. and Jayasuriya, K. (1998) 'The political rationalities of regionalism: APEC and the EU in comparative perspective', *The Pacific Review* 11(3): 311–336.

Beeson, M. and Li, F. (2014) *China's Regional Relations: Evolving Foreign Policy Dynamics* (Boulder, CO: Lynne Rienner).

Beeson, M. and Li, F. (2015) 'What consensus? Geopolitics and policy paradigms in China and the US', *International Affairs* 91(1): 93–109.

Beeson, M. and Stone, D. (2013a) 'The changing fortunes of a policy entrepreneur: The case of Ross Garnaut', *Australian Journal of Political Science* 48(1): 1–14.

Beeson, M. and Stone, D. (2013b) 'The European Union model's influence in Asia after the Global Financial Crisis', *European Journal of East Asian Studies* 12: 167–190.

Beeson, M. and Xu, S. (forthcoming) 'China's evolving role in global governance: The AIIB and the limits of an alternative international order', in K. Zeng (ed.), *Handbook of the International Political Economy of China* (Cheltenham: Edward Elgar).

Beeson, M. and Zeng, J. (2017) 'Realistic relations? How the evolving bilateral relationship is understood in China and Australia', *Pacific Focus* 32(2): 159–181.

Beeson, M. and Zeng, J. (forthcoming) 'The BRICS and global governance: China's contradictory role', *Third World Quarterly.*

Bell, D.A. (2015) *The China Model: Political Meritocracy and the Limits of Democracy* (Princeton: Princeton University Press).

Bell, D. (2017) 'China's corruption clampdown risks policy paralysis', *Financial Times,* May 2.

Bell, S. (2011) 'Do we really need a new "constructivist institutionalism" to explain institutional change?', *British Journal of Political Science* 41(4): 883–906.

Bell, S. and Feng, H. (2013) *The Rise of the People's Bank of China: The Politics of Institutional Change* (Cambridge, MA: Harvard University Press).

Bell, S. and Hindmoor, A. (2009) *Rethinking Governance: The Centrality of the State in Modern Society* (Melbourne: Cambridge University Press).

Bell, S. and Hindmoor, A. (2015) *Masters of the Universe, Slaves of the Market* (Cambridge, MA: Harvard University Press).

Bellamy, A.J. (2009) 'Realizing the responsibility to protect', *International Studies Perspectives* 10(2): 111–128.

Bellamy, A.J., Williams, P.D., and Griffin, S. (2010) *Understanding Peacekeeping* (Cambridge: Polity Press).

Benner, T., Gaspers, J., Ohlberg, M., Poggetti, L., and Shi-Kupper, K. (2018) *Authoritarian Advance: Responding to China's Growing Political Influence in Europe* (Berlin: GPPi).

Berger, M.T. (2006) 'From nation-building to state-building: The geopolitics of development, the nation-state system and the changing global order', *Third World Quarterly* 27(1): 5–25.

Berger, P. and Luckmann, T. (1967) *The Social Construction of Reality: A Treatise in the Sociology Knowledge* (London: Penguin).

Berger, S. (2005) *How We Compete: What Companies around the World are Doing to Make It in Today's Global Economy* (New York: Double Day).

Berggruen, N. and Gardels, N. (2013) *Intelligent Governance for the 21st Century: A Middle Way between West and East* (Cambridge: Polity Press).

Bergsten, C.F. (2008) 'A partnership of equals', *Foreign Affairs* 87(4): 57–69.

Bernauer, T., Boehmelt, T., and Koubi, V. (2013) 'The democracy-civil society paradox in global environmental governance', *Global Environmental Politics* 13(1): 88–107.

Bernstein, R. and Munro, R.H. (1997) *The Coming Conflict with China* (New York: Vintage).

Bevir, M. and Rhodes, R.A. (2010) *The State As Cultural Practice* (Oxford: Oxford University Press).

Biel, R. (2000) *The New Imperialism-Crisis and Contradictions in North-South Relations* (London: Zed Books).

Biermann, F. and Pattberg, P. (2008) 'Global environmental governance: Taking stock, moving forward', *Annual Review of Environment and Resources* 33(1): 277–294.

Bisley, N. (2012) 'APEC: Asia-Pacific Economic Cooperation', in M. Beeson and R. Stubbs (eds), *The Routledge Handbook of Asian Regionalism* (London: Routledge): 350–363.

Blackburn, R. (2008) 'The subprime crisis', *New Left Review* 50(March–April): 63–106.

Blackwill, R.D. and Harris, J.M. (2016) *War by Other Means: Geoeconomics and Statecraft* (Cambridge, MA: Harvard University Press).

Blaut, J.M. (1993) *The Colonizer's View of the World* (New York: Guilford Press).

Block, F. (1977) *The Origins of the International Economic Disorder* (Berkeley: University of California Press).

Block, F. and Evans, P. (2005) 'The state and the economy', in N.J. Smelser and R. Swedberg (eds), *The Handbook of Economic Sociology* (Princeton: Princeton University Press): 505–526.

Bloomfield, A. (2012) 'Time to move on: Reconceptualizing the strategic culture debate', *Contemporary Security Policy* 32(July): 1–25.

Blyth, M. (2002) *Great Transformations: Economic Ideas and Institutional Change in the Twentieth Century* (Cambridge: Cambridge University Press).

Blyth, M. (2013) *Austerity: The History of a Dangerous Idea* (Oxford: Oxford University Press).

Boas, T. and Gans-Morse, J. (2009) 'Neoliberalism: From new liberal philosophy to anti-liberal slogan', *Studies in Comparative International Development* 44(2): 137–161.

Bohman, J. (1998) 'Survey article: The coming of age of deliberative democracy', *Journal of Political Philosophy* 6(4): 400–425.

Boli, J. and Thomas, G.M. (1999) 'INGOs and the organisation of world culture', in J. Boli and G.M. Thomas (eds), *Constructing World Culture: International Nongovernmental Organizations Since 1875* (Stanford: Stanford University Press): 13–48.

Booth, K. (ed.) (2011) *Realism and World Politics* (London: Routledge).

Booth, K. and Wheeler, N.J. (2008) *The Security Dilemma: Fear, Cooperation, and Trust in World Politics* (London: Red Globe Press).

Börzel, T.A., Dimitrova, A., and Schimmelfennig, F. (2017) 'European Union enlargement and integration capacity: Concepts, findings, and policy implications', *Journal of European Public Policy* 24(2): 157–176.

Börzel, T.A. and Risse, T. (eds) (2016) *The Oxford Handbook of Comparative Regionalism* (Oxford: Oxford University Press).

Bradsher, K. (2010) 'Amid tension, China blocks vital exports to Japan', *New York Times*, September 22.

Bradsher, K. (2018) 'Trump's charm and threats may not be working on China. Here's why', *New York Times*, May 21.

Bradsher, K. and Myers, S.L. (2018) 'Trump's trade war is rattling China's leaders', *New York Times*, August 14.

Braithwaite, J. and Drahos, P. (2000) *Global Business Regulation* (Cambridge: Cambridge University Press).

Braudel, F. (1992) *The Structures of Everyday Life: The Limits of the Possible* (Berkeley: University of California Press).

Bräutigam, D. and Tang, X. (2012) 'Economic statecraft in China's new overseas special economic zones: Soft power, business or resource security?', *International Affairs* 88(4): 799–816.

Bräutigam, D. and Tang, X. (2014) '"Going global in groups": Structural transformation and China's special economic zones overseas', *World Development* 63: 78–91.

Braw, E. (2018) 'Europe's security concerns over Chinese investments need to be addressed', *South China Morning Post*, February 2.

Bremmer, I. (2010) *The End of the Free Market: Who Wins the War between States and Corporations?* (New York: Penguin).

Bremmer, I. (2012) *Every Nation for Itself: Winners and Losers in a G-Zero World* (New York: Portfolio/Penguin).

Bremmer, I. (2017a) 'The mixed fortunes of the BRICS countries, in 5 facts', *Time*, September 1.

Bremmer, I. (2017b) 'How China's economy is poised to win the future', *Time*, November 2.

Bremmer, I. (2018) 'It's official: China wants its share of global leadership', *Australian Financial Review*, January 15.

Brenner, N. (2004) *New State Spaces: Urban Governance and the Rescaling of Statehood* (Oxford: Oxford University Press).

Breslin, S. (2007) *China and the Global Economy* (London: Red Globe Press).

Breslin, S. (2011a) 'East Asia and the global/transatlantic/Western crisis', *Contemporary Politics* 17(2): 109–117.

Breslin, S. (2011b) 'The "China model" and the global crisis: From Friedrich List to a Chinese mode of governance?', *International Affairs* 87(6): 1323–1343.

Breslin, S. (2013) 'China and the global order: Signaling threat or friendship?', *International Affairs* 89(3): 615–634.

Breslin, S. and Higgott, R. (2000) 'Studying regions: Learning from the old, constructing the new', *New Political Economy* 5(3): 333–352.

Brewster, R. (2018) 'Trump is breaking the WTO. Will China want to save it?', *Washington Post*, May 2.

Brødsgaard, K.E. (2012) 'Politics and business group formation in China: The party in control?', *The China Quarterly* 211: 624–648.

Brooks, S.G. and Wohlforth, W.C. (2016) 'The rise and fall of the great powers in the twenty-first century: China's rise and the fate of America's global position', *International Security* 40(3): 7–53.

Brown, K. (2014) *The New Emperors: Power and the Princelings in China* (London: I.B. Tauris).

Browne, A. (2018) 'China builds bridges and highways while the U.S. mouths slogans', *Wall Street Journal*, January 30.

Brownlee, J. (2007) *Authoritarianism in an Age of Democratization* (Cambridge: Cambridge University Press).

Buckley, C. (2016) 'China's antigraft enforcers take on a new role: Policing loyalty', *New York Times*, October 22.

Buranelli, Costa F. (forthcoming) 'Spheres of influence as negotiated hegemony – the case of Central Asia', *Geopolitics* 1–26.

Burley, A.M. (1993) 'Regulating the world: Multilateralism, international law, and the projection of the New Deal regulatory state', in J.G. Ruggie (ed.), *Multilateralism Matters: The Theory and Praxis of an Institutional Form* (New York: Columbia University Press): 125–156.

Bush, R.C. (2016) *Hong Kong in the Shadow of China: Living with the Leviathan* (Washington, DC: Brookings Institution Press).

Buzan, B. (2012) 'How regions were made, and the legacies for world politics: An English School reconnaissance', in T.V. Paul (ed.), *International Relations Theory and Regional Transformation* (Cambridge: Cambridge University Press): 22–46.

Buzan, B. and Little, R. (2000) *International Systems in World History: Remaking the Study of International Relations* (Oxford: Oxford University Press).

Cabrera, L. (2006) *Political Theory of Global Justice: A Cosmopolitan Case for the World State* (London: Routledge).

Cabrera, L. (2010) 'World government: Renewed debate, persistent challenges', *European Journal of International Relations* 16(3): 511–530.

Cai, H. and Treisman, D. (2006) 'Did government decentralization cause China's economic miracle?', *World Politics* 58: 505–535.

Cai, Y. (2008) 'Power structure and regime resilience: Contentious politics in China', *British Journal of Political Science* 38(3): 411–432.

Callahan, W.A. (2008) 'Chinese visions of world order: Post-hegemonic or a new hegemony?', *International Studies Review* 10(4): 749–761.

Callahan, William A. (2010) *China: The Pessoptimist Nation* (Oxford: Oxford University Press).

Callick, R. (2017) 'China congress: Xi Jinping recruits the entire power elite', *The Australian*, October 19.

Callick, R. (2018) 'Xi's new China sweeping away the rule of state', *The Australian*, March 23.

Campbell, K.M., Gulledge, J., McNeill, J.R., Podesta, J., Ogden, P., Fuerth, L., Woolsey, R.J., Lennon, A.T., Smith, J., and Weitz, R. (2007) *The Age of Consequences: The Foreign Policy and National Security Implications of Global Climate Change* (Washington, DC: Center for Strategic and International Studies).

Camroux, D. (2012) 'The East Asia Summit: Pan-Asian multilateralism rather than intra-Asian regionalism', in M. Beeson and R. Stubbs (eds), *The Routledge Handbook of Asian Regionalism* (London: Routledge): 375–383.

Capoccia, G. and Kelemen, R.D. (2007) 'The study of critical junctures: Theory, narrative, and counterfactuals in historical institutionalism', *World Politics* 59(April): 341–369.

Carr, E.H. (1998 [1939]) *The Twenty Years Crisis, 1919–1939* (New York: Harper and Row).

Carson, R. (2002) *Silent Spring* (New York: Houghton Mifflin Harcourt).

Carter, N. (2007) *The Politics of the Environment*, 2nd edn (Cambridge: Cambridge University Press).

Castells, M. (1996) *The Rise of the Network Society* (Oxford: Blackwell).

Castles, F. (1998) *Comparative Public Policy: Patterns of Post-War Transformation* (Cheltenham: Edward Elgar).

Cerny, P.G. (1996) 'International finance and the erosion of state policy capacity', in P. Gummett (ed.), *Globalisation and Public Policy* (Cheltenham: Edward Elgar): 82–104.

Cerny, P.G. (1998) 'Neomedievalism, civil war and the new security dilemma: Globalisation as durable disorder', *Civil Wars* 1(1): 36–64.

Cerny, P.G. (2010) *Rethinking World Politics: A Theory of Transnational Neopluralism* (Oxford: Oxford University Press).

Cha, V.D. (2016) *Powerplay: The Origins of the American Alliance System* (Princeton: Princeton University Press).

Chan, G., Lee, P.K., and Chan, L.H. (2012) *China Engages Global Governance: A New World Order in the Making?* (London: Routledge).

Chan, S. (2009) 'Commerce between rivals: Realism, liberalism, and credible communication across the Taiwan Strait', *International Relations of the Asia Pacific* 9(3): 435–467.

Chang, G.G. (2002) *The Coming Collapse of China* (London: Arrow).

Chang, H.J. (2002) *Kicking Away the Ladder: Development Strategy in Historical Perspective* (London: Anthem Books).

Chang, H.J. and Grabel, I. (2005) 'Reclaiming development from the Washington Consensus', *Journal of Post Keynesian Economics* 27(2): 273–291.

Checkel, J.T. (1999) 'Norms, institutions, and national identity in contemporary Europe', *International Studies Quarterly* 43(1): 83–114.

Chellaney, B. (2012) 'Asia's worsening water crisis', *Survival* 54(2): 143–156.

Chen, A. (2002) 'Capitalist development, entrepreneurial class, and democratization in China', *Political Science Quarterly* 117(3): 401–422.

Chen, G.C. and Lees, C. (2016) 'Growing China's renewables sector: A developmental state approach', *New Political Economy* 21(6): 574–586.

Cheng, J.Y.S. (2011) 'The Shanghai Co-operation Organization : China's initiative in regional institutional building', *Journal of Contemporary Asia* 41(4): 632–656.

Cheng, Y.N. (2010) 'The Chinese model of development: An international perspective', *Social Sciences in China* 31(2): 44–59.

Chin, G. (2014) 'The BRICS-led Development Bank: Purpose and Politics beyond the G20', *Global Policy* 5(3): 366–373.

Chin, G. and Thakur, R. (2010) 'Will China change the rules of global order?', *The Washington Quarterly* 33(4): 119–138.

Chin, J. (2018) 'China spends more on domestic security as Xi's powers grow', *Wall Street Journal*, March 6.

Christoff, P. (2010) 'Cold climate in Copenhagen: China and the United States at COP15', *Environmental Politics* 19(4): 637–656.

Christoff, P. and Eckersley, R. (2013) *Globalization and the Environment* (Lanham, MD: Rowman & Littlefield).

Chwieroth, J.M. (2007) 'Testing and measuring the role of ideas: The case of neoliberalism in the International Monetary Fund', *International Studies Quarterly* 51(1): 5–30.

Clarke, J.S. (2016) 'Where does the $8bn UN peacekeeping budget go?', *The Guardian*, April 6.

Clarke, M. (2017) 'The Belt and Road Initiative: China's new grand strategy?', *Asia Policy* 24(1): 71–79.

Clarke, M. (2018) 'In Xinjiang, China's "neo-totalitarian" turn is already a reality', *The Diplomat*, 41, April.

Cockett, R. (1994) *Thinking the Unthinkable: Think-Tanks and the Economic Counter-Revolution 1931–1983* (New York: Harper Collins).

Coe, N.M., Dicken, P., and Hess, M. (2008) 'Global production networks: Realizing the potential', *Journal of Economic Geography* 8(3): 271–295.

Cohen, J.E. (1995) *How Many People Can the Earth Support?* (New York: W.W. Norton).

Colander, D. (2011) 'How economists got it wrong: A nuanced account', *Critical Review: A Journal of Politics and Society* 23(1): 1–27.

Colander, D., Goldberg, M., Haas, A., Juselius, K., Kirman, A., Lux, T., and Sloth, B. (2009) 'The financial crisis and the systemic failure of the economics profession', *Critical Review: A Journal of Politics and Society* 21(2): 249–267.

Coll, S. (2017) 'The strongman problem, from Modi to Trump', *The New Yorker*, January 18.

Collier, P. (2007) *The Bottom Billion: Why the Poorest Countries Are Failing and What Can Be Done about It* (Oxford: Oxford University Press).

Cooley, A. (2015) 'Countering democratic norms', *Journal of Democracy* 26(3): 49–63.

Cooper, A.F. (2010) 'The G20 as an improvised crisis committee and/or a contested "steering committee" for the world', *International Affairs* 86(3): 741–757.

Cooper, A.F., Higgott, R.A., and Nossal, K.R. (1993) *Relocating Middle Powers: Australia and Canada in a Changing World Order* (Carlton: Melbourne University Press).

Cooper, D.A. (2011) 'Challenging contemporary notions of middle power influence: Implications of the proliferation security initiative for "middle power theory"', *Foreign Policy Analysis* 7(3): 317–336.

Cooper, N., Brady, E., Steen, H., and Bryce, R. (2016) 'Aesthetic and spiritual values of ecosystems: Recognising the ontological and axiological plurality of cultural ecosystem "services"', *Ecosystem Services* 21: 218–229.

Cox, R.W. (1986) 'Social forces, states and world orders: Beyond international relations theory', in R.O. Keohane (ed.), *Neorealism and Its Critics* (New York: Columbia University Press): 204–254.

Cox, R.W. (1987) *Production, Power, and World Order: Social Forces in the Making of History* (New York: Columbia University Press).

Crawford, B. (2007) *Power and German Foreign Policy: Embedded Hegemony in Europe* (London: Red Globe Press).

Crilly, R. (2017) 'Donald Trump pulls US out of Paris Climate Accord to "put American workers first"', *The Telegraph,* June 2.

Crook, C. (2018) 'Europe's Italian problem is bigger than Brexit', *Bloomberg*, May 21.

Crotty, J. (2009) 'Structural causes of the global financial crisis: A critical assessment of the "new financial architecture"', *Cambridge Journal of Economics* 33(4): 563–580.

Culpepper, P.D. and Reinke, R. (2014) 'Structural power and bank bailouts in the United Kingdom and the United States', *Politics & Society* 42(4): 427–454.

Cutler, A.C., Haufler, V., and Porter, T. (1999) 'Private authority and international affairs', in A.C. Cutler et al. (eds), *Private Authority and International Affairs* (New York: State University of New York): 3–28.

Daalder, I. and Kagan, R. (2016) 'The U.S. can't afford to end its global leadership role', *Foreign Policy in the U.S. Presidential Debates* 22.

Dai, X. and Renn, D. (2016) 'China and international order: The limits of integration', *Journal of Chinese Political Science* 21(2): 177–197.

Dauvergne, P. (1997) *Shadows in the Forest: Japan and the Politics of Timber in Southeast Asia* (Cambridge, MA: MIT Press).

Davenport, C. (2018) 'How Andrew Wheeler, the new acting E.P.A. chief, differs from Scott Pruitt', *New York Times*, July 5.

de Jonquieres, G. (2014) *The Problematic Politics of China's Economic Reform Plans* (No. 5/2014). Brussels.

de Soto, H. (2000) *The Mystery of Capital* (New York: Basic Books).

de Vries, C.E. (2018) *Euroscepticism and the Future of European Integration* (Oxford: Oxford University Press).

Deng, Y. (2008) *China's Struggle for Status: The Realignment of International Relations* (Cambridge: Cambridge University Press).

Dent, C.M. (2010) 'Free trade agreements in the Asia-Pacific a decade on: Evaluating the past, looking to the future', *International Relations of the Asia Pacific* 10(2): 201–245.

Desai, R.M., Olofsgård, A., and Yousef, T.M. (2009) 'The logic of authoritarian bargains', *Economics & Politics* 21(1): 93–125.

Deudney, D.H. (2007) *Bounding Power: Republican Security Theory from the Polis to the Global Village* (Princeton: Princeton University Press).

Deutsch, K. (1969) *Political Community and the North Atlantic Area: International Organization in the Light of Historical Experience* (Princeton: Princeton University Press).

Dicken, P. (2011) *Global Shift: Mapping the Changing Contours of the Global Economy*, 6th edn (New York: Guilford Press).

Diehl, P.F., Reifschneider, J., and Hensel, P.R. (1996) 'United Nations intervention and recurring conflict', *International Organization* 50(4): 683–700.

Dieter, H. (2008) 'ASEAN and the emerging monetary regionalism: A case of limited contribution', *The Pacific Review* 21(4): 489–506.

Dimitrov, R.S. (2016) 'The Paris agreement on climate change: Behind closed doors', *Global Environmental Politics* 16(3): 1–11.

Dinan, D., Nugent, N., and Paterson, W.E. (2017) *The European Union in Crisis* (London: Red Globe Press).

Dinda, S. (2004) 'Environmental Kuznets Curve hypothesis: A survey', *Ecological Economics* 49(4): 431–455.

Dirlik, A. (2012) 'The idea of a "Chinese model": A critical discussion', *China Information* 26(3): 277–302.

Dobbin, F., Simmons, B., and Garrett, G. (2007) 'The global diffusion of public policies: Social construction, coercion, competition, or learning?', *Annual Review of Sociology* 33: 449–472.

Donnan, S. (2018) 'US says China WTO membership was a mistake', *Financial Times*, January 20.

Donnelly, J. (2006) 'Sovereign inequalities and hierarchy in anarchy: American power and international society', *European Journal of International Relations* 12(2): 139–170.

Dower, J.W. (1986) *War without Mercy: Race and Power in the Pacific War* (New York: Pantheon).

Down, I. and Wilson, C.J. (2013) 'A rising generation of Europeans? Life-cycle and cohort effects on support for "Europe"', *European Journal of Political Research* 52(4): 431–456.

Doyle, M.W. (1986) *Empires* (Ithaca, NY: Cornell University Press).

Drew, E. (2017) 'The madness of king Donald', *Project Syndicate*, December 4.

Dreyer, J.T. (2015) 'The "Tianxia trope": Will China change the international system?', *Journal of Contemporary China* 24(96): 1015–1031.

Drezner, D.W. (2005) 'Globalization, harmonization, and competition: The different pathways to policy convergence', *Journal of European Public Policy* 12(5): 841–859.

Drezner, D.W. (2007) *All Politics Is Global: Explaining International Regulatory Regimes* (Princeton: Princeton University Press).

Dryzek, J.S. (1997) *The Politics of the Earth: Environmental Discourses* (Oxford: Oxford University Press).

Dryzek, J.S. (2012) 'Global civil society: The progress of post-Westphalian politics', *Annual Review of Political Science* 15(1): 101–119.

Dryzek, J.S., Downes, D., Hunold, C., Schlosberg, D., and Hernes, H.K. (2003) *Green States and Social Movements: Environmentalism in the United States, United Kingdom, Germany, and Norway* (Oxford: Oxford University Press).

Dueck, C. (2015) *The Obama Doctrine: American Grand Strategy Today* (Oxford: Oxford University Press).

Dunlap, R.E. and McRight, A.M. (2011) 'Organized climate change denial', in J.S. Dryzek, R.B. Norgaard, and D.

Schlosberg (eds), *The Oxford Handbook of Climate Change and Society* (Oxford: Oxford University Press): 144–160.

Dyer, G. (2010) *Climate Wars: The Fight for Survival as the World Overheats* (Oxford: Oneworld).

Easterly, W. (2006) *The White Man's Burden: Why the West's Efforts to Aid the Rest Have Done so Much Ill and so Little Good* (New York: Penguin).

Eaton, S. and Kostka, G. (2014) 'Authoritarian environmentalism undermined? Local leaders' time horizons and environmental policy implementation in China', *The China Quarterly* 218: 359–380.

Eccleston, R., Kellow, A., and Carroll, P. (2015) G20 endorsement in post crisis global governance: More than a toothless talking shop? *The British Journal of Politics & International Relations* 17(2): 298–317.

Eckersley, R. (2000) 'Deliberative democracy, ecological representation and risk', in M. Saward (ed.), *Democratic Innovation: Deliberation, Representation and Association* (London: Routledge): 117–132.

Eckersley, R. (2004) *The Green State: Rethinking Democracy and Sovereignty* (Cambridge, MA: MIT Press).

The Economist Intelligence Unit (2017) 'The road ahead: China's automobile market', October 2, www.eiu.com/industry/article/815926465/the-road-ahead-chinas-automobile-market/2017-10-02

The Economist (2013) 'The post industrial future is nigh', February 19.

The Economist (2018a) 'Decades of optimism about China's rise have been discarded', March 1.

The Economist (2018b) 'A threatened trade war between China and America may be on hold', May 24.

Economy, E.C. (2004) *The River Runs Black: The Environmental Challenge to China's Future* (Ithaca, NY: Cornell University Press).

Elvin, M. (1973) *The Pattern of the Chinese Past* (Stanford: Stanford University Press).

Embury-Dennis, T. (2018) 'Trump's environment chief Scott Pruitt suggests climate change could be good for humanity', *The Independent*, February 8.

Emmers, R. and Tan, S.S. (2011) 'The ASEAN regional forum and preventive diplomacy: Built to fail?', *Asian Security* 7(1): 44–60.

Emmerson, D. (1984) 'Southeast Asia: What's in a name?', *Journal of Southeast Asian Studies* 15(1): 1–21.

Erlanger, S. (2017) 'As Trump era arrives, a sense of uncertainty grips the world', *New York Times*, January 16.

Evans, P. (1995) *Embedded Autonomy: States and Industrial Transformation* (Princeton: Princeton University Press).

Fairbank, J.K. (1968) *The Chinese World Order: Traditional China's Foreign Relations* (Cambridge, MA: Harvard University Press).

Fairbank, J.K., Reischauer, E.O., and Craig, A.M. (1965) *East Asia: The Modern Transformation* (Boston: Houghton Mifflin).

Falk, R. (1993) 'The making of global citizenship', in J. Brecher et al. (eds), *Global Visions: Beyond New World Order* (Montreal: Black Rose Books): 39–50.

Farrell, H. (2018) 'Donald Trump says trade wars are "good, and easy to win." He's flat-out wrong', *Washington Post*, March 2.

Fawcett, L. (2017) 'Regions and regionalism', in M. Beeson and N. Bisley (eds), *Issues in 21st Century World Politics*, 3rd edn (London: Red Globe Press): 97–112.

Fawn, R. (2009) '"Regions" and their study: Where from, what for and where to?', *Review of International Studies* 35(Supplement S1): 5–34.

Felter, C. and Labrador, R.C. (2018) 'Brazil's corruption fallout', *Council on Foreign Relations*, www.cfr.org/backgrounder/brazils-corruption-fallout

Ferchen, M. (2013) 'Whose China model is it anyway? The contentious search for consensus', *Review of International Political Economy* 20(2): 390–420.

Ferguson, N. (2004) *Colossus: The Price of America's Empire* (New York: Penguin).

Ferguson, N. (2017) 'Another global financial crisis is imminent, and here are four reasons why', *South China Morning Post*, November 20.

Findlay, R. and O'Rourke, K. (2007) *Power and Plenty: Trade, War, and the World Economy* (Princeton: Princeton University Press).

Fischer, F. (1990) *Technocracy and the Politics of Expertise* (Newbury Park, CA: Sage).

Fisher, M. (2018) 'Turkey's crisis exposes the perils of strongman rule', *New York Times*, August 14.

Flannery, N. (2018) 'Is Trump really going to end NAFTA?', *Forbes*, March 12, www.forbes.com/sites/nathanielparish-flannery/2018/03/12/is-trump-really-going-to-end-nafta/#b78523e7a0e2

Fleming, S., Donnan, S., and Manson, K. (2018) 'Gary Cohn's departure leaves economic nationalists in the ascendant', *Financial Times*, March 8.

Folly, M.H. (1984) 'Breaking the vicious circle: Britain, the United States, and the genesis of the North Atlantic Treaty', *Diplomatic History* 12: 59–77.

Foot, R. (2014) '"Doing some things" in the Xi Jinping era: The United Nations as China's venue of choice', *International Affairs* 90(5): 1085–1100.

Foot, R., MacFarlane, S.N., and Mastanduno, M. (2003) 'Introduction', in R. Foot, S.N. MacFarlane, and M. Mastanduno (eds), *US Hegemony and International Organizations* (Oxford: Oxford University Press): 265–272.

Ford, J. (2018) 'Carillion shows the perils of capitalism without capital', *Financial Times*, January 22.

Forsythe, M. (2017) 'China aims to spend at least $360 billion on renewable energy by 2020', *New York Times*, January 5.

Foster, J.B., Clark, B., and York, R. (2010) *The Ecological Rift: Capitalism's War on the Earth* (New York: Monthly Review Press).

Foucault, M. (1980) *Power/Knowledge* (New York: Pantheon Books).

Foucault, M. (1991) 'Governmentality', in G. Burchell et al. (eds), *The Foucault Effect: Studies in Governality* (New York: Harvester Wheatsheaf).

Frank, A.G. (1998) *ReOrient: Global Economy in the Asian Age* (Berkeley: University of California Press).

Frank, A.G. and Gills, B.K. (1996) *The World System: Five Hundred Years or Five Thousand?* (London: Routledge).

Friedberg, A.L. (2011) *A Contest for Supremacy: China, America, and the Struggle for Mastery in Asia* (New York: W.W. Norton).

French, H.W. (2017) *Everything under the Heavens: How the Past Helps Shape China's Push for Global Power* (New York: Knopf).

Frieden, J.A. (2006) *Global Capitalism: Its Fall and Rise in the Twentieth Century* (New York: W.W. Norton).

Friedman, U. (2018) 'John Bolton's radical views on North Korea', *The Atlantic*, March 23.

Fröbel, F., Heinrichs, J., and Kreye, O. (1977) 'The tendency towards a new international division of labor: The utilization of a world-wide labor force for manufacturing oriented to the world market', *Review (Fernand Braudel Center)* 1(1): 73–88.

Froitzheim, M., Söderbaum, F., and Taylor, I. (2011) 'The limits of the EU as a peace and security actor in the Democratic Republic of the Congo', *Africa Spectrum* 46(3): 45–70.

Fuchs, D.A. (2007) *Business Power in Global Governance* (Boulder, CO: Lynne Rienner).

Fukuyama, F. (1992) *The End of History and the Last Man* (New York: Free Press).

Fukuyama, F. (2011) *The Origins of Political Order: From Prehuman Times to the French Revolution* (New York: Farrar, Strauss and Giroux).

Fukuyama, F. (2013) 'What is governance?', *Governance* 26(3): 347–368.

Gaddis, J.L. (1972) *The United States and the Origins of the Cold War, 1941–1947* (New York: Columbia University Press).

Gaddis, J.L. (1982) *Strategies of Containment: A Critical Appraisal of Postwar American Security Policy* (Oxford: Oxford University Press).

Gallagher, M.E. (2002) '"Reform and openness" – Why China's economic reforms have delayed democracy', *World Politics* 54(3): 338–372.

Gamble, A. (2009) 'The western ideology', *Government and Opposition* 44(1): 1–19.

Gao, C. (2017a) 'China, US fight over China's market economy status', *The Diplomat*, December 2.

Gao, C. (2017b) '"A community of shared future": One short phrase for UN, one big victory for China?', *The Diplomat*, November 5.

Gao, M. (2018) *Constructing China: Clashing Views of the People's Republic* (London: Pluto Press).

Gareis, S.B. (2012) *The United Nations*, 2nd edn (London: Palgrave Macmillan).

Garnaut, R. (2011) *The Garnaut Review 2011: Australia in the Global Response to Climate Change* (Cambridge: Cambridge University Press).

Gartzke, E. (2007) 'The capitalist peace', *American Journal of Political Science* 51(1): 166–191.

Gat, A. (2007) 'The return of authoritarian great powers', *Foreign Affairs* 86(4): 59–69.

Gaudreau, M. and Cao, H. (2015) 'Political constraints on adaptive governance', *Journal of Environment & Development* 24(4): 418–444.

Gereffi, G. (2005) 'The global economy: Organization, governance, and development', in N.J. Smelser and R. Swedberg (eds), *Handbook of Economic Sociology* (Princeton: Princeton University Press): 160–182.

Gereffi, G., Humphrey, J., and Sturgeon, T.J. (2005) 'The governance of global value chains', *Review of International Political Economy* 12(1): 78–104.

Germain, R.D. (2004) 'Globalising accountability within the international organisation of credit: Financial governance and the public sphere', *Global Society* 18(3): 217–242.

Gerschenkron, A. (1966) *Economic Backwardness in Historical Perspective* (Cambridge, MA: Belknap Press).

Gerzhoy, G. and Miller, N. (2016) 'Donald Trump thinks more countries should have nuclear weapons. Here's what the research says', *Washington Post*, April 6.

Gibbon, P., Bair, J., and Ponte, S. (2008) 'Governing global value chains: An introduction', *Economy and Society* 37(3): 315–338.

Gilley, B. (2014) *The Nature of Asian Politics* (Cambridge: Cambridge University Press).

Gills, J. and Schwartz, J. (2017) 'Earth sets a temperature record for the third straight year', *New York Times*, January 18.

Gilpin, R. (1981) *War and Change in World Politics* (Cambridge: Cambridge University Press).

Glanville, L. (2013) 'The myth of "traditional" sovereignty', *International Studies Quarterly* 57(1): 79–90.

Glassman, J. (2005) 'On the borders of Southeast Asia: Cold War geography and the construction of the other', *Political Geography* 24: 784–807.

Gleeson, D. (2015) 'Big pharma is the real winner in TPP plan', *The Drum*, ANBC News, June 11.

Gleick, P.H. (2014) 'Water, drought, climate change, and conflict in Syria', *Weather, Climate, and Society* 6(3): 331–340.

Glyn, A., Hughes, A., Lipietz, A., and Singh, A. (1990) 'The rise and fall of the golden age', in S. Marglin and J. Schor (eds), *The Golden Age of Capitalism: Reinterpreting the Postwar Experience* (Oxford: Clarendon Press): 39–125.

Goldstein, J.S. (2011) *Winning the War on War: The Decline of Armed Conflict Worldwide* (New York: Penguin).

Gomez, E.T. (2002) *Political Business in East Asia* (London: Routledge).

Gong, G.W. (1984) *The Standard of 'Civilisation' in International Society* (Oxford: Clarendon Press).

Gore, A. (2013) *The Future* (London: W.H. Allen).

Gourevitch, P.A. (2005) *Political Power and Control: The New Global Politics of Corporate Governance* (Princeton: Princeton University Press).

Gowa, J. (1983) *Closing the Gold Window: Domestic Politics and the End of Bretton Woods* (Ithaca, NY: Cornell University Press).

Grant, R.W. and Keohane, R.O. (2005) 'Accountability and abuses of power in world politics', *American Political Science Review* 99(1): 29–43.

Green, J.F. and Colgan, J. (2013) 'Protecting sovereignty, protecting the planet: State delegation to international organizations and private actors in environmental politics', *Governance* 26(3): 473–497.

Green, M.J. (2017) *By More than Providence: Grand Strategy and American Power in the Asia Pacific since 1783* (New York: Columbia University Press).

Grieco, J.M. (1999) 'Realism and regionalism: American power and German and Japanese institutional strategies during and after the Cold War', in E.B. Kapstein and M. Mastanduno (eds), *Unipolar Politics: Realism and State Strategies after the Cold War* (New York: Columbia University Press): 319–353.

Grigg, A. (2017) 'Security push likely to anger China', *Australian Financial Review*, April 21.

Grimes, W.W. (2009) *Currency and Contest in East Asia: The Great Power Politics of Financial Regionalism* (Ithaca, NY: Cornell University Press).

Guo, Y. (2012) 'Classes without class consciousness and class consciousness without classes: The meaning of class in the People's Republic of China', *Journal of Contemporary China* 21(77): 723–739.

Guttmann, R. (1994) *How Credit-Money Shapes the Economy: The United States in a Global System* (New York: M E Sharpe).

Haacke, J. (2003) *ASEAN's Diplomatic and Security Culture: Origins, Developments and Prospects* (London: Routledge Curzon).

Haas, R.N. (2018) 'Liberal world order, R.I.P', *Project Syndicate*, March 21.

Habermas, J. (1985) *The Theory of Communicative Action: Reason and the Rationalization of Society*, vol. 1 (Boston: Beacon Press).

Hacker, J.S. and Pierson, P. (2010) 'Winner-take-all politics: Public policy, political organization, and the precipitous rise of top incomes in the United States', *Politics Society* 38(2): 152–204.

Hall, P.A. (1989) *The Political Power of Economic Ideas: Keynesianism across Nations* (Princeton: Princeton University Press).

Hall, P.A. and Soskice, D. (eds) (2001) *Varieties of Capitalism: The Institutional Foundations of Comparative Advantage* (Oxford: Oxford University Press).

Halper, S. (2010) *The Beijing Consensus: How China's Authoritarian Model Will Dominate the Twenty-First Century* (New York: Basic Books).

Hamilton, C. (2010) *Requiem for a Species: Why We Resist the Truth about Climate Change* (London: Earthscan).

Hanlon, R.J. (2017) 'Thinking about the Asian Infrastructure Investment Bank: Can a China-led development bank improve sustainability in Asia?', *Asia & the Pacific Policy Studies* 4(3): 541–554.

Harpaz, M.D. (2016) 'China's coherence in international economic governance', *Journal of Chinese Political Science* 21, (2): 123–147.

Harvey, C. (2016) 'Research shows – yet again – that there's no scientific debate about climate change', *Wall Street Journal*, April 15.

Harvey, D. (2007) *A Brief History of Neoliberalism* (Oxford: Oxford University Press).

Harvey, D. (2010) *The Enigma of Capital and the Crises of Capitalism* (Oxford: Oxford University Press).

Hatch, W. and Yamamura, K. (1996) *Asia in Japan's Embrace: Building a Regional Production Alliance* (Cambridge: Cambridge University Press).

Haugen, R.A. (1995) *The New Finance: The Case Against Efficient Markets* (New York: Prentice Hall).

Hay, C. (2007) *Why We Hate Politics* (Cambridge: Polity Press).

He, B. and Warren, M.E. (2011) 'Authoritarian deliberation: The deliberative turn in Chinese political development', *Perspectives on Politics* 9(2): 269–289.

Heilbroner, R. (1990) 'Economics as ideology', in W. Samuels (ed.), *Economics as a Discourse: An Analysis of the Language of Economists* (Boston: Kluwer Academic Publishers): 101–116.

Heilmann, S. (2007) 'Policy experimentation in China's economic rise', *Studies in Comparative International Development* 43(1): 1–26.

Heilmann, S. and Perry, E.J. (2011) 'Embracing uncertainty: Guerrilla policy style and adaptive governance in China', in S. Heilmann and E.J. Perry (eds), *Mao's Invisible Hand: The Political Foundations of Adaptive Governance in China* (Cambridge, MA: Harvard University Press): 1–29.

Heilmann, S. and Shih, L. (2013) *The Rise of Industrial Policy in China, 1978–2012* (Trier: University of Trier).

Hein, J.E. and Jenkins, J.C. (2017) 'Why does the United States lack a global warming policy? The corporate inner circle versus public interest sector elites', *Environmental Politics* 26(1): 97–117.

Held, D. (2000) 'Regulating globalization? The reinvention of politics', *International Sociology* 15(2): 394–408.

Held, D. (2004) *Global Covenant: The Social Democratic Alternative to the Washington Consensus* (Cambridge: Polity Press).

Held, D. (2016) 'Climate change, migration and the cosmopolitan dilemma', *Global Policy* 7(2): 237–246.

Held, D., McGrew, A., Goldblatt, D., and Perraton, J. (1999) *Global Transformations: Politics, Economics and Culture* (Stanford: Stanford University Press).

Helleiner, E. (1994) *States and the Reemergence of Global Finance* (Ithaca, NY: Cornell University Press).

Helleiner, E. (2010) 'What role for the new Financial Stability Board? The politics of international standards after the crisis', *Global Policy* 1(3): 282–290.

Helleiner, E. and Pagliari, S. (2011) 'The end of an era in international financial regulation? A postcrisis research agenda', *International Organization* 65(1): 169–200.

Helm, D. (2008) 'Climate-change policy: Why has so little been achieved?', *Oxford Review of Economic Policy* 24(2): 211–238.

Hemmer, C. and Katzenstein, P.J. (2002) 'Why is there no NATO in Asia? Collective identity, regionalism, and the origins of multilateralism', *International Organization* 56(3): 575–607.

Henning, C.R. (2002) *East Asian Financial Cooperation* (Washington, DC: Institute for International Economics).

Hettne, B. (1999) 'Globalization and the new regionalism: The second great transformation', in B. Hettne et al. (eds), *Globalism and the New Regionalism* (London: Macmillan): 1–24.

Higgott, R.A. (1998) 'The Asian economic crisis: A study in the politics of resentment', *New Political Economy* 3(3): 333–356.

Hilde, T.C. (2012) 'Uncertainty and the epistemic dimension of democratic deliberation in climate change adaptation', *Democratization* 19(5): 889–911.

Hirst, P. and Thompson, G. (1996) *Globalization in Question* (Oxford: Polity Press).

Hobson, J.M. (1997) *The Wealth of States* (Cambridge: Cambridge University Press).

Hobson, J.M. (2004) *The Eastern Origins of Western Civilization* (Cambridge: Cambridge University Press).

Hobson, J.M. (2007) 'Reconstructing international relations through world history: Oriental globalization and the global–dialogic conception of inter-civilizational relations', *International Politics* 44(4): 414–430.

Hobson, J.M. (2012) *The Eurocentric Conception of World Politics: Western International Theory, 1760–2010* (Cambridge: Cambridge University Press).

Hobson, J.M. and Sharman, J.C. (2005) 'The enduring place of hierarchy in world politics: Tracing the social logics of hierarchy and political change', *European Journal of International Relations* 11(1): 63–98.

Hockenos, P. (2017) 'Germany is a coal-burning, gas-guzzling climate change hypocrite', *Foreign Policy*, November 13.

Hodge, A. (2017) 'Donald Trump is bulldozing allies of Obama's China pivot', *The Australian*, January 14.

Hogan, M.J. (1987) *The Marshall Plan: America, Britain, and the Reconstruction of Western Europe, 1947–1952* (Cambridge: Cambridge University Press).

Homer-Dixon, T.F. (1999) *Environment, Scarcity, and Violence* (Princeton: Princeton University Press).

Hopewell, K. (2018) 'What is "Made in China 2025" – And why is it a threat to Trump's trade goals?', *Washington Post*, May 3.

Hornby, L. (2017) 'Communist party asserts control over China Inc', *Financial Times*, October 4.

Howard, L.M. (2008) *UN Peacekeeping in Civil Wars* (Cambridge: Cambridge University Press).

Howland, D. (2015) 'An alternative mode of international order: The international administrative union in the nineteenth century', *Review of International Studies* 41(1): 161–183.

Hsü, I. (1983) *The Rise of Modern China*, 3rd edn (Hong Kong: Oxford University Press).

Hsueh, R. (2011) *China's Regulatory State: A New Strategy for Globalization* (Ithaca, NY: Cornell University Press).

Hsueh, R. (2016) 'State capitalism, Chinese-style: Strategic value of sectors, sectoral characteristics, and globalization', *Governance* 29(1): 85–102.

Huang, C. (2015) 'China seeks role for yuan in AIIB to extend currency's global reach', *South China Morning Post*, April 14.

Huang, K. (2018) 'Beijing warns of pro-independence turmoil in ties with Taipei in 2018', *South China Morning Post*, January 1.

Hughes, R. (2012) *The Fatal Shore: The Epic of Australia's Founding* (New York: Vintage).

Hung, H.F. (2009) 'America's head servant?', *New Left Review* 60(November–December): 5–25.

Hunt, E.K. (1979) *History of Economic Thought: A Critical Perspective* (Belmont, CA: Wadsworth).

Hunt, M.H. (1987) *Ideology and US Foreign Policy* (New Haven, CT: Yale University Press).

Huntington, S.P. (1968) *Political Order in Changing Societies* (New Haven, CT: Yale University Press).

Huntington, S.P. (1996) *The Clash of Civilizations and the Remaking of World Order* (New York: Simon & Schuster).

Hurrell, A. (1995) 'Explaining the resurgence of regionalism in world politics', *Review of International Studies* 21(4): 331–358.

Hurrell, A. (2001) 'Global inequality and international institutions', *Metaphilosophy* 32(1/2): 34–57.

Hurrell, A. (2005) 'Power, institutions, and the production of inequality', in M. Barnett and R. Duvall (eds), *Power in Global Governance* (Cambridge: Cambridge University Press): 33–58.

Hurrell, A. (2010) 'Regional powers and the global system from a historical perspective', in D. Flemes (ed.), *Regional Leadership in the Global System: Ideas, Interests, and Strategies of Regional Powers* (Farnham: Ashgate): 15–27.

Ikenberry, G.J. (1992) 'A world-economy restored – Expert consensus and the Anglo-American postwar settlement', *International Organization* 46(1): 289–321.

Ikenberry, G.J. (1996) 'The future of international leadership', *Political Science Quarterly* 111(3): 385–402.

Ikenberry, G.J. (2001) *After Victory: Institutions, Strategic Restraint, and the Rebuilding of Order after Major Wars* (Princeton: Princeton University Press).

Ikenberry, G.J. (2003) 'State power and the institutional bargain: America's ambivalent economic and security multilateralism', in R. Foot, S.N. MacFarlane, and M. Mastanduno (eds), *US Hegemony and International Organizations: The United States and Multilateral Institutions* (Oxford: Oxford University Press): 49–70.

Ikenberry, G.J. (2011) 'The future of the liberal world order', *Foreign Affairs* 90(3): 56–68.

Ikenberry, G.J. and Lim, D.J. (2017) *China's Emerging Institutional Statecraft: The Asian Infrastructure Investment Bank and the Prospects for Counter-Hegemony* (Washington, DC: Brookings Institute).

Ikenberry, G.J., Mastanduno, M., and Wohlforth, W.C. (2009) 'Introduction: Unipolarity, state behavior, and systemic consequences', *World Politics* 61(1): 1–27.

Ip, G. (2018) 'A costly, deadly obsession with coal', *Wall Street Journal*, June 6.

IPCC (International Panel on Climate Change). (2007) *Climate Change 2007: The Physical Science Basis* (Geneva: IPCC Secretariat).

Jackson, R. (1990) *Quasi-States: Sovereignty, International Relations and the Third World* (Cambridge: Cambridge University Press).

Jacques, M. (2009) *When China Rules the World: The Rise of the Middle Kingdom and the End of the Western World* (London: Allen Lane).

James, H. (2001) *The End of Globalization: Lessons from the Great Depression* (Cambridge, MA: Harvard University Press).

Jayasuriya, K. (2004) 'The new regulatory state and relational capacity', *Policy and Politics* 32(4): 487–501.

Jayasuriya, K. (2008) 'Regionalising the state: Political topography of regulatory regionalism', *Contemporary Politics* 14(1): 21–35.

Jayasuriya, K. (2009) 'Regulatory regionalism in the Asia-Pacific: Drivers, instruments and actors', *Australian Journal of International Affairs* 63(3): 335–347.

Jervis, R. (2008) 'Unipolarity', *World Politics* 61(1): 188–213.

Johnson, C. (1982) *MITI and the Japanese Miracle: The Growth of Industry Policy 1925–1975* (Stanford: Stanford University Press).

Johnston, A.I. (1995) *Cultural Realism: Strategic Culture and Grand Strategy in Chinese History* (Princeton: Princeton University Press).

Johnston, A.I. (2008) *Social States: China in International Relations, 1980–2000* (Princeton: Princeton University Press).

Jones, D.M. and Paasi, A. (eds) (2017) *Regional Worlds: Advancing the Geography of Regions* (London: Routledge).

Jones, D.M. and Smith, M.L.R. (2007) 'Making process, not progress: ASEAN and the evolving East Asian regional order', *International Security* 32(1): 148–184.

Jopson, B. (2017) 'With alumni in the White House, Goldman sees an opening', *Financial Times*, August 23.

Kahler, M. (2000) 'Legalization as a strategy: The Asia-Pacific case', *International Organization*, 54(3): 549–571.

Kahler, M. (2004) 'Defining accountability up', *Government and Opposition* 39(2): 142–158.

Kahler, M. (2010) 'Asia and the reform of global governance', *Asian Economic Policy Review* 5(2): 178–193.

Kahler, M. (2013) 'Rising powers and global governance: Negotiating change in a resilient status quo', *International Affairs* 89(3): 711–729.

Kang, D.C. (2010) 'Hierarchy and legitimacy in international systems: The tribute system in early modern East Asia', *Security Studies* 19(4): 591–622.

Kant, I. (2003 [1795]) *To Perpetual Peace: A Philosophical Sketch* (Indianapolis: Hackett Publishing).

Kapstein, E. (1994) *Governing the Global Economy: International Finance and the State* (Cambridge, MA: Harvard University Press).

Kastner, S.L. (2016) 'Is the Taiwan strait still a flash point? Rethinking the prospects for armed conflict between China and Taiwan', *International Security* 40(3): 54–92.

Katada, S.N., Roberts, C., and Armijo, L.E. (2017) 'The varieties of collective financial statecraft: The BRICS and China', *Political Science Quarterly* 132(3): 403–433.

Katz, R. (1998) *Japan: The System That Soured* (Armonk, NY: M.E. Sharpe).

Kaplan, R.D. (2012) *The Revenge of Geography: What the Map Tells US about the Coming Conflicts and the Battle against Fate* (New York: Random House).

Katzenstein, P.J. (1996) *Cultural Norms and National Security: Police and Military in Postwar Japan* (Ithaca, NY: Cornell University Press).

Katzenstein, P. and Tsujinaka, Y. (1995) '"Bullying", "buying", and "binding": US-Japanese transnational relations and domestic structures', in T. Risse-Kappen (ed.), *Bringing Transnational Actors Back In: Non-State Actors, Domestic Structures and International Institutions* (Cambridge: Cambridge University Press): 79–111.

Kaufman, A.A. (2010) 'The "century of humiliation," then and now: Chinese perceptions of the international order', *Pacific Focus* 25(1): 1–33.

Keane, J. (2003) *Global Civil Society?* (Cambridge: Cambridge University Press).

Kehoe, J. (2018) 'US report: China "debt trap" on Australia's doorstep', *Australian Financial Review*, May 13.

Kenis, P. and Schneider, V. (1991) 'Policy networks and policy analysis: Scrutinizing a new analytical toolbox', in B. Marin and R. Mayntz (eds), *Policy Networks: Empirical Evidence and Theoretical Considerations* (Boulder, CO: Westview): 25–59.

Kennan, G. (1997) 'The sources of Soviet conduct', in J.F. Hoge and F. Zakaria (eds), *The American Encounter: The United States and the Making of the Modern World* (New York: Basic Books): 155–169.

Kennedy, S. (2010) 'The myth of the Beijing Consensus', *Journal of Contemporary China* 19(65): 461–477.

Kennedy, S. (2012) 'China in global governance: What kind of status quo power?', in S. Kennedy, and S. Cheng, (eds),

The Growing Role of Chinese in Global Governance (Bloomington, IN: Research Center for Chinese Politics and Business): 9–21.

Keohane, R.O. (1989) 'International institutions: Two approaches', *International Studies Quarterly* 32(4): 379–396.

Keohane, R.O. and Nye, J.S. (1977) *Power and Interdependence: World Politics in Transition* (Boston: Little, Brown & Co).

Keohane, R.O. and Victor, D.G. (2011) 'The regime complex for climate change', *Perspectives on Politics* 9(1): 7–23.

Keynes, J.M. (1958) *General Theory of Employment, Interest and Money* (New York: Harcourt Brace).

Keynes, J.M. (2004 [1919]) *The Economic Consequences of the Peace* (New York: Dover).

Khanna, P. (2016) 'Rise of the Titans', *Foreign Policy*, March/April (No. 217): 50–55.

Kimmelmann, M. (2017) 'Rising waters threaten China's rising cities', *The New York Times*, April 7.

Kindleberger, C.P. (1973) *The World in Depression 1929–1939* (Berkeley: University of California Press).

Kirshner, J. (2008) 'Dollar primacy and American power: What's at stake?', *Review of International Political Economy* 15(3): 418–438.

Kirshner, J. (2013) 'Bringing them all back home? Dollar diminution and U.S. power', *The Washington Quarterly* 36(3): 27–45.

Kirshner, J. (2014) *American Power after the Financial Crisis* (Ithaca, NY: Cornell University Press).

Kivimäki, T. (2014) *The Long Peace of East Asia* (Farnham: Ashgate).

Klein, B.P. and Cukier, K.N. (2009) 'Tamed tigers, distressed dragon', *Foreign Affairs* 88(4): 8–16.

Kohli, A. (2004) *State-Directed Development: Political Power and Industrialization in the Global Periphery* (Cambridge: Cambridge University Press).

Konczal, M. (2018) 'Why are Democrats helping Trump dismantle Dodd-Frank?', *New York Times*, March 6.

Kooiman, J. (1993) *Modern Governance: New Government-Society Interactions* (London: Sage).

Koppel, J.G.S. (2010) *World Rule: Accountability, Legitimacy, and the Design of Global Governance* (Chicago: University of Chicago Press).

Kovel, J. (2007) *The Enemy of Nature: The End of Capitalism or the End of the World?* 2nd edn (London: Zed Books).

Krasner, S.D. (1999) *Sovereignty: Organized Hypocrisy* (Princeton: Princeton University Press).

Krastev, Ivan (2016) 'Why Putin tolerates corruption', *New York Times*, May 15.

Krauthammer, C. (1990–1991) 'The unipolar moment', *Foreign Affairs* 70(1): 23–33.

Kreppel, A. (2006) 'Understanding the European Parliament from a federalist perspective: The legislatures of the USA and EU compared', *Comparative Federalism: The European Union and the United States* 245–274.

Kröger, S. (2007) 'The end of democracy as we know it? The legitimacy deficits of bureaucratic social policy governance', *European Integration* 29(5): 565–582.

Kruathammer, C. (2009) 'Decline is a choice: The new liberalism and the end of American ascendancy', *Weekly Standard* 15(5).

Krugman, P. (2012) 'Economics in crisis', *New York Times*, March 5.

Kunz, D.B. (1997) *Butter and Guns: America's Cold War Economic Diplomacy* (New York: Free Press).

Kupchan, C.A. and Trubowitz, P.L. (2007) 'Dead center: The demise of liberal internationalism in the United States', *International Security* 32(2): 7–44.

Kuttner, R. (2018) *Can Democracy Survive Capitalism?* (New York: W.W. Norton).

LaFeber, W. (1997) *The Clash: US-Japanese Relations Throughout History* (New York: W.W. Norton).

Lake, D.A. (1999) *Entangling Relations: America's Foreign Policy and Its Century* (Princeton: Princeton University Press).

Lake, D.A. (2003) 'The new sovereignty in international relations', *International Studies Quarterly* 5: 303–323.

Lake, D.A. (2010) 'Rightful rules: Authority, order, and the foundations of global governance', *International Studies Quarterly* 54(3): 587–613.

Lamy, P. (2012) 'Global governance: From theory to practice', *Journal of International Economic Law* 15(3): 721–728.

Lardy, N.R. (2002) *Integrating China into the Global Economy* (Washington, DC: Brookings Institute).

Latham, M.E. (2010) *The Right Kind of Revolution: Modernization, Development, and US Foreign Policy from the Cold War to the Present* (Ithaca, NY: Cornell University Press).

Latham, R. (1997) *The Liberal Moment: Modernity, Security, and the Making of Postwar International Order* (New York: Columbia University Press).

Layne, C. (2012) 'This time it's real: The end of unipolarity and the Pax Americana', *International Studies Quarterly* 56(1): 203–213.

Layne, C. (2017) 'The US foreign policy establishment and grand strategy: How American elites obstruct strategic adjustment', *International Politics* 54(3): 260–275.

Leakey, R.E. and Lewin, R. (1995) *The Sixth Extinction: Patterns of Life and the Future of Humankind* (New York: Doubleday).

Leffler, M.P. (1992) *A Preponderance of Power: National Security, the Truman Administration, and the Cold War* (Stanford: Stanford University Press).

Legro, J.W. (2005) *Rethinking the World: Great Power Strategies and International Order* (Ithaca, NY: Cornell University Press).

Lenz, T. and Marks, G. (2016) 'Regional institutional design', in T.A. Borzel and T. Risse (eds), *The Oxford Handbook of Comparative Regionalism* (Oxford: Oxford University Press): 513–537.

Levi-Faur, D. (2005) 'The global diffusion of regulatory capitalism', *The ANNALS of the American Academy of Political and Social Science* 598(1): 12–32.

Levine, D.J. and Barder, A.D. (2014) 'The closing of the American mind: "American School" International Relations and the state of grand theory', *European Journal of International Relations* 20(4): 863–888.

Li, Q. and Reuveny, R. (2006) 'Democracy and environmental degradation', *International Studies Quarterly* 50(4): 935–956.

Li, S., Sato, H., and Sicular, T. (2013) *Rising Inequality in China: Challenges to a Harmonious Society* (Cambridge: Cambridge University Press).

Li, X., Brodsgaard, K.E., and Jacobsen, M. (2009) 'Redefining Beijing Consensus: Ten economic principles', *China Economic Journal* 2(3): 297–311.

Lieberthal, K.G. (1992) 'Introduction: The "fragmented authoritarianism" model and its limitations', in K.G. Lieberthal and D.M. Lampton (eds), *Bureaucracy, Politics, and Decision Making in Post-Mao China* (Berkeley: University of California Press): 1–30.

Liff, A.P. and Ikenberry, G.J. (2015) 'Racing toward tragedy? China's rise, military competition in the Asia Pacific, and the security dilemma', *International Security* 39(2): 52–91.

Lin, J.Y. (2011) 'China and the global economy', *China Economic Journal* 4(1): 1–14.

Lin, J.Y. (2012) 'From flying geese to leading dragons: New opportunities and strategies for structural transformation in developing countries', *Global Policy* 3(4): 397–409.

Lincoln, E.J. (1990) *Japan's Unequal Trade* (Washington, DC: Brookings Institute).

Lind, J.M. (2010) *Sorry States: Apologies in International Politics* (Ithaca, NY: Cornell University Press).

Lindsay, J.M. (2011) 'George W. Bush, Barack Obama and the future of US global leadership', *International Affairs* 87(4): 765–779.

Linklater, A. (1998) *The Transformation of Political Community* (Oxford: Polity Press).

Lipschutz, R.D. (2005) *Globalisation, Governmentality and Global Politics* (London: Routledge).

Liu, G. (2017) *Chinese Foreign Policy in Transition* (London: Routledge).

Liu, M. (2015) *The China Dream: Great Power Thinking and Strategic Posture in the Post-American Era* (New York: CN Times).

Liu, X. (2016) 'China will play a greater part in a world shared by all', *The Telegraph*, January 20.

Lo, K. (2015) 'How authoritarian is the environmental governance of China?', *Environmental Science & Policy* 52: 152–159.

Lock, E. (2010) 'Refining strategic culture: Return of the second generation', *Review of International Studies* 36(3): 685–708.

Lovett, A.W. (1996) 'The United States and the Schuman Plan. A study in French diplomacy 1950–1952', *The Historical Journal* 39(2): 425–455.

Lucas, E. (2014) *The New Cold War: Putin's Russia and the Threat to the West* (London: Macmillan).

Luce, E. (2017) *The Retreat of Western Liberalism* (New Yok: Atlantic Monthly Press).

Luce, E. (2018) 'America's political journey into tribalism', *Financial Times*, January 24.

Luck, E. (2003) 'American exceptionalism and international organizations: Lessons from the 1990s', in R. Foot, N. MacFarlane, and M. Mastanduno (eds), *US Hegemony and the International Organization* (Oxford: Oxford University Press): 25–48.

Lukin, A. (2018) *China and Russia: The New Rapprochement* (Cambridge: Polity Press).

Lundestad, G. (1986) 'Empire by invitation? The United States and Western Europe, 1945–1952', *Journal of Peace Research* 23(3): 263–277.

Luttwak, E. (1990) 'From geopolitics to geoeconomics', *The National Interest* (Summer): 17–23.

Luttwak, E.N. (1993) *Endangered American Dream: How to Stop the United States from Becoming a Third-World Country and How to Win the Geo-Economic Struggle for Industrial Supremacy* (New York: Simon and Schuster).

Lynas, M. (2008) *Six Degrees: Our Future on a Hotter Planet* (London: Harper).

MacFarlane, N. and Menon, A. (2014) 'The EU and Ukraine', *Survival* 56(3): 95–101.

Maddison, A. (2007) *Contours of the World Economy, 1–2030 AD* (Oxford: Oxford University Press).

Maier, C.S. (1981) 'The two postwar eras and the conditions for stability in twentieth-century Western Europe', *American Historical Review*, 86(2): 327–352.

Malone, D. (2004) *The UN Security Council: From the Cold War to the 21st Century* (Boulder, CO: Lynne Rienner).

Manger, M.S. (2012) 'Vertical trade specialization and the formation of North-South PTAs', *World Politics*, 64(4): 622–658.

Mann, J. (2017) 'The adults in the room', *New York Review of Books*.

Mann, M. (1993) *The Sources of Social Power: The Rise of Classes and Nation States, 1760–1914* (Cambridge: Cambridge University Press).

Mann, T.E. and Ornstein, N.J. (2012) *It's Even Worse than It Looks: How the American Constitutional System Collided with the New Politics of Extremism* (New York: Basic Books).

Manners, I. (2002) 'Normative power Europe: A contradiction in terms?',

JCMS: Journal of Common Market Studies 40(2): 235–258.

Manson, K. and Fleming, S. (2018) 'Trump replaces McMaster with Bolton in day of turmoil', *Financial Times*, March 23.

Markusen, A. (1992) 'Dismantling the cold war economy', *World Policy Journal* 9(3): 389–399.

Marsh, D. and Smith, M. (2000) 'Understanding policy networks: Towards a dialectical approach', *Political Studies* 48(1): 4–21.

Martin, P. (2005) 'A global answer to global problems', *Foreign Affairs* 84(3): 2–6.

Mastanduno, M. (1998) 'Economics and security in statecraft and scholarship', *International Organization* 52(4): 825–854.

Mastanduno, M. (2009) 'System maker and privilege taker: U.S. power and the international political economy', *World Politics* 61(1): 121–154

Mattis, J. (2018) *Sharpening the American Military's Competitive Edge* (Washington, DC: Department of Defense).

Mattli, W. (1999) *The Logic of Regional Integration: Europe and Beyond* (Cambridge: Cambridge University Press).

Mattli, W. and Woods, N. (2009) 'In whose benefit? Explaining regulatory change in global politics', in W. Mattli and N. Woods (eds), *The Politics of Global Regulation* (Princeton: Princeton University Press): 1–43.

Mazower, M. (2012) *Governing the World: The History of an Idea* (London: Allen Lane).

McCarthy (2018) 'Does the US really need a huge boost in military spending?', *The Guardian*, February 9.

McDougall, W.A. (1997) *Promised Land, Crusader State: The American Encounter with the World since 1776* (Boston: Mariner Books).

McGregor, R. (2010) *The Party: The Secret World of China's Communist Rulers* (New York: HarperCollins).

McGregor, R. (2017) *Asia's Reckoning: China, Japan, and the Fate of US Power in the Pacific Century* (New York: Viking).

McLannahan, B. (2017) 'Goldman Sachs: Occupying Washington again', *Financial Times*, January 20.

McMahon, D. (2018) *China's Great Wall of Debt: Shadow Banks, Ghost Cities, Massive Loans, and the End of the Chinese Miracle* (Boston: Houghton Mifflin Harcourt)

McMahon, R.J. (1999) *The Limits of Empire: The United States and Southeast Asia since World War II* (New York: Columbia University Press).

McMichael, P. (2012) *Development and Social Change: A Global Perspective*, 5th edn (Newbury Park, CA: Pine Forge Press).

McNeil, W.H. (1982) *The Pursuit of Power: Technology, Armed Force, and Society since A.D. 1000* (Chicago: University of Chicago Press).

Mead, W.R. (2001) *Special Providence: American Foreign Policy and How It Changed the World* (New York: Alfred Knopf).

Mead, W.R. (2018) 'Kim needs the clout nuclear arms bring to his hermit kingdom', *The Australian*, April 26.

Meadows, D.H., Randers, J., and Meadows, D. (1974) *The Limits to Growth: A Report for the Club of Rome's Project on the Predicament of Mankind* (New York: Universe Books).

Mearsheimer, J.J. (1994/95) 'The false promise of institutions', *International Security* 19(3): 5–49.

Mearsheimer, J.J. (2010) 'The gathering storm: China's challenge to US power in Asia', *The Chinese Journal of International Politics* 3(4): 381–396.

Medrano, J.D. (2010) *Framing Europe: Attitudes to European Integration in Germany, Spain, and the United Kingdom* (Princeton: Princeton University Press).

Menon, A. (2008) *Europe: The State of the Union* (London: Atlantic Books).

Mertha, A. (2009) '"Fragmented authoritarianism 2.0": Political pluralization in the Chinese policy process', *The China Quarterly* 200: 995–1012.

Mertha, A. (2012) 'Domestic institutional challenges facing China's leadership on the eve of the 18th Party Congress', *Asia Policy* 14(1): 1–20.

Meseguer, C. (2005) 'Policy learning, policy diffusion, and the making of a new order', *The ANNALS of the American Academy of Political and Social Science* 598(1): 102–124.

Migdal, J.S. (1988) *Strong States and Weak Societies: State-Society Relations and State Capabilities in the Third World* (Princeton: Princeton University Press).

Miller, J. (2018) 'Trump's tax cuts incentivized corporate offshoring', *The American Prospect*, March 1.

Miller, T. (2017) *China's Asian Dream: Empire Building along the New Silk Road* (London: Zed Books).

Milliken, J. and Krause, K. (2002) 'State failure, state collapse, and state reconstruction: Concepts, lessons and strategies', *Development and Change* 33(5): 753–774.

Milward, A.S. (1984) *The Reconstruction of Western Europe, 1945–51* (London: Routledge).

Minsky, H.P. (1986) *Stabilizing the Unstable Economy* (New Haven, CT: Yale University Press).

Mitchell, A. and Diamond, L. (2018) 'China's surveillance state should scare everyone', *The Atlantic*, February 2.

Mitzen, J. (2013) *Power in Concert: The Nineteenth-century Origins of Global Governance* (Chicago: University of Chicago Press).

Mo, Z. (2018) 'Under neo-totalitarianism, there is no "civil society" in China', *China Change*, February 4.

Modelski, G. and Thompson, W. (1996) *Leading Sectors and World Powers: The Coevolution of Global Economics and Politics* (Columbia: University of South Carolina Press).

Mokyr, J. (2017) *A Culture of Growth: The Origins of the Modern Economy* (Princeton: Princeton University Press).

Montinola, G., Qian, Y., and Weingast, B.R. (1995) 'Federalism, Chinese style – the political basis for economic success in China', *World Politics* 48(1): 50–81.

Moran, D.D., Lenzen, M., Kanemoto, K., and Geschke, A. (2013) 'Does ecologically unequal exchange occur?', *Ecological Economics* 89: 177–186.

Moravcsik, A. (1991) 'Negotiating the Single European Act: National interests and conventional statecraft in the European Community', *International Organization* 45(1): 19–56.

Moravcsik, A. (1997) 'Taking preferences seriously: A liberal theory of international politics', *International Organization* 51(04): 513–553.

Morgenthau, H.J. (1973) *Politics Among Nations*, vol. 4 (New York: Knopf).

Morris-Suzuki, T. (1996) *The Technological Transformation of Japan: From the Seventeenth to the Twenty-First Century*, vol. 24 (London: Routledge).

Mozur, P. (2017) 'China's top ideologue calls for tight control of internet', *New York Times*, December 3.

Mueller, J. (2010) 'Capitalism, peace, and the historical movement of ideas', *International Interactions* 36(2): 169–184.

Mueller, J.E. (1989) *Retreat from Doomsday: The Obsolescence of Major War* (New York: Basic Books).

Mügge, D. (2011) 'Limits of legitimacy and the primacy of politics in financial governance', *Review of International Political Economy* 18(1): 52–74.

Murphy, C.N. (2000) 'Global governance: Poorly done and poorly understood', *International Affairs* 76(4): 789–803.

Myers, S.L. (2018a) 'With Xi's power grab, China joins new era of strongmen', *New York Times*, February 26.

Myers, S.L. (2018b) 'Trump's trade threats put China's leader on the spot', *New York Times*, March 22.

Nagy, S.R. (2016) 'What China expects from Trump', *Asia and the Pacific Policy Society*, December 2.

Narine, S. (2002) *Explaining ASEAN: Regionalism in Southeast Asia* (Boulder, CO: Lynne Rienner).

Naughton, B. (2010) 'China's distinctive system: Can it be a model for others?', *Journal of Contemporary China* 19(65): 437–460.

Naughton, B. (2015) 'China and the two crises', in T.J. Pempel and K. Tsunekawa (eds), *Two Crises, Different Outcomes: East Asia And Global Finance* (Ithaca, NY: Cornell University Press): 110–134.

Navarro, P. (2006) *The Coming China Wars: Where They Will Be Fought and How They Will Be Won* (Upper Saddle River, NJ: FT Press).

Navarro, P. (2018) 'Donald Trump is standing up for American interests', *Financial Times*, April 9.

Newell, P. (2012) *Globalization and the Environment: Capitalism, Ecology and Power* (Cambridge: Polity Press).

Newman, E. (2010) 'Critical human security studies', *Review of International Studies* 36(01): 77–94.

Nonini, D.M. (2008) 'Is China becoming neoliberal?', *Critique of Anthropology* 28(2): 145–176.

North, D.C. and Thomas, R.P. (1973) *The Rise of the Western World: A New Economic History* (Cambridge: Cambridge University Press).

North, D.C., Wallis, J.J., and Weingast, B.R. (2009) *Violence and Social Orders: A Conceptual Framework for Interpreting Recorded Human History* (New York: Cambridge University Press).

Northedge, F.S. (1986) *The League of Nations: Its Life and Times, 1920–1946* (Leicester: Leicester University Press).

Nye, J.S. (1990) *Bound to Lead: The Changing Nature of American Power* (New York: Basic Books).

O'Brien, F. (2017) 'China to overtake US economy by 2032 as Asian might builds: Report', *Sydney Morning Herald*, December 26.

O'Brien, R. and Williams, M. (2010) *Global Political Economy: Evolution and Dynamics*, 3rd edn (London: Red Globe Press).

O'Connor, J. (1979) *The Fiscal Crisis of the State* (New Brunswick, NJ: Transaction Publishers).

O'Hanlon, M.E. (2015) 'Dollars at work: What defense spending means for the U.S. economy', *Brooking Institute*, August 19.

Ohmae, K. (1990) *The Borderless World: Power and Strategy in the Interlinked Economy* (New York: Harper Business).

Oliver, C. (2016) 'Enthusiasm for EU in sharp decline throughout Europe, not just UK', *Financial Times*, June 8.

O'Neill, K. (2017) *The Environment and International Relations* (Cambridge: Cambridge University Press).

Oreskes, N. and Conway, E.M. (2010) *Merchants of Doubt: How a Handful of Scientists Obscured the Truth on Issues from Tobacco Smoke to Global Warming* (New York: Bloomsbury Press).

Organski, A.F.K. (1968) *World Politics* (New York: Knopf).

Ortmann, S. and Thompson, M.R. (2014) 'China's obsession with Singapore: Learning authoritarian modernity', *The Pacific Review* 27(3): 433–455.

Osnos, E. (2018) 'Trump vs. the "Deep State"', *The New Yorker*, May 21.

OUSTR (Office of the United States Trade Representative. (2018) US-China Trade Facts (Washington), https://ustr.gov/countries-regions/china-mongolia-taiwan/peoples-republic-china

Ozgercin, K. (2012) 'Seeing like the BIS on capital rules: Institutionalising self-regulation in global finance', *New Political Economy* 17(1): 97–116.

Paasi, A. (2003) 'Region and place: Regional identity in question', *Progress in Human Geography* 27(4): 475–485.

Page, J., Wei, L., and Wong, C.H. (2017) 'China digs in heels, girds for Trump's unpredictability', *Wall Street Journal*, January 16.

Panda, A. (2018) 'US nuclear weapons modernization', *Council on Foreign Relations*, February 7.

Pant, H. (2013) 'The BRICS fallacy', *The Washington Quarterly* 36(3): 91–105.

Parenti, C. (2011) *Tropic of Chaos: Climate Change and the New Geography of Violence* (New York: Nation Books).

Park, J. (2013) 'Political rivals and regional leaders: Dual identities and Sino-Japanese relations within East Asian cooperation', *The Chinese Journal of International Politics* 6(1): 85–107.

Paterson, M. (2009) 'Post-hegemonic climate politics?', *British Journal of Politics and International Relations* 11: 140–158.

Patrick, S. (2009) 'Prix fixe and à la Carte: Avoiding false multilateral choices', *The Washington Quarterly* 32(4): 77–95.

Patrick, S. (2014) 'The unruled world: The case for good enough global governance', *Foreign Affairs* 93(1): 58–73.

Patrick, S.P. (2012) '(Almost) everyone agrees: The U.S. should ratify the Law of the Sea Treaty', *The Atlantic*, June 10.

Patton, M. (2016) 'China's economy will overtake the U.S. in 2018', *Forbes*, April 29.

Pauly, L.W. (1997) *Who Elected the Bankers? Surveillance and Control in the World Economy* (Ithaca, NY: Cornell University Press).

Peck, J. and Zhang, J. (2013) 'A variety of capitalism ... with Chinese characteristics?', *Journal of Economic Geography* 13(3): 357–396.

Pei, M. (2006) *China's Trapped Transition: The Limits of Developmental Autocracy* (Cambridge, MA: Harvard University Press).

Pei, M. (2016) *China's Crony Capitalism* (Cambridge, MA: Harvard University Press).

Peterson, J. (2017) 'Juncker's political European Commission and an EU in crisis', *Journal of Common Market Studies* 55(2): 349–367.

Phillips, T., Holmes, O., and Bowcott, O. (2016) 'Beijing rejects tribunal's ruling in South China Sea case', *The Guardian*, July 13.

Pierson, P. (2000) 'Increasing returns, path dependence, and the study of politics', *American Political Science Review* 94(2): 251–267.

Pieterse, J.N. (2004) *Globalization or Empire?* (London: Routledge).

Piketty, T. (2014) *Capital in the Twenty-First Century* (Cambridge, MA: Belknap Press).

Pinker, S. (2012) *The Better Angels of Our Nature: Why Violence Has Declined* (New York: Viking).

Pinker, S. (2018) *Enlightenment Now: The Case for Reason, Science, Humanism, and Progress* (New York: Viking).

Plesch, D. and Weiss, T. (2015) '1945's lesson: "Good enough" global governance ain't good enough', *Global Governance* 21: 197–204.

Polidano, C. (2000) 'Measuring public sector capacity', *World Development* 28(5): 805–822.

Polillo, S. and Guillen, M.F. (2005) 'Globalization pressures and the state: The worldwide spread of central bank independence', *American Journal of Sociology* 110(6): 1764–1802.

Pollard, R.A. (1985) *Economic Security and the Origins of the Cold War, 1945–1950* (New York: Columbia University Press).

Pomeranz, K. and Topik, S. (1999) *The World that Trade Created: Society, Culture, and the World Economy* (Armonk, NY: M.E. Sharpe).

Porter, T. (2002) 'Politics, institutions, constructivism and the merging international regime for financial regulation', *The Review of Policy Research* 19(1): 54–79.

Posen, B.R. (2003) 'Command of the commons: The military foundation of US hegemony', *International Security* 28(1): 5–46.

Prebisch, R. (1962) 'The economic development of Latin America and its principal problems', *Economic Bulletin for Latin America* 7(1): 1–22.

Przeworski, A., Alvarez, M.E., Cheibub, J.A., and Limongi, F. (2000) *Democracy and Development: Political Institutions and Well-Being in the World, 1950–1990* (Cambridge: Cambridge University Press).

Pyle, K.B. (2007) *Japan Rising: The Resurgence of Japanese Power and Purpose* (New York: Public Affairs).

Qi, Y. and Lu, J. (2018) 'China's coal consumption has peaked', *Brookings Institution*, January 22.

Qi, Y. and Zhang, L. (2014) 'Local environmental enforcement constrained by central-local relations in China', *Environmental Policy and Governance* 24(3): 204–215.

Qin, Y. (2009) 'Development of international relations theory in China', *International Studies* 46(1–2): 185–201.

Qin, Y. (2011) 'Development of international relations theory in China: Progress through debates', *International Relations of the Asia-Pacific* 11(2): 231–257.

Qin, Y. (2018) *A Relational Theory of World Politics* (Cambridge: Cambridge University Press).

Qiu, J. (2006) 'The politics of history and historical memory in China-Japan relations', *Journal of Chinese Political Science* 11(1): 25–53.

Quahe, S. (2018) 'EU in crisis: What implications for climate and energy policy?', *Asia Europe Journal* 16(2): 169–182.

Quiggin, J. (2012) 'What have we learned from the Global Financial Crisis?', *Australian Economic Review* 44(4): 355–365.

Rachman, G. (2018a) 'Mid-sized powers must unite to preserve the world order', *Financial Times*, May 28.

Rachman, G. (2018b) 'America rejects the world it made', *Financial Times*, January 29.

Radaelli, C.M. (2017) *Technocracy in the European Union* (London: Routledge).

Ramo, J.C. (2004) *The Beijing Consensus* (London: The Foreign Policy Centre).

Ravalliona, M. (2008) 'Are there lessons for Africa from China's success against poverty?', *World Development* 37(2): 303–313.

Ravenhill, J. (2000) 'APEC adrift: Implications for economic regionalism in Asia and the Pacific', *The Pacific Review* 13(2): 319–333.

Reilly, J. (2014) 'A wave to worry about? Public opinion, foreign policy and China's anti-Japan protests', *Journal of Contemporary China* 23(86): 197–215.

Reinhart, C.M. and Rogoff, K.S. (2009) *This Time Is Different: Eight Centuries of Financial Folly* (Princeton: Princeton University Press).

Reinicke, W.H. (1998) *Global Public Policy: Governing Without Government?* (Washington, DC: Brookings Institute).

Reus-Smit, C. (2012) 'International relations, irrelevant? Don't blame theory', *Millennium – Journal of International Studies* 40(3): 525–540.

Rhodes, E. (2003) 'The imperial logic of Bush's liberal agenda', *Survival* 45(1): 131–154.

Rhodes, R. (1997) *Understanding Governance: Policy Networks, Governance, Reflexivity and Accountability* (Buckingham: Open University Press).

Ribot, J. (2002) *Democratic Decentralization of Natural Resources: Institutionalizing Popular Participation* (Washington, DC: World Resources Institute).

Ripsman, N.M. (2005) 'Two stages of transition from a region of war to a region of peace: Realist transition and liberal endurance', *International Studies Quarterly* 49(4): 669–693.

Risse-Kappen, T. (1994) 'Ideas do not float freely: Transnational coalitions, domestic structures, and the end of the cold war', *International Organization* 48(2): 185–214.

Roberts, J.T. and Parks, B.C. (2007) *A Climate of Injustice: Global Inequality, North-South Politics, and Climate Policy* (Cambridge, MA: MIT Press).

Robinson, W.I. (2004) *A Theory of Global Capitalism: Production, Class, and State in A Transnational World* (Baltimore: Johns Hopkins University Press).

Rodan, G. (2009) 'New modes of political participation and Singapore's nominated members of parliament', *Government and Opposition* 44(4): 438–462.

Rodrik, D. (1997) *Has Globalization Gone Too Far?* (Washington, DC: Institute of International Economics).

Rodrik, D. (2006) 'Goodbye Washington consensus? Hello Washington confusion? A review of the World Bank's economic growth in the 1990s: Learning from a decade of reform', *Journal of Economic Literature* 44(4): 973–987.

Rodrik, D. (2018) 'Trump's trade gimmickry', *Project Syndicate*, March 9.

Root, H.L. (2009) *Alliance Curse: How America Lost the Third World* (Washington, DC: Brookings Institution Press).

Rose, N. (1993) 'Government, authority and expertise in advanced liberalism', *Economy and Society* 22(3): 283–299.

Rose, N. and Miller, P. (1992) 'Political power beyond the state: Problematics of government', *British Journal of Sociology* 43(2): 271–303.

Rosecrance, R. (1986) *The Rise of the Trading State: Commerce and Conquest in the Modern World* (New York: Basic Books).

Rosenau, J.N. (1990) *Turbulence in World Politics: A Theory of Change and Continuity* (Princeton: Princeton University Press).

Rosenau, J.N. (1992) 'Governance, order, and change in world politics', in J.N. Rosenau and E.-O. Czempiel (eds), *Governance without Government: Order and Change in World Politics* (Cambridge: Cambridge University Press): 1–29.

Rosenau, J.N. (1995) 'Governance in the twenty-first century', *Global Governance* 13: 13–43.

Rosenau, J.N. (2002) 'NGOs and fragmented authority in globalizing space', in Y.H.J. Ferguson and R.J. Barry (eds), *Political Space: Frontiers of Change and Governance in a Globalizing World* (New York: State University of New York Press): 261–279.

Rosenberg, J. (2010) 'Basic problems in the theory of uneven and combined development. Part II: Unevenness and political multiplicity', *Cambridge Review of International Affairs* 23(1): 165–189.

Ross, M.L. (1999) 'The political economy of the resource curse', *World Politics* 51(2): 297–322.

Rostow, W.W. (1960) *The Stages of Economic Growth: A Non-Communist Manifesto* (Cambridge: Cambridge University Press).

Rozman, G. (2004) *Northeast Asia's Stunted Regionalism: Bilateral Distrust in the Shadow of Globalisation* (Cambridge: Cambridge University Press).

Ruggie, J.G. (1982) 'International regimes, transactions and change: Embedded liberalism in the postwar economic order', *International Organization* 36(2): 379–415.

Ruggie, J.G. (1998) 'What makes the world hang together? Neo-utilitarianism and the social constructivist challenge', *International Organization* 52(4): 855–885.

Ruggie, J.G. (1993) 'Multilateralism: The anatomy of an institution', in J.G. Ruggie (ed.), *Multilateralism Matters: The Theory and Praxis of an Institutional Form* (New York: Columbia University Press): 3–47.

Russett, B.M. (1995) *Grasping the Democratic Peace: Principles for a post-Cold War World* (Princeton: Princeton University Press).

Sabel, C.F. and Zeitlin, J. (2010) *Experimentalist Governance in the European Union: Towards a New Architecture* (Oxford: Oxford University Press).

Samuels, G. (2017) 'Erdogan: Turkey does not need the EU', *The Times*, July 12.

Sanger, D.E. and Perlez, J. (2017) 'Trump hands the Chinese a gift: The chance for global leadership', *The New York Times*.

Sbragia, A. (2008) 'Comparative regionalism: What might it be?', *Journal of Common Market Studies* 46(s1): 29–49.

Schweller, R. (2018) 'Three cheers for Trump's foreign policy', *Foreign Affairs*, September/October.

Self, P. (1993) *Government by the Market: The Politics of Public Choice* (London: Macmillan).

Sender, H. and Stacey, K. (2017) 'China takes "project of the century" to Pakistan', *Financial Times*, May 18.

Shambaugh, D. (2002) *Modernizing China's Military: Progress, Problems, and Prospects* (Berkeley: University of California Press).

Shambaugh, D. (2013) *China Goes Global: The Partial Power* (Oxford: Oxford University Press).

Shapiro, J. (2001) *Mao's War against Nature: Politics and the Environment in Revolutionary China* (Cambridge: Cambridge University Press).

Shen, S. (2016) 'How China's "Belt and Road" compares to the Marshall Plan', *The Diplomat*, February 6.

Shih, C.Y. and Huang, C.C. (2013) 'Preaching self-responsibility: The Chinese style of global governance', *Journal of Contemporary China* 22(80): 351–365.

Shue, H. (2011) 'Face reality? After you! A call for leadership on climate change', *Ethics & International Affairs* 25(01): 17–26.

Shear, M.D. and Steinhauer, J. (2017) 'Trump to seek $54 billion increase in military spending', *New York Times*, February 27.

Shirouzu, N. and Takada, K. (2014) 'Two years after protests, "China risk" still haunts Japan firms', *Reuters*, September 12.

Shue, H. (2011) 'Face reality? After you!? A call for leadership on climate change', *Ethics & International Affairs* 25(01): 17–26.

Shultz, G.P., Perry, W.J. Kissinger, H.A., and Nunn, S. (2007) 'A World Free of Nuclear Weapons', *Wall Street Journal*, January 4.

Sikka, P. and Willmott, H. (2010) 'The dark side of transfer pricing: Its role in tax avoidance and wealth retentiveness', *Critical Perspectives on Accounting* 21(4): 342–356.

Silke, A. (2003) *Terrorists, Victims and Society: Psychological Perspectives on Terrorism and Its Consequences* (New York: John Wiley & Sons).

Simmons, B.A. and Elkins, Z. (2004) 'The globalization of liberalization: Policy diffusion in the international political economy', *American Political Science Review* 98(1): 171–189.

Sinclair, T.J. (2005) *The New Masters of Capital: American Bond Rating Agencies and the Politics of Creditworthiness* (Ithaca, NY: Cornell University Press).

Sinderbard, R. (2017) 'How Kellyanne Conway ushered in the era of "alternative facts"', *Washington Post*, January 22.

Singer, A. and Wildavsky, M. (1993) *The Real World Order: Zones of Peace/Zones of Turmoil* (Chatham, NJ: Chatham House Publishers).

Singer, P. (2002) *One World: Ethics of Globalisation* (New Haven, CT: Yale University Press).

Sit, R. (2018) 'Trump meets every criteria for an authoritarian leader, Harvard political scientists warn', *Newsweek*, May 4.

Skidelsky, R. (2009) *Keynes: The Return of the Master* (New York: Public Affairs).

Skidmore, D. (2011) *The Unilateralist Temptation in American Foreign Policy* (New York: Routledge).

Slaughter, A.M. (2017) *The Chessboard and the Web: Strategies of Connection in a Networked World* (New Haven, CT: Yale University Press).

Smith, A. (1981) *An Inquiry into the Nature and Causes of the Wealth of Nations* (Indianapolis: Liberty Fund).

Smith, K.E. (2013) *European Union Foreign Policy in a Changing World* (Cambridge: Polity Press).

Smith, N. (2008) *Uneven Development: Nature, Capital, and the Production of Space*, 3rd edn (London: Verso).

Smith, S. (2002) 'The United States and the discipline of international relations: "Hegemonic country, hegemonic discipline"', *International Studies Review* 4(2): 67–85.

Smith, T. (1994) *America's Mission: The United States and the Worldwide Struggle for Democracy in the Twentieth Century* (Princeton: Princeton University Press).

Smyth, J. (2016) 'Return of Australia "history wars"', *Financial Times*, April 1.

Snyder, J. (2009) 'One world, rival theories', *Foreign Policy*, October 26.

Snyder, J. (2017) 'The modernization trap', *Journal of Democracy* 28(2), 77–91.

Söderbaum, F. (2012) 'Theories of regionalism', in M. Beeson and R. Stubbs (eds), *The Routledge Handbook of Asian Regionalism* (London: Routledge): 11–21.

Solomon, S. (1995) *The Confidence Game: How Unelected Central Bankers are Governing the Changed World Economy* (New York: Simon & Schuster).

Special Correspondent (2017) 'The resistible rise of Xi Jinping', *Foreign Policy*, October 19.

Sperling, J. (2010) 'National security cultures, technologies of public goods supply and security governance', in E.J. Kirchner and J. Sperling (eds), *National Security Cultures: Patterns of Global Governance* (London: Routledge): 1–17.

Spruyt, H. (1994) *The Sovereign State and Its Competitors* (Princeton: Princeton University Press).

Starrs, S. (2017) 'International organizations: Can they break free from states?', in M. Beeson and N. Bisley (eds), *Issues in 21st Century World Politics*, 2nd edn (London: Red Globe Press): 68–82.

Startin, N. (2015) 'Have we reached a tipping point? The mainstreaming of Euroscepticism in the UK', *International Political Science Review* 36(3): 311–323.

Steinfeld, E.S. (2010) *Playing Our Game: Why China's Rise Doesn't Threaten the West* (New York: Oxford University Press).

Steinhardt, H.C. and Wu, F. (2016) 'In the name of the public: Environmental protest and the changing landscape of popular contention in China', *The China Journal* (75): 61–82.

Stephen, M.D. (2014) 'Rising powers, global capitalism and liberal global governance: A historical materialist account of the BRICS challenge', *European Journal of International Relations* 20(4): 912–938.

Stephens, P. (2018) 'Donald Trump shatters international trust in America', *Financial Times*, May 3.

Stevis, M. and Thomas, A. (2015) 'Greek, German tensions turn to open resentment as referendum looms', *Wall Street Journal*, July 4.

Stiglitz, J.E. (2002) *Globalization and Its Discontents* (New York: W.W. Norton).

Stiglitz, J.E. (2007) *Making Globalization Work* (New York: W.W. Norton).

Stockmann, D. and Gallagher, M.E. (2011) 'Remote control: How the media sustain authoritarian rule in China', *Comparative Political Studies* 44(4): 436–467.

Stokes, D. (2014) 'Achilles' deal: Dollar decline and US grand strategy after the crisis', *Review of International Political Economy* 21(5): 1071–1094.

Stokes, D. and Waterman, K. (2017) 'Trump's bilateralism and US power in East Asia', *The Diplomat*, August 9.

Stone, D. (2008) 'Global public policy, transnational policy communities, and their networks', *Policy Studies Journal* 36(1): 19–38.

Stone-Fish, I. (2014) 'Is China still a "developing" country?', *Foreign Policy*, September 25.

Strange, S. (1970) 'International economics and international relations: A case of mutual neglect', *International Affairs* 46(2): 304–315.

Strange, S. (1996) *The Retreat of the State: The Diffusion of Power in the World Economy* (Cambridge: Cambridge University Press).

Strauss, D. (2018) 'Hidden value in phones could "cut US trade deficit in half"', *Financial Times*, May 18.

Streeck, W. (2014) *Buying Time: The Delayed Crisis of Democratic Capitalism* (London: Verso Books).

Stubbs, R. (2005) *Rethinking Asia's Economic Miracle* (London: Red Globe Press).

Szamosszegi, A. and Kyle, C. (2011) *An Analysis of State-Owned Enterprises and State Capitalism in China* (Washington, DC: Capital Trade).

Tabb, W.K. (1995) *The Postwar Japanese System: Cultural Economy and Economic Transformation* (New York: Oxford University Press).

Taleb, N.N. (2007) *The Black Swan: The Impact of the Highly Improbable* (New York: Random House).

Tan, C.K. (2018) 'China spending puts domestic security ahead of defense', *Nikkei Asian Review*, March 14.

Tang, S. (2010) 'Social evolution of international politics: From Mearsheimer to Jervis', *European Journal of International Relations* 16(1): 31–55.

Tang, S. (2013) *The Social Evolution of International Politics* (Oxford: Oxford University Press).

Tang, S. (2018) 'China and the future international order(s)', *Ethics & International Affairs* 32(1): 31–43.

Taniguchi, R. and Babb, S. (2009) 'The global construction of development models: The US, Japan and the East Asian miracle', *Socio-Economic Review* 7(2): 277–303.

Tankersley, J. (2016) 'American Dream collapsing for young adults, study says, as odds plunge that children will earn more than their parents', *Washington Post*, December 8.

Tatke, S. (2017) 'Once a force to be reckoned with, Germany's Green Party is wobbling on the political stage, *The Wire*, June 30.

Teets, J.C. (2014) *Civil Society Under Authoritarianism: The China Model* (Cambridge: Cambridge University Press).

Temin, P. (1989) *Lessons from the Great Depression* (Cambridge, MA: MIT Press).

Teschke, B. (2003) *The Myth of 1648: Class, Geopolitics, and the Making of Modern International Relations* (London: Verso).

Tett, G. (2009) *Fool's Gold: How Unrestrained Greed Corrupted a Dream, Shattered Global Markets and Unleashed a Catastrophe* (London: Little, Brown & Co).

Tiezzi, S. (2014) 'China doesn't want to be number one', *The Diplomat*, May 8.

Tilly, C. (1990) *Coercion, Capital, and European States* (Oxford: Blackwell).

Tovey, A. (2016) '$1,570,000,000,000: how much the world spent on arms this year', *The Telegraph*, December 12.

Toye, J. (2014) 'Assessing the G77: 50 years after UNCTAD and 40 years after the NIEO', *Third World Quarterly* 35(10): 1759–1774.

Trachtenberg, M. (1999) *A Constructed Peace: The Making of the European Settlement, 1945–63* (Princeton: Princeton University Press).

Trubowitz, P. (1998) *Defining the National Interest: Conflict and Change in American Foreign Policy* (Chicago: University of Chicago Press).

Tsai, K.S. (2007) *Capitalism without Democracy: The Private Sector in Contemporary China* (Ithaca, NY: Cornell University Press).

Ulaş, L. (2016) 'Cosmopolitanism, self-interest and world government', *Political Studies* 64(1S): 105–120.

Underhill, G.R.D. and Zhang, X. (2008) 'Setting the rules: Private power, political underpinnings, and legitimacy in global monetary and financial governance', *International Affairs* 84(3): 535–554.

US Government (2002) *National Security Strategy* (Washington, DC: Department of Defense)

Van Ness, P. (1970) *Revolution and Chinese Foreign Policy: Peking's Support for Wars of National Liberation* (Berkeley: University of California Press).

Vasudevan, R. (2009) 'Dollar hegemony, financialization, and the credit crisis', *Review of Radical Political Economics* 41(3): 291–304.

Väyrynen, R. (2006) 'Introduction: Contending views.', in R. Väyrynen (ed.), *The Waning of Major War: Theories and Debates* (London: Routledge): 1–30.

Vermeiren, M. (2013) 'The crisis of US monetary hegemony and global economic adjustment', *Globalizations* 10(2): 245–259.

Vermeiren, M. and Dierckx, S. (2012) 'Challenging global neoliberalism? The global political economy of China's capital controls', *Third World Quarterly* 33(9): 1647–1668.

Vogel, E.F. (1979) *Japan as No 1: Lessons for America* (Cambridge, MA: Harvard University Press).

Vogel, E.F. (2011) *Deng Xiaoping and the Transformation of China* (Cambridge, MA: Belknap Press).

Volcovici, V. and Mason, J. (2017) 'Trump signs order dismantling Obama-era climate policies', *Reuters*, March 28.

Volodzko, D. (2017) 'China wins its war against South Korea's US THAAD missile shield – Without firing a shot', *South China Morning Post*, November.

Vucetic, S. (2011) *The Anglosphere: A Genealogy of A Racialized Identity in International Relations* (Stanford: Stanford University Press).

Wade, R. (1990) *Governing the Market: Economic Theory and the Role of Government in East Asian Industrialization* (Princeton: Princeton University Press).

Wade, R. (1996) 'Japan, the World Bank, and the art of paradigm maintenance: The East Asian Miracle in political perspective', *New Left Review* 217(May/June): 3–36.

Wade, R. (2000) 'Wheels within wheels: Rethinking the Asian crisis and the Asian model', *Annual Review of Political Science* 3: 85–115.

Wade, R. and Veneroso, F. (1998) 'The Asian crisis: The high debt model versus the Wall Street-Treasury-IMF complex', *New Left Review* 228(Mar/Apr): 3–23.

Waever, O. (2017) 'International leadership after the demise of the last superpower: System structure and stewardship', *Chinese Political Science Review* 2(4): 452–476.

Wagstyl, S., Beesley, A., Barker, A., and Politi, J. (2017) 'Trump flexes muscle against pillars of postwar order', *Financial Times*, January 17.

Wallace, H. (1996) 'The institutions of the EU: Experience and experiments', *Policy-Making in the European Union*, 3: 37–68.

Wallace, H., Wallace, W., and Pollack, M.A. (eds) (2000) *Policy-Making in the European Union* (Oxford: Oxford University Press).

Wallerstein, I. (1979) *The Capitalist World-Economy* (Cambridge: Cambridge University Press).

Walt, S.M. (1985) 'Alliance formation and the balance of world power', *International Security* 9(4): 3–43.

Walter, A. (2008) *Governing Finance: East Asia's Adoption of International Standards* (Ithaca, NY: Cornell University Press).

Walter, C.E. and Howie, F.J.T. (2011) *Red Capitalism: The Fragile Financial Foundations of China's Extraordinary Rise* (Singapore: Wiley).

Walters, F.P. (1965) *A History of the League of Nations* (Oxford: Oxford University Press).

Waltz, K.N. (1979) *Theory of International Politics* (New York: McGraw-Hill).

Wang, H. and French, E. (2014) 'China in global economic governance', *Asian Economic Policy Review* 9(2): 254–271.

Wang, J. (2012) '"Marching Westwards": The Rebalancing of China's Geostrategy', *International and Strategic Studies* 731–711.

Wang, L. and Zheng, J. (2010) 'China and the changing landscape of the world economy', *Journal of Chinese Economic and Business Studies* 8(3): 203–214.

Webber, D. (2014) 'How likely is it that the European Union will disintegrate? A critical analysis of competing theoretical perspectives', *European Journal of International Relations*, 20(2), 341–365.

Webber, M., Croft, S., Howorth, J., Terriff, T., and Krahmann, E. (2004) 'The governance of European security', *Review of International Studies* 30(1): 3–26.

Weiss, T.G. (2013) *Global Governance: Why? What? Whither?* (Cambridge: Polity Press): p xv.

Wendt, A. (1992) 'Anarchy is what states make of it: The social construction of power politics', *International Organization* 46(2): 391–425.

Wendt, A. (2003) 'Why a world state is inevitable', *European Journal of International Relations* 9(4): 491–542.

White, H. (2012) *The China Choice: Why America Should Share Power* (Melbourne: Black Inc).

White House (2012) 'Fact Sheet: East Asia Summit Outcomes' (Washington), www.whitehouse.gov/the-press-office/2012/11/20/fact-sheet-east-asia-summit-outcomes

Wildau, G. (2017) 'China bank overseer launches "regulatory windstorm"', *Financial Times,* April 19.

Wildau, G. and Mitchell, T. (2016) 'China: Renminbi stalls on road to being a global currency', *Financial Times*, December 11.

Williamson, J. (1993) 'Democracy and the "Washington consensus"', *World Development,* 21(8), 1329–1336.

Wilson, J.D. (forthcoming) 'The evolution of China's Asian Infrastructure Investment Bank: From a revisionist to status-seeking agenda', *International Relations of the Asia-Pacific.*

Wilson, P.H. (2011) *The Holy Roman Empire 1495–1806*, 2nd edn (Basingstoke: Macmillan).

Witte, G. and Birnbaum, M. (2018) 'In Eastern Europe, the E.U. faces a rebellion more threatening than Brexit', *Washington Post*, April 5.

Wohlforth, W.C. (1999) 'The stability of a unipolar world', *International Security* 24(1): 5–41.

Wolf, M. (2017) 'The long and painful journey to world disorder', *Financial Times*, January 5.

Wolf, M. (2018) 'Why so little has changed since the financial crash', *Financial Times*, September 4.

Wong, C.H. (2016) '"Panama Papers" put Beijing's corruption fight under fresh scrutiny', *Financial Times*, April 5.

Wong, C.H. (2017) 'China's President Xi casts country as guardian of globalization', *Wall Street Journal*, May 14.

Wong, C.H. (2018) 'China's Communist Party proposal sets stage for Xi to hold onto power', *Wall Street Journal*, February 25.

Wood, E.M. (2002) *The Origin of Capitalism: A Longer View* (London: Verso).

Woods, L. (1993) *Asia-Pacific Diplomacy: Nongovernmental Organizations and International Relations* (Vancouver: UBC Press).

Woods, N. (1999) 'Good governance in international organizations', *Global Governance* 5(1): 39–61.

Woods, N. (2010) 'Global governance after the financial crisis: A new multilateralism or the last gasp of the great powers?', *Global Policy* 1(1): 51–63.

World Bank (1993) *The East Asian Miracle: Economic Growth and Public Policy* (Oxford: Oxford University Press).

World Bank (1994) *Governance: The World Bank's Experience* (Washington, DC: World Bank).

World Bank (1997) *World Development Report 1997: The State in a Changing World* (New York: Oxford University Press).

World Bank and Development Research Centre of the State Council (2012) *China 2030: Building a Modern, Harmonious and Creative High-Income Society* (Washington, DC: World Bank).

Wright, R. (2000) *Nonzero: The Logic of Human Destiny* (New York: Pantheon Books).

Wright, T. (2010) *Accepting Authoritarianism: State-Society Relations in China's Reform Era* (Stanford: Stanford University Press).

Wynne, B. (2010) 'Strange weather, again: Climate science as political art', *Theory, Culture & Society* 27(2–3): 289–305.

Xi, J. (2014a) *The Governance of China* (Beijing: Foreign Language Press).

Xi, J. (2014b) *New Asian Security Concept for New Progress in Security Cooperation.* Ministry of Foreign Affairs of the People's Republic of China, www.fmprc.gov.cn/mfa_eng/zxxx_662805/t1159951.shtml.

Xi, J. (2018) *Openness for Greater Prosperity, Innovation for a Better Future.* Boao Forum for Asia Annual Conference, Boao.

Yahuda, M. (2006) 'The limits of economic interdependence: Sino-Japanese relations', in A.I. Johnston and R.S. Ross (eds), *New Directions in the Study of China's Foreign Policy* (Stanford: Stanford University Press): 162–185.

Yan, X. (2011a) 'How China can defeat America', *New York Times*, November 20.

Yan, X. (2011b) *Ancient Chinese Thought, Modern Chinese Power* (Princeton: Princeton University Press).

Yang, J. (2015) 'Vulgarisation of Keynesianism in China's response to the global financial crisis', *Review of International Political Economy* 22(2): 360–390.

Yeophantong, P. (2013) 'Governing the world: China's evolving conceptions of responsibility', *The Chinese Journal of International Politics* 6(October): 329–364.

Yeung, H.W.c. (2009) 'Regional development and the competitive dynamics of global production networks: An East Asian perspective', *Regional Studies* 43(3): 325–351.

Yeung, H.W.c. (2013) 'Governing the market in a globalizing era: Developmental states, global production networks and inter-firm dynamics in East Asia', *Review of International Political Economy* 21, 70–101.

Yeung, H.W.c. (2016) *Strategic Coupling: East Asian Industrial Transformation in the New Global Economy* (Ithaca, NY: Cornell University Press).

Youwei (2015) 'The end of reform in China: Authoritarian adaptation hits a wall', *Foreign Affairs* (May/June).

Yu, Y., Feng, K., and Hubacek, K. (2014) 'China's unequal ecological exchange', *Ecological Indicators* 47: 156–163.

Zahid, M. (2010) *Muslim Brotherhood and Egypt's Succession Crisis: The Politics of Liberalisation and Reform in the Middle East* (New York: I.B. Tauris).

Zalasiewicz, J., Williams, M., Steffen, W., and Crutzen, P. (2010) 'The new world of the Anthropocene', *Environmental Science & Technology* 44(7): 2228–2231.

Zelko, F. (2013) *Make It a Green Peace! The Rise of Countercultural Environmentalism* (Oxford: Oxford University Press).

Zeng, J. (2015) *The Chinese Communist Party's Capacity to Rule: Ideology, Legitimacy and Party Cohesion* (London: Palgrave Macmillan).

Zeng, J. (2016) 'Constructing new type of great power relations: The state of debate in China (1998–2014)', *British Journal of Politics and International Relations* 18(2): 422–442

Zhan, X. and Tang, S.Y. (2013) 'Political opportunities, resource constraints and policy advocacy of environmental NGOs in China', *Public Administration* 91(2): 381–399.

Zhang, F. (2015) *Chinese Hegemony: Grand Strategy and International Institutions in East Asian History* (Stanford: Stanford University Press).

Zhang, X. and James, K. (2017) 'From wealth to power: China's new economic statecraft', *The Washington Quarterly* 40(1): 185–203.

Zhao, S. (2015) 'Rethinking the Chinese world order: The imperial cycle and the rise of China', *Journal of Contemporary China* 24(96): 961–982.

Zhao, S. 2016. 'China and the evolving world order: A stakeholder or a revolutionary power?', *The ASEAN Forum*, June 22.

Zhao, T. (2009) 'A political world philosophy in terms of all-under-heaven (Tian-Xia)', *Diogenes* 56(1): 5–18.

Zhao, Z. (1998) 'Soft versus structured regionalism: Organizational forms of cooperation in Asia-Pacific', *Journal of East Asian Affairs* 12: 96–134.

Zhixu, M. (2018) 'Under neo-totalitarianism, there is no "civil society" in China', *China Change*, February 4.

Zhong, Y. and Hwang, W. (2015) 'Pollution, institutions and street protests in urban China', *Journal of Contemporary China* 25(98): 216–232.

Zhuang, P., Wu, W. and Huang, K. (2016) 'US opposition to AIIB "strategic mistake", says senior Trump adviser', *South China Morning Post*, November 10.

Zoellick, R.B. (2005) *Whither China: From Membership to Responsibility?* New York, http://2001-2009.state.gov/s/d/former/zoellick/rem/53682.htm

Zubok, V.V.M. and Pleshakov, C. (1997) *Inside the Kremlin's Cold War* (Cambridge, MA: Harvard University Press).

Zumbrun, J. and Emont, J. (2018) 'China's financial reach leaves eight countries vulnerable, study finds', *Wall Street Journal*, March 4.

Index

254   *Index*

CPSIA information can be obtained
at www.ICGtesting.com
Printed in the USA
LVHW051205310523
748362LV00008B/407

9 781137 588609